MARILYN

The Tragic Venus

Other Books by EDWIN P. HOYT

MARILYN
The Tragic Venus

New Edition

by
EDWIN P. HOYT

Chilton Book Company
RADNOR, PENNSYLVANIA

Library of Congress Cataloging in Publication Data

Hoyt, Edwin Palmer.
   Marilyn, the tragic Venus.

   1.   Monroe, Marilyn, 1926-1962.   I.   Title.
PN2287.M69H6   1973   791.43'028'0924 [B]   73-9951
ISBN   0-8019-5915-2

Foreword and Acknowledgments

ON beginning this study of an American motion picture star, the author had fewer preconceptions than most writers might be expected to have. I had never seen Marilyn Monroe in the flesh. I had never seen a Marilyn Monroe motion picture.

My interest in Marilyn was kindled by the manner of her death and the obvious shock it brought to so many different types of people, who seemed to care so much about this strange girl. The emotional bath that swirled across America in the days following her death was unmatched since the scandal of Ingrid Bergman and Roberto Rossellini. But where Bergman and Rossellini had outraged the virtue—or the public protestations of virtue—of the American movie-goers, Marilyn had simply left the scene abruptly and tragically, without saying goodby.

The facts that Marilyn did not say goodby and that psychiatrists and responsible citizens were called in by the Los Angeles authorities to deliberate, godlike, and decide how Marilyn died: these were interesting to a student of the American scene. The phenomenon of Marilyn was interesting, this non-movie-goer also discovered. The verdict of death by suicide somehow did not seem satisfactory. It was too abrupt. It was not meaningful. It did not square with the actions or attitudes of Joe DiMaggio. It did not fit somehow, unless something important was left out or something important was being concealed.

There was another reason for undertaking the study of Marilyn Monroe's life and times. I have a continuing interest in money, power, and fame.

As far as men were concerned, I had discovered in my studies of the Vanderbilts and others that money was really the least important of all three commodities or possessions. Money might be the original goad, but soon power surpassed it in the eyes of the attainer; then power, too, palled, and the interest was focused on prestige; and finally, once they had been attained, almost solely on accomplishment for its own sake. Morgans, Vanderbilts, Astors, Rockefellers have lived by this pattern. I was curious to see how a woman would react if, starting from nowhere, she was to achieve money, fame, and power.

And so I began my study of Marilyn Monroe.

One interesting aspect to this study was the claim, made on every side, that "so much has been written" about Marilyn. True, so much has been written, and so little truth has been revealed. Marilyn was a difficult subject to catch. She had adopted all the tricks of protective coloration of the artist: the deliberate untruth, the half-truth, and the misleading statement. She told the truth, too, the naive truth which was a hallmark of her conversation. The concealments and untruths were usually handled for her by others, and the myths were allowed to flower and grow, which they did, unencumbered. These untruths and myths are not confined to the famous. They exist about most people in varying degrees. For nearly all people are one thing to one person and quite something else to the next. All of us, apparently, are complex people who have as many images as a chameleon.

It was interesting to this author to discover in Marilyn the same drives one finds in captains of industry and in politicians. Marilyn never did care for the money, however; that was a major difference. She did not even really want the power, although she felt for a time, and I believe quite wrongly, that she would flourish under her own rule better than under the direction of others. She never did discover that she could not rule herself. She left the influences of Hollywood for the East. She was always grateful to Arthur Miller for taking her out of the sinkholes of Hollywood and letting her find her way among the theatrical people of New York. She accepted the influence of Lee Strasberg on her life gladly, and that influence ruled her

[vi]

until her death. She might have gone on, as the Strasbergs suggested, to prove herself a great actress in the best traditions of the theater. Poor Marilyn, she never had the chance.

The study of Marilyn's life convinced me that, in the essentials of the American dream, women are more idealistic than men, they honor accomplishment for its own sake more than men. Or perhaps they are more naive than men and not so convinced of the basic evil of mankind. Marilyn gave evidence of conviction that mankind was evil, and yet she never ceased to place her trust in her fellow man, as she did with Lee Strasberg and a line of advisers who stood behind him.

Those who knew Marilyn well at the end of her life say they are convinced that Marilyn did not commit suicide, that she died by accident by her own hand, and of this the author, too, is convinced. She undoubtedly was depressed; she took sleeping pills in excessive amounts; it was a habit with her. Her friends and protectors said that she was "allergic" to sleeping pills. Some of them also said that she was "allergic" to alcohol, and that is why she seemed so visibly affected by it on occasion. A few, commenting on parts of this manuscript, lamented the author's telling of tales that indicated that Marilyn drank to excess from time to time. She did so, however; it was a part of her character. If the "excess" in her case was less than it might have been in another's, that is really not at issue. The question was whether and how much Marilyn drank. The answer was: too much.

Marilyn's relationships with men created many confusions and much misunderstanding. She was Johnny Hyde's mistress. She was the mistress of Joseph Schenck, chairman of the board of Twentieth Century Fox, and she had affairs with many others and slept casually with many, many men. So by ordinary moral standards, Marilyn's conduct left much to be desired. But those who knew Marilyn well at various times in her life hesitated to judge her by ordinary moral standards. Nunnally Johnson said she would sleep with men as a way of saying "thank you." He said she was not very sexy. Others said she was really very sexy indeed. On one occasion toward the end of her career, Spyros Skouras was concerned about Marilyn's night life. She had been, he heard, mixed up with two or three very young men—had affairs with them. Skouras suggested that this was not particularly helpful for Marilyn's career, since so much still depended on public reaction to her film presence. Marilyn said that she liked men, that when she had a man in her bed she did not feel the need for sleeping pills.

That is the kind of anecdote which aroused the open hostility of some who were close to Marilyn at the end of her career. Perhaps, actually, they did not know the promiscuous Marilyn, the amoral Marilyn. More likely, they were interested in protecting her, in creating an image of a Marilyn who never was, to live down through the ages. Why? Because that is the way people are.

But this was Marilyn. She was amoral and promiscuous, and she did like men. And she was as unsexy as a girl could be at times, too. She was a human being. She was a human being in Hollywood, where all the fleshly emotions are drawn larger than life. She was a woman of the entertainment world, where, as Lee Strasberg put it to the author, nothing exists except in the eye of the beholder. The actor, said Strasberg, does not exist except in his reputation. He has nothing tangible to offer. And so this may explain why there is so much desire on the part of Marilyn's friends to create the image of a Marilyn without the woman in it.

It was the woman as well as the actress who would have kept Marilyn from committing suicide. She had tried suicide any number of times—but these were all theatrical suicides, attempted when she knew there was someone on hand to prevent the sleeping pills from taking their deadly effect. Marilyn was not the type for suicide. She had too much to live for at the moment she died. She had been convinced by the Strasbergs that she would become one of the great dramatic actresses of all times.

Without any pretense of expert knowledge, the author suspects that Marilyn was always a better actress than she was given credit for being or than she allowed herself to be. Much of the effect of striving for perfection that she created was overdrawn, but there was a good deal of truth in it too. She could put on an emotional scene in a dressing room which would do credit to a Garbo or a Bette Davis. She could turn off the emotions, too, if

[viii]

something said by one of her advisers struck the proper chord. Milton Greene proved that—at one time one of the Hollywood commentators claimed that Greene had some magnetic, Svengali influence over Marilyn; if so, it was her capacity for self-hypnotism.

Like most actors and actresses, Marilyn acted most of the time. Her life was a succession of roles (housewife, movie star, dramatic actress, poor little rich girl), and the eagerness with which she threw herself into them may account for some of the conflicting testimony from people who considered themselves her friends.

As is the case in anyone's life, all the friends of Marilyn are not friends among themselves; many of them have no use for one another, and, as is the case in the entertainment industry, the dislikes are volubly aired. This also lends itself to creating confusion for the biographer who is attempting to draw a picture of a subject. In Marilyn's case, it really lent itself to much delay, more than anything else. Some of the subjects for interview, such as the Strasbergs, were very late in consenting to be interviewed. Some, like Darryl Zanuck, were never available, although this did not make as much difference as one might believe. I became interested, however, in the anomalous situation whereby Marilyn and those close to her at the last felt that Zanuck and Twentieth Century Fox were her enemies, and Spyros Skouras and others at Fox said they were her friends. Thus what appears to be an inordinate interest of the author in Darryl Zanuck showed through. In the end, various people in Hollywood gave what seems to be an adequate answer to this odd question. It was not Darryl Zanuck who created so much difficulty for Marilyn, but some of Darryl Zanuck's staff, whose watchdog proclivities were very strong. Marilyn thought Zanuck disliked her. One reason might be that she could never get through the palace guard to the busy chief of the studio. It would be enough to give anyone pause.

One must accept Marilyn's instinctive belief that she was mistreated and disliked by her studio, without pinning it on Zanuck or any other. Marilyn spent a good part of one day of her two-day interview with Richard Meryman in a gloomy monologue of complaint against the wrongs Fox had done her over the years. But accepting this verdict does not mean accepting its total truth—one need only realize that this is how Marilyn felt about it. That really is all that is important because it was her life, not the life of Fox Studios, that was under examination.

The search for truth in matters regarding the motion picture business, as in writing the story of Marilyn Monroe, turned out to be the most difficult the author has undertaken in some twenty years of reporting and research in many climes, foreign and domestic. Compared to Hollywood tales the propaganda of the Chinese Nationalist Government of Chiang Kai-shek two decades ago now seems totally objective. It is not so much that everyone in Hollywood is dishonest (although the outlander must beware lest he be cozened), but memories fade and are strengthened by repetition of stories told long ago, in which the stories often undergo complete metamorphosis. Furthermore, it seems that nearly everyone connected with the motion picture industry has been rubbed against ham, and so the part played by the teller of the tale is always the starring role. This universality of leading roles tends to be confusing, as when there are four different versions of one story—which the author encountered at least once. The story with two entirely opposite versions turned out to be so common as to cause not a lifted eyebrow, as the tale of the exposure of Marilyn's participation in the nude-calendar incident.

One tale, by far the most dramatic, had it that when producers Jerry Wald and Norman Krasna were about ready to release *Clash by Night*, suddenly Wald began receiving mysterious telephone calls from a stranger who wanted ten thousand dollars. Otherwise, said the blackmailer, he would spill the beans that one of the featured players in the movie, Marilyn Monroe, had posed for the nude calendar that was that year decorating the walls of many establishments frequented by men. Since the Hays office was very powerful and very sticky about nudity, the producers were worried. They called in Perry Lieber, head of publicity at RKO, and discussed it with him.

"Excelsior!" said Perry Lieber. The only answer to this challenge was complete honesty. Whereupon Perry Lieber is said to have picked up the telephone and called Aline Mosby of United Press Associations and tipped her off that Marilyn had misbehaved. And Aline Mosby, it is said, then called Twentieth Century Fox's publicity department, and the cat was out of the bag. Various mean, unkindly officials of Twentieth Century Fox began browbeating Marilyn, telling her to deny everything and threatening to break her contract under the morals clause. Marilyn quivered and worried and called Sidney Skolsky, and he told her to be honest and face the music, and she did.

That story is infinitely preferable to the story that Aline Mosby simply came to Twentieth Century Fox Studios one day and in the course of a routine interview asked Marilyn about the nude calendar, and that Marilyn casually admitted that she had posed for it because she needed the money. But when the author asked Perry Lieber about his part in this affair, Perry Lieber said he had never telephoned Aline Mosby and had never talked about the calendar with Marilyn and had never had anything to do with Marilyn as far as he could remember. So the author made a judgment and used the less dramatic tale, which was told to him by Sonia Wolfson, the press agent in attendance on Marilyn and Miss Mosby during the interview. There was little further checking to be done; Miss Mosby had disappeared from Hollywood to foreign lands and was not available for comment, and Sidney Skolsky apparently does not discuss Marilyn.

The matter of communication in Hollywood makes the French or Korean telephone system seem child's play. If the outsider wishes to telephone an insider, he calls the Screen Actors Guild or the Directors Guild or the other organization to which the person belongs. The Guild telephone operator puts him onto a secretary, who gives him the number of the person's agent or lawyer or accountant, and the accountant or lawyer or agent may or may not give the caller the number of the person. In case of a player, the chances of getting through are almost nil. In case of a director, they are slightly better: at least a secretary will talk to the caller—after all, he might be a producer with money and a script. Telephone numbers, difficult as they are to come by, are easy to acquire compared to addresses. The author wrote letters to more than one hundred people not readily available by telephone. Most of these were sent care of various guilds and unions and perhaps were forwarded. Half a dozen replies were received, and one long distance telephone call across the country from William Lundigan. Like Marilyn, most Hollywoodians do not write many letters, it seems.

At the motion picture studios the publicity departments were most helpful. I am indebted to everyone at Twentieth Century Fox publicity, from Harry Brand and Perry Lieber down to the office boys who run the errands. Specifically, Frank Neal, Bill Smith, John Campbell, Sonia Wolfson, and all the secretaries and copying machine operators and file clerks seem to have done something for me at one time or another. Howard Strickling at Metro-Goldwyn-Mayer was very helpful in a number of ways. I am indebted to Spyros Skouras, Chairman of the Board of Twentieth Century Fox, for much information. Pat Newcomb, Marilyn's public relations representative, gave me information and a number of leads on sources. Florabel Muir, Hollywood correspondent of the New York *Daily News*, was very helpful. Nunnally Johnson, who wrote and produced two of Marilyn's movies and wrote the original script for her last movie, gave me a wealth of detail concerning several periods of Marilyn's life in which he knew her well. Richard Sale, director of *Ticket to Tomahawk* told me a great deal about Marilyn's early Hollywood life. Lee and Paula Strasberg took time from their busy schedule to see the author. Dr. Marianne Kris was very kind.

The late Harpo Marx was helpful, regarding the very brief association of the Marx Brothers with Marilyn in *Love Happy*. A number of officials of the Los Angeles public school system attempted to help the author track down information about Marilyn's brief educational career, but without success because of local laws which guard the educational records of all individuals from public view, apparently in perpetuity. It will be unfortunate for future biographers and historians if we ever elect a President who attended the Los Angeles public schools.

I am in debt to Frank H. Ricketson, Jr., President of Fox Intermountain Theaters for information and for opening several doors. Mrs. Allan Snyder was helpful. Information from Allan

Snyder came from a statement he made for the Twentieth Century Fox publicity files after Marilyn's death. At the time of the preparation of the film *Marilyn*, the Fox publicity department searched out many in the film industry who had known Marilyn and asked them to recall anecdotes. These were most valuable, although some of the accounts clashed with those of other people; such are the ways of human memory.

Agnes Flanagan, who was Marilyn's hair stylist on a number of movies and who did Marilyn's hair for her in the last few months, was most generous in sharing recollections. So was Hazel Washington, Hollywood columnist and Marilyn's studio maid in a number of pictures. The editors of the Los Angeles *Times* allowed me to use the *Times* library and clippings to check certain aspects of Marilyn's career. I am also indebted to the librarians of the *Times* and to the librarians of the Los Angeles *Herald Express* for information. The librarians of the New York Public Library were helpful, as they always are.

Joseph Mankiewicz of New York and Hollywood very kindly wrote me a detailed letter concerning Marilyn and contributed an anecdote. Fred Karger, orchestra leader and musical director, was very frank in discussing his relationship with Marilyn and told me a great deal about her life at several points. Billy Wilder was extremely busy during my stay in Hollywood, but he took time out from editing his current motion picture to discuss her with me and to confirm certain remarks he had made earlier. Robin French, actor's agent, told me something of Marilyn's relationship with Hugh French, and helped give the picture of Marilyn that the author received. John Springer, Marilyn's public relations counsel in New York from 1959 until her death, was most helpful and gracious. Richard Meryman of *Life*, who conducted the very revealing interview or personality profile of Marilyn in the summer of 1962, gave me much insight into her last days. Don Boutyette, Hollywood publicist, told me several stories about Marilyn's brief association with Columbia Pictures, where he was then working as a publicist.

The problem of professional ethics is a troublesome one, even when the subject of a biography is dead and there are no living relatives. Although Marilyn's mother was alive at the time of the preparation of this book, she was incompetent. This created problems, too. Lawyers Aaron Frosch and Milton Rudin of New York and Los Angeles refused to discuss Marilyn's affairs as a matter of professional ethics, or even to give matters of public record. Dr. Ralph Greenson of Los Angeles, Marilyn's psychiatrist, took the same position. So, apparently, did Dr. Hyman Engelberg of Los Angeles, who did not respond either to letters or telephone calls.

Quite understandably, neither Joe DiMaggio nor Arthur Miller, Marilyn's former husbands, wished to discuss their private affairs with a biographer. No attempt was made to invade the privacy of James Dougherty, her first husband, since he had already told his story to others a number of times.

Among the people who knew Marilyn well there was considerable reluctance to talk about her, for a number of reasons. Part of it was affection. Mrs. Milton H. Greene told me that she could not bear even to look at Marilyn's picture because Marilyn's death was still so great a cause of disturbance to her. Lee and Paula Strasberg were difficult to reach in the beginning, but most gracious when we met. John Springer told me quite frankly that he was worried about what I was going to write, because so many unpleasant and scurrilous words had been written about Marilyn. Among those who were close to her—even many with whom Marilyn had broken—there was a protectiveness that I have never encountered in dealing with any other personality, living or dead. Marilyn's magnetism off-stage was strongest in arousing this feeling when she lived. It continued, obviously, long after her death, long after she could be of use to anyone.

Emmaline Snively was very frank with me in discussing Marilyn's opening gambits in the world of Hollywood, especially in telling that little tale of Snively's venture into press agentry. Mrs. Agnes Fowler helped me track down a number of people whom I had almost given up after combating the system the Hollywoodians have perfected to assure their insulation from the outside world.

Milton H. Greene was most helpful, and gave generously of his time in talking to me about his association with Marilyn. James Haspiel, an ardent fan of Marilyn's during the last years of her life, was kind enough to read the manuscript and comment on it.

I am very much indebted to the secretary of Dr. Max Cutler of Beverly Hills, who spent hours trying to locate Natasha Lytess for me. We never were successful, other than to discover that she seemed to be in Europe.

Many other people were involved in this book, in one way or another. Darryl Zanuck's relationship with Marilyn was not a very close one, obviously, but there is no question about her fear of him, or her feeling that he disliked her intensely; neither of which has ever been satisfactorily explained. Toward the end Marilyn exhibited all the symptoms of paranoia about Twentieth Century Fox, but she always had felt persecuted by Twentieth Century. Mr. Zanuck's almost continual residence in Europe during the period in which this book was prepared and the author's inability to get through to him during the brief period in which he was in New York accounts for the absence of the Zanuck view of Marilyn's attitude.

The above was written a decade ago, but I have seen no reason to change it, or a line of the book about Marilyn, for every word of it is as it was. Marilyn's story grows more poignant through the years; her pictures are now a part of the American folk art. When I was doing the book, in 1963 and 1964, the judgments on Marilyn were tentative. Some who regarded her as a great comedienne were not quite sure how this judgment would go down in history. But as any youths who have seen the revivals of the Monroe films on television will tell you, she was, indeed, a very funny actress. Much of this ability was projected in spite of the people around her and her directors, who bought her and used her, primarily because she was the sex goddess.

In the 1970s Sex is the goddess and there is no Venus figure in sight; Gina Lollabrigida is the closest to it, and she is getting along. Raquel Welch comes to mind, but compared to Marilyn she is very cold potatoes. As for the rest, they can be put down as a succession of snits, some of them trying to achieve the Monroe type of stardom, but not many, because the motion picture world is so fragmented that there is no room, apparently, for a Marilyn any more. To be what Marilyn was to her audience, a girl today would have to be black-Jewish-Chinese-Japanese-Chicano and native American Indian—rolled into one. She could not even keep up with the hair styles let alone the ambience.

But somehow there seems to be a wind of change stirring in the canyons of California and the forests of Vermont. In the very recent past the interest in Marilyn has grown much stronger, there have been more magazine articles retracing the old story, more revived pictures, more still photographs dredged from somewhere. The Marilyn claque has never died, but it is in the way of being reborn. To me this is a fine thing, because in spite of all her troubles Marilyn was a good soul, and her pictures left the world a little happier place in which to live.

EDWIN P. HOYT
Bomoseen, Vt.
April, 1973

MARILYN

The Tragic Venus

Chapter One

ONE summer's night amid lights that twinkle along boulevards sprawling outward from the center of Los Angeles toward the Pacific Ocean, the world changed a little. Another light was snuffed out; a woman died in a lonely bare bedroom of a house on the western side of the city.

The woman was artificially blonde. She had no family to speak of, almost no friends, and only a handful of friendly acquaintances. No sycophants surrounded her because she had little money, although she earned money easily and spent it lavishly. She was a friendly, shy creature who sometimes impressed strangers as vulgar, sometimes as lost and bewildered, sometimes as lush and inviting. She was known to cry at the sight of a dead animal on the roadside, and she was known to keep scores, dozens, hundreds of people waiting for as long as three hours while she primped in the privacy of her apartment. Her doctors had told her she was emotionally ill, and sometimes she seemed to agree: she consulted a succession of psychiatrists. She lived with death constantly but did not fear death nearly so much as she feared insanity. The idea that she might go mad harried her.

She had grown up in the most insecure of circumstances— an unwanted child of an unbalanced woman, shuttled between foster homes and an orphanage. Insecurity lay at the center of her character, so deep-seated that it affected her every action.

She feared and abhorred rejection of any kind; she was so sensitive that a changed tone of voice was enough to disturb her so that she could not concentrate.

People who were in position to have known her well differed widely in evaluation of her character. She thrived in an atmosphere of conflict and animosity, said one. She detested animosity and conflict, said another.

She had suffered through three unhappy marriages, making only part of that unhappiness for herself. Yet she did not speak ill of her former husbands in the way it would hurt them most —publicly. She loved children as well as animals and wished desperately to bear a child, but she had miscarried several times and some of her doctors were convinced that she was incapable of carrying a child to parturition. As a woman, then, she regarded herself as a failure. She had not yet become a great performer, or even the most important actress in the only world she knew, the screen world. She had never won an important award for acting, and her name sometimes aroused laughter when acting ability was attributed to her. By some standards, notably her own, she was not beautiful or even striking. She was so unsure of herself that she paid huge sums to acting coaches to tell her what to do. In her chosen profession she had barely begun. And yet, when she died so suddenly that warm summer's night of August 4, 1962, the blinding glare of the publicity revealed the fact that she was the best-loved woman in the world. Not just the best-known personality in the international world of film production. No, she was literally the most famous woman on earth.

First came the headlines and announcements on radio and television, from Red Square to Times Square to Dalhousie Square.

MARILYN IS DEAD, they shrieked. Sometimes they said MM.

On that first morning, a Sunday in America, the news was shock enough. Not only in America, but the world over, MM

[4]

was a symbol of modern woman; she occupied a place in the hearts of men matched only in modern times by Charlie Chaplin, whose woeful little Charlie or Charlot had also captured the people of the world. Marilyn knew the extent of her popularity and position, as did a handful of others in the amusement business. One of her cherished ambitions was someday to make a movie with Charlie Chaplin. From time to time she talked about it, and the idea never failed to bring a smile of anticipation and satisfaction to Marilyn's face.

On this Sunday the shock traveled around the world. With it came the insatiable hunger of the world press for details, and the tragedy deepened into mystery, mystery that was perhaps unavoidable given the circumstances of Marilyn's life.

There is no glamour in death, and when it comes suddenly in an American metropolis, there is no privacy or dignity in death either. Within a few hours after the news was known, prying eyes were spying out the most intimate details of Marilyn's life and habits. But in this case it was as though a camera had invaded a private home to spy on the people there —only to find them gone. For without Marilyn the details were so much dross. There was no one to direct the flow of information in an orderly fashion, and the reportorial search for facts and motivations deteriorated into mystery, confusion, and maudlin speculation.

The mystery of Marilyn Monroe's death began late on the afternoon of August 4. It was a pleasant Saturday afternoon, and Marilyn had been sunbathing on the grounds of her house with Patricia Newcomb, who handled her personal publicity. Pat Newcomb was trying to cure a case of bronchitis, and Marilyn had invited her for a day in the sun around the swimming pool. Marilyn's was a handsome house, but by Hollywood standards it was not grand or even very expensive. It was a middle-income house for the area, the kind that a writer might own, or a doctor, or a successful salesman. The theme was Spanish-American, low and cool. The house was set back from Fifth Helena Drive in Brentwood, not far below Sunset Boulevard. The area was most respectable, but not in the height of fashion. Fashion dictated that film idols maintain houses along the gentle curves of the wide avenues of Beverly Hills, where mansions stand jammed side by side among the palm trees like so many development houses; or that the movie greats buy huge estates that sit in solitude on the sides of the mountains overlooking the city; or that they disdain California altogether and move to Spanish *fincas* or Irish castles.

Marilyn did none of those things. If she did not have the money to live splendidly, she could have borrowed the money. In past years she had done so, living in the best hotels or renting mansions in Beverly Hills. But in 1962 Marilyn was settling down, beginning to accept a new role in her life and planning for the future—rather than living every day as a surprise gift that must be spent lavishly. Marilyn had bought this house a few months before for $77,500, using some cash, but assuming a mortgage for about half the value. Hers was not an unusual purchase among Hollywood personalities, even those with the highest earning power, for while money talk is common in Hollywood, large sums of cash are more elusive, and financial commitments are always heavy for those in the charmed circle. Marilyn was far from penniless—broke but potentially solvent—and she would remain thus as long as she retained her earning capacity. On that day, August 4, she had been offered a starring role in a projected Broadway musical (which never was produced), and not long before she had rejected a Las Vegas night club's offer for an engagement at fifty-five thousand dollars per week. A huge figure? Yes, *but*. The "but" came when an agent's ten per cent commission was extracted off the top, and the "star" began to buy wardrobe, to pay for travel, to hire servants, and to pay for the personal services that maintained the glamour of stardom. Marilyn paid seventy to one hundred dollars to her hairdressers to arrange her hair. She paid one hundred to two hundred dollars to her makeup man. These were not exorbitant charges in the film industry, but they did tend to carve large chunks from a flat weekly paycheck. Add the costs of maintenance at Las Vegas, the costs of her personal publicity service, the cost of federal and state income taxes, and the infrequency with which such an engagement might be repeated. To go to Las Vegas, Marilyn would have to transport her secretary, her press agent, hairdresser, makeup man, acting coach, and personal maid. She might dispense with the personal maid at home in Los Angeles. The hairdresser, in his own bailiwick, could be available on call. Secretary and press agent lived at home. The acting coach came from New York—at Marilyn's expense—when necessary. But in Las Vegas they would all be on expenses all day long, and the expenses were Marilyn's. That cost, of course, does not include her personal expenditures. To play Las Vegas she would need an entire new professional wardrobe. She had just purchased an evening gown of white sequins from her favorite Hollywood designer, Jean Louis, for sixteen hundred dollars, and it had been fitted to her that very day at home. One would have to multiply this figure at least ten times over to ascertain the cost of wardrobe for a Marilyn Monroe production.

A production is what it would be, and thus it must be regarded. For a Las Vegas appearance would conjure forth the fabricated Marilyn Monroe, the composite image created by a combination of endless publicity and careful acting on the part of the woman who was the nucleus of the creature. The private Marilyn Monroe did not need a maid to do her nails or a hairdresser to do her hair or a body-makeup man to embellish face and form. She did not require or want a large or expensive wardrobe; she was happy enough in a pair of blue jeans and a cotton shirt and sandals. At that moment of her death, Marilyn was badly in need of a manicure and pedicure. When she remained at home, she limited herself to about a hundred dollars a month for spending money and was quite

[7]

happy with so small an amount. Her household expenses were meager by Hollywood standards. In the month preceding this last day she had spent just over two hundred dollars for wines, liquors, and cocktail snacks. When she drank, she preferred champagne, although at the end she was also drinking vodka.

For a number of years the gowns Marilyn wore at public appearances were created for that purpose only or were borrowed from the studio. So were the shoes and accessories. So were the limousines. And so, often, were the escorts.

A solo performance at a Las Vegas night club would mean that Marilyn, and she alone, would be the center of attraction for long minutes; a crowded hundred faces would be staring whitely at her, and a broken strap or a dropped line might mean instant, searing laughter at, and not with, her. At Marilyn's most courageous, unworried by emotional problems, she would cringe at the prospect. In the summer of 1962, bedeviled by insecurity and sleeplessness, drugged often with liquor and sleeping pills, it was small wonder to any who knew her that Marilyn Monroe would reject what was apparently, but only apparently, so advantageous an offer.

They talked about this offer and other matters, she and Pat Newcomb. The relationship between them was not exactly that of employer-employee, not exactly that of equal friends. Pat Newcomb worked for the Arthur Jacobs Public Relations Agency, and she was assigned by that agency to Marilyn. The employer-employee relationship, then, was once-removed. There were other reasons for something like friendship to develop. Pat Newcomb was younger, in her early thirties, attractive, and far better educated and polished than Marilyn. These factors helped bridge gaps. Pat Newcomb could also be tough with the press and interlopers. One might say she could "play the heavy" when it was necessary to protect Marilyn. The star appreciated protection, for she was very nearly defenseless if caught unawares.

And yet most of the conversations between Marilyn and

[8]

Pat Newcomb in some way mirrored Marilyn's business affairs. It was Pat Newcomb's job to set up appointments for photographers who wanted to take publicity pictures. Pat Newcomb made the arrangements for interviews, as one a few weeks before with *Life's* Richard Meryman.

Pat had come to the house on Friday evening. She and Marilyn had gone for dinner to a small restaurant a few blocks from the house and had spent a quiet leisurely evening. It was not unusual for Marilyn to eat in a restaurant. She kept little food in the house, and she was never very conscious of food, then or before. Her meals were irregular. Her housekeeper did not normally stay overnight. On Saturday, Pat Newcomb and Marilyn spent most of the day near the swimming pool, working and relaxing in the sun. The talked of a pleasant future.

Marilyn had been involved in a serious dispute with Twentieth Century Fox Film Corporation, concerning an unfinished movie. The movie had been suspended and the film company had begun suit against her for three quarters of a million dollars for breach of contract. But that action was taken two months before, and in August it was apparent the picture could not proceed without Marilyn. There were plans for an amicable settlement which would bring her back to the production lot, for Spyros Skouras, head of Twentieth Century Fox, had intervened to stop the quarreling. Two other film producers were seeking Marilyn's services or co-operation. Several magazines were negotiating for articles and picture spreads on Marilyn. There was no question about her status as the reigning Hollywood glamour queen, and the magazines, as a group, knew they were not wrong about that. They created the image. They maintained it. With particular devotion they clung to Marilyn, defending her position against all comers. The Kim Novaks and Jayne Mansfields and Brigitte Bardots were waiting in the wings, but they were still in the wings. Marilyn was not ready to yield the stage.

[9]

Marilyn was thirty-six years old that August, thirty-six years, two months, and three days old. She had never been more attractive. Always she had a tendency to put on weight, particularly on hips, belly, and the chest; when she weighed more than she should Marilyn looked pasty and overripe—strange because her face remained slender while her body grew heavy. The camera tended to hide such liabilities if the shooting angles were correct, and so producers and directors had liked Marilyn a little fatter than she liked herself. At one time, when Marilyn was working under her first seven-year contract for Twentieth Century Fox, she was reducing under a doctor's care, on her own volition, when the studio telephoned the doctor and complained that he was leading Marilyn straight to ruin. So Marilyn often appeared in films carrying twenty pounds more than the doctor ordered.

But not now, not in the summer of 1962. She had gone to the studio for costume design and other testing at the weight she liked and had proved herself more beautiful and more glamorous than before. Her girlishness was unlined. She "came through" as they said in Hollywood. She weighed 117 pounds and she stood five feet five and a half inches tall in her stocking feet.

She was healthy and relatively happy. She had suffered from gallstones and had gone to the hospital thirteen months earlier to have her gallbladder removed. She avoided most fatty foods thereafter. She had always preferred lean beef anyhow, when she thought about food. And this might not be for many hours at a time, depending on her mood.

Among the items of conversation in the Monroe household that day was the coming of some of the furniture that Marilyn had bought in Mexico. Earlier in the summer she and her housekeeper, Mrs. Eunice Murray, and Pat Newcomb had travelled to Mexico on a furniture-buying trip. In Mexico City the press had nearly mobbed Marilyn and she had staged a press conference that was jammed with reporters and photographers.

Marilyn and Mrs. Murray had gone off poking around for furniture and Pat Newcomb had remained in Mexico City. Then they had all come home. It was not to be long before all the new furniture would be delivered and the house would lose its half-deserted look. The furniture leaned to heavy mission-style chests and carvings; it was tasteful and attractive and above all, comfortable. Marilyn was slowly assembling the household belongings that she wanted for herself, accepting the fact that she had no one else to please.

As evening came on, Pat Newcomb packed her overnight case and prepared to go home to her apartment in Beverly Hills. She was to return to the house the next day. When they parted Marilyn remarked that she would see Pat Newcomb on Sunday. They planned to attend a movie.

Pat left because she understood that Marilyn's psychiatrist was coming to the house to pay a professional call. Marilyn had been consulting psychiatrists off and on for about eight years. The current one was Dr. Ralph Greenson of Beverly Hills, and, since the latest trouble with Twentieth Century Fox, Marilyn had been leaning heavily on him. Marilyn saw Dr. Greenson nearly every day and had done so since the first of July. She was not sleeping well. She was addicted to sleeping pills, but she knew the addiction was harmful, and she was doing her best to break the habit. She had not been very successful in this effort; she required the frequent attentions of Dr. Greenson, and much attention from her general physician, Dr. Hyman Engelberg.

On this August evening Dr. Greenson either came or telephoned. (No one seemed quite sure which.) Marilyn decided to go to bed early and, apparently, without dinner. (That was not unusual for her.) At around seven o'clock she received a telephone call from Peter Lawford, the actor, who invited her to the Lawford house in Santa Monica for dinner. She declined. She told Lawford that she wanted to get to bed early. The casual invitation was not unusual either because Marilyn was on intimate terms with the Lawfords. They were part of the Rat Pack, begun by Humphrey Bogart and perpetuated by Frank Sinatra. They had introduced her to the Robert Kennedys and had in a way been responsible for one of the events that Marilyn felt to be a high point in her career—her appearance at the Madison Square Garden rally for President John F. Kennedy on his birthday on May 29.

A little later Marilyn talked by telephone with Joe DiMaggio, Jr., the son of one of her former husbands. She was very fond of young DiMaggio, as she was fond of all the children of the families into which she had made her way, or of nearly all the people she met who would accept her for herself and were not concerned with what she could do for them or what they could get from her. She found that small children, in their innocence, did not go far beyond personalities, and so Marilyn was always at home with children, when she might be frightened or made miserable by their parents. Joe DiMaggio, Jr., was no longer a small child, but a grown man in the Marine Corps at Camp Pendleton. After the divorce of more than half a dozen years before, she had continued to keep in touch with the youngster.

Marilyn was asleep when young DiMaggio's call came through, and Mrs. Murray answered the telephone. The housekeeper woke Marilyn and asked her if she wanted to talk with the boy. Marilyn said she did and then carried her telephone on its long cord into a bedroom across the hall from her room. Later she wandered back with the telephone still in hand and completed the call in her own bedroom.

That is all that witnesses saw of Marilyn's last day, but other facts about her last hours came to light later. Mrs. Murray did not always stay at the house. Her presence there on this night indicated that Marilyn was disturbed and that Dr. Greenson, Mrs. Murray's sponsor, knew that Marilyn was disturbed.

Marilyn took sleeping pills at some time during the evening. Perhaps she had taken them and they had begun to affect her when Peter Lawford called. Lawford said she refused the invitation because she was tired, and that her voice sounded tired on the telephone.

At some time during the early part of the night perhaps there was another telephone call, or perhaps Marilyn made a call, or tried to. One or the other event certainly occurred. At some time, apparently, Marilyn took more sleeping pills, and the combination began to build up.

Midnight came. Mrs. Murray saw a light under Marilyn's door. This was unusual but not alarming. Just after three o'clock in the morning Mrs. Murray awoke and saw that the light was still burning. She tried the door to the room and discovered that the door was locked. She knocked. There was no answer. She walked outside onto the terrace and approached Marilyn's bedroom from the French windows that opened onto the terrace. They, too, were locked. She saw Marilyn lying on her stomach. Marilyn did not respond to Mrs. Murray's rapping on the glass. Mrs. Murray saw then that Marilyn was clutching the telephone receiver in her hand, lying motionless, and the housekeeper became worried.

Mrs. Murray telephoned Dr. Greenson. Dr. Greenson said he was coming to the house. He also told Mrs. Murray to call Dr. Engelberg. She did.

At 3:40 in the morning Dr. Greenson arrived, broke the French window with a fireplace poker and gained admission to Marilyn's room. He found her cold and lifeless. Ten minutes later Dr. Engelberg arrived. At 4:25 in the morning the police were called. An hour later the coroner's office was notified. At 7:45 A.M. the black death wagon was dispatched by the coroner's office. The body of Marilyn Monroe was bundled onto a narrow tubular stretcher, wrapped securely in a blue blanket, and the stretcher was taken to the Los Angeles County Morgue, where the body would be chopped and sliced and examined. Marilyn had become Los Angeles County Coroner's Case No. 81128.

Between the time of discovery of the body and that dispatch into impersonal official hands, the affairs of Marilyn Monroe disintegrated. She had no one to protect her. Those who might wish to protect Marilyn were either unavailable or were denied the power. Those concerned were either doing a routine job or were more interested in protecting themselves. It was all quite natural. Marilyn was dead but life continued.

The monster that destroyed the illusion of one Marilyn Monroe was the press. The press need not have been a monster; the newspaper men and women and photographers were doing what they knew quite well how to do. These professionals were used to working with other professionals in this job of publicity. They expected certain perquisites and favors as their due; they also expected to be denied certain other favors and requests. Among the newspaper and magazine representatives were scandal-mongers and shady characters, but among them also were respectable and respected reporters, writers, and photographers.

From the beginning, at three o'clock in the morning, it was apparent that no one person was really in charge, to bring about an orderly public end to the career of Marilyn Monroe.

Two doctors were involved. The psychiatrist said he had been treating Marilyn to help her overcome her sleeplessness. The general practitioner said he had been prescribing medication for Marilyn. It is apparent that knowledge of Marilyn's motivation in terms explainable to the press and the public required disclosure of more intimate medical details. These were never made available. The doctors took refuge behind professional ethics and declined to discuss her affairs more than necessary for the conduct of administrative justice.

There was some delay between the times of arrival of the two doctors at the Fifth Helena house and the telephone call that had to be made to the police department. The call was not made for an hour. At 4:25 in the morning Dr. Engelberg called Los Angeles Police Headquarters to report the death. His call was transferred to the West Los Angeles division, and police officers were dispatched. The press, of course, was then alerted, and it became obvious that a number of police would have to be sent to the scene to preserve order.

When the police arrived, they took the charitable position that Marilyn had accidentally taken an overdose of sleeping tablets. But when the coroner's officers arrived and interviewed Dr. Greenson, he indicated that Marilyn had been very depressed on the previous evening. The coroner's men suggested that she had committed suicide.

The press did not understand any of these and other vagaries, and no one seemed to be very much interested in bringing light to the reporters. When Pat Newcomb arrived, she was denied access to the house. Mortuary and coroner's officers had followed a Los Angeles practice in case of sudden death and had sealed all entrances to the residence.

The secrecy, expected by students of sudden death in Hollywood, created difficulties for the photographers and reporters. Pat Newcomb was upset, and in the course of the morning she lost her temper in the face of questions, which made matters no better.

Had Pat Newcomb or anyone else been permitted to answer questions and deal with the press in a sane fashion, the death of Marilyn Monroe might have been explained. As it was, the reporters left the scene feeling that more had been concealed about Marilyn's passing than had been revealed.

For one thing, how had Mrs. Murray telephoned to Dr. Greenson if Marilyn lay on her bed, face down, beneath a champagne-colored blanket, with the telephone receiver clutched in her hand? The telephone obviously was inoperative if a receiver of any extension was off the hook. (Why was it not revealed that there were *two* telephone lines into the house, a private line and a private-private line?)

To whom had Marilyn been trying to telephone, if at all? The reporters asked police, coroner's men, the doctors, Miss Newcomb, and Milton Rudin, Marilyn's lawyer, when he arrived. No one answered the question. Some reporters suspected that someone must have confiscated a piece of paper on which a tell-tale telephone number was written in Marilyn's hand. Some reporters came to the conclusion that Marilyn had called for help, as she had done on other occasions when she had taken overdoses of sleeping tablets. If so, this time, however, the call went unanswered. No one ever convinced them to the contrary.

Who was Mrs. Murray? It was known that Dr. Greenson had brought her into Marilyn's life, and Mrs. Murray said that she had more than a housekeeper's freedom in the house. Forever, reporters had looked for Svengalis in Marilyn's career. In the more popular press that hint was duly registered.

How did Dr. Engelberg call the police? No toll calls were made from Marilyn's house and Marilyn's West Los Angeles number was a toll call to downtown Los Angeles. (The second telephone again.)

The telephone was the most significant part of the mystery, and around it grew the evil roots of conjecture. Something was being concealed—much was being concealed. Why? No one stopped to reason that concealment flowed from carelessness, administrative procedures, the ethics of the professional men involved, and the very important matter that there was no one close enough to Marilyn to take charge of her affairs, even at this belated hour.

In the evil way that gossip spreads, some of the newspapermen began to embroider a story which would fill the holes. They decided that Marilyn had been trying to call a very dear friend. Some settled on Robert Kennedy, Attorney General of the United States of America.

[16]

Why Robert Kennedy? Because Marilyn had recently come to know the Robert Kennedys and had been seen with them. Much was made of the friendship of Marilyn for Peter and Patricia Lawford, since Mrs. Lawford was the sister of Attorney General Robert Kennedy and of President John F. Kennedy.

Such a solution to the tragedy of Marilyn Monroe appealed to the political enemies of the Kennedys and to the sense of drama of many others in America. It was not long before that rumor spread across Los Angeles, permeating every cranny of the motion picture colony and beyond. For in Hollywood nothing can be allowed to be simple if it can be made complex. It was not the kind of tale that the victims could deny. All the Kennedys could do was ignore it.

But on August 5, 1962, the rumors were only beginning. The troublesome matter to the officials of the city and county of Los Angeles was the different interpretation put on Marilyn's death by two of the city's official departments. This situation was one that officialdom could not abide and so it was decided that an inquest would be held, a post-mortem investigation to determine the cause of Marilyn's death. Physically, there was very little doubt about the cause except in the minds of the suspicious who had a great amount of imagination and practically no information. Marilyn died from an overdose of narcotics. The inquisitors, a distinguished panel of medical men, decided that Marilyn had died from an overdose of barbiturates, and they presumed to call her death a suicide.

When this information was duly printed across the world, and when an account appeared in *Time* magazine, a physician in Canon City, Colorado, wrote a letter to that magazine which raised a vital point known to doctors who deal with habitual users of sleeping potions.

"In nearly a third of a century of practice," wrote Dr. H. Paul Johnson, "I have seen patients in a semi-stuporous condition after the first dose repeat it one or several times, with no self-destructive intent because they were not fully conscious."

Hollywood knew how to illustrate that story: not long before Marilyn's death, officials at the Metro-Goldwyn-Mayer studio received an anguished call from one of the performing artists who were working at the studio. He had taken a dose of sleeping tablets, he said. He had been waked up by the telephone not long before, and without thinking, he had taken another dose of sleeping pills. He had just realized it, and now he was calling for help. Would the studio send a doctor immediately? The studio did so, but by the time the doctor arrived, the victim of the overdose of sleeping pills was comatose. He never recovered consciousness.

So the story and the possibilities were well known in Hollywood, and there the questions of Marilyn's death brought the numb reaction from among her peers that indicated they knew it could happen to any one of them.

Accident or suicide? The only certain knowledge was the death of Marilyn Monroe.

As the initial shock wore off and officials and professional men refused further information, the newspapers and wire services found interest but no story. No responsible newspaper could afford to print the rumors that were circulating about Hollywood. No reporter could prove any of those rumors to be founded on fact.

For a day or so the story of Marilyn's life succeeded that of her death. At the funeral the strongest character of Marilyn's life stepped back into it, if too late to help her. There was no one else to take over, so Joe DiMaggio took over. He shocked the Hollywood community, which he had grown to despise, by barring all Hollywood from the funeral. Hollywood had expected a huge orgy of grief and was willing—eager—to show how much everyone in the film colony loved, adored, and worshipped Marilyn Monroe. But only thirty-one mourners were allowed to attend the funeral, and not one of these represented the film world, except the personal staff that Marilyn had gathered around her.

The news, the shock, evaporated quickly enough and the story disappeared from the front pages. But the story could not be finished until the moralizers had their say. The moralizers were the editorialists who had succeeded the ministerial alliance as spiritual leaders of a largely unchurched world.

With all her faults she grossed forty-three million dollars for "the manipulators," wrote Lincoln Kirstein in the *Nation*. (The figure was far larger than that.)

No one forced Marilyn to go to Hollywood. Hollywood did well by her and she did well by Hollywood, said the *National Review*.

Marilyn was accountable for her own life and her over-dose of sleeping pills, sniffed the *Christian Century*, "but Hollywood and Americans who live everywhere else were and are also accountable before God for the elevation and eventual destruction of this woman."

In life and death Marilyn was made to order for the moralizers. They did not disappoint their audiences. The fingers pointed and the alarums were sounded all across the world, and then there was silence; but it was not the silence of forgetfulness, it was the silence of plain people who did not moralize, who accepted, watched the world go by, and remembered. They remembered Marilyn Monroe. Marilyn's personal star was sunk in the pavement of Hollywood Boulevard's sidewalk, on the south side of the street, east of Highland Avenue, between the stars of Edward Arnold and Ginger Rogers. Her name appeared on the side of a star-studded office building a few blocks away on Sunset Boulevard. A year after her death and two years after death, the anniversary was recalled by writers for press agencies. Two years after death her likeness was used by the promoters of the Hollywood wax museum to advertise their wares on Los Angeles streets; Clare Boothe Luce chose this second anniversary to write an article for *Life*, explaining Marilyn.

Dead, Marilyn was still the reigning queen of Hollywood. The vacuum was unfilled. *Time*, in examining the newer crop of female actresses in the cinema world, indicated that the Marilyn Monroe type was passé. That is true in the sense that Marilyn was not replaced, but every studio in Hollywood was looking, and some, such as Twentieth Century Fox, were looking at high school girls still too young to come under contract—physical stand-ins for Marilyn Monroe.

Marilyn was not replaced, and she would not be.

Why should the world remember such a woman, when Elizabeth Taylor was yet on the scene, when a score of younger motion picture personalities were waiting to step into the tight bodice of her deserted gown?

Was Marilyn Monroe the victim of "ballyhoo and sensation," as Sir Laurence Olivier remarked bitterly on hearing of her death?

Was Hedda Hopper right when she said, "In a way we are all guilty. We built her up to the skies, we loved her, but left her lonely and afraid when she needed us most"?

Was she the sacrificial lamb destroyed on the altar of capitalism, as *Izvestia* trumpeted from Moscow?

Was she an ambitious, designing female, struggling to the top by any means available, and then taking the quick way out when she found herself aging and alone, as Clare Boothe Luce indicated so sardonically?

Was she the creature of her times, the image of Everywoman and what she might become, given her fill of the heady brews of success in twentieth-century America?

Or was hers a unique story that could never be duplicated in America or elsewhere?

Chapter Two

WHO was the woman who became Marilyn Monroe, and were did she come from? To say that the girl was named Norma Jean Baker means nothing at all. To say that she was born and brought up in Los Angeles in the lower middle class and that she was born into the motion picture business says something rather more, but still does not tell much about the woman.

The story of Marilyn Monroe, movie actress, did not begin with her birth or her childhood or at any time prior to the summer of 1945—although her past was to haunt her later. The story began one day in June, 1945, when the young woman walked into the office of Emmaline Snively of the Blue Book Models Agency.

At that time Miss Snively kept her offices at an impressive address—the Ambassador Hotel on Wilshire Boulevard. The Ambassador was one of *the* hotels. The film capital had not yet spread so far south and west as to put the Ambassador out of bounds, and such institutions as the Beverly Hilton Hotel and its complex of stores and offices were not yet built. For a model agency in Hollywood the Ambassador was, in 1945, a very good address in an area where such things counted high with the young clients who paid the fees to learn, and with the business clients who paid the fees to employ the girls once they had learned what Miss Snively had to teach them.

Miss Snively was a bouncy little woman in her forties who knew her way about in the mazes of the motion picture and modelling businesses. There were a number of ways in which young women could make money by modelling. One, which held no interest at all for Marilyn and for which she was then totally unsuited, was high fashion. Miss Snively provided high fashion models for salons and photographers and clothing concerns. She also provided product models, and for this kind of work the face and figure of the girl who would be Marilyn Monroe were well suited. She weighed 118 pounds, she was nineteen years old, and her measurements were thirty-six inches around the bust, twenty-four at the waist, and thirty-four at the hips. She was a slightly top-heavy size twelve.

On the sunny June day when Marilyn appeared at the Ambassador, Miss Snively saw a girl wearing a white shark-skin dress with a green-and-orange yoke. She had obviously washed it carefully, ironed it skillfully, and had cleaned her white shoes. Miss Snively did not know it then, but there was the entire wardrobe for modelling purposes of her latest applicant.

Emmaline Snively looked the girl over carefully. The figure was excellent. The legs were good, although she was not long-legged or the "leggy" type. The hair was of a shade which in Hollywood is euphemistically termed California blonde—not blonde at all but slightly sunbleached brunette. On the other hand, the girl's hair was too curly, too long and had a vaguely untidy look.

Miss Snively asked her applicant to walk slowly across the room. The girl, who would develop the most famous walk in the world, did so and wobbled on her high heels. Miss Snively asked the girl to stand. The girl whose open-legged stance would become a trademark did so—her knees locked, throwing

[22]

her pelvis back and her chest forward in the gesture that was natural and typical and was to become known to millions of movie-goers. Yet it was a pose less than graceful for a model.

Miss Snively saw that she had here a diamond in the rough, but very rough. The girl who would be Marilyn had been recommended by a photographer who said she possessed some elusive but highly photogenic quality. She had a healthy look about her and a "nice girl" look. She was what Miss Snively automatically thought of as the "little girl" type, suitable for hair preparations, wrist watches, cultured pearls—anything where the advertiser or exhibitor would want to show off his product on the girl next door.

Miss Snively agreed to teach the art of modelling (she called it a science) to the girl who would be Marilyn Monroe. The Blue Book Models Agency fee for a three-month course was one hundred dollars. Marilyn did not have one hundred dollars but Miss Snively was more or less used to that among the young women who came to her, and she arranged to have Marilyn pay off the fee from money she would earn.

So the course began. Marilyn's first job was not one that required a model but one that required a pretty young girl. She was a hostess for one of the exhibitors at the 1945 home show in the Pan-Pacific auditorium. This paid Miss Snively's one hundred dollars, and from that time on the money the girl earned was to be her own. She earned about fifteen dollars an hour, when she worked.

It was apparent to all in Miss Snively's establishment that Marilyn was a very special type of model. She was sent out on a clothes job and failed completely, because she did not have the knack of showing off clothes. People looked at the girl, not the dress. She was sent out to do another job where she was to pose in a nightgown. The purpose was to advertise a new Douglas Aircraft Company airplane, the DC-4, with which sleeper service was inaugurated on American Airlines that year. She was very successful in this task, for she did just what the advertising agency wanted: she brought sex appeal to an airplane.

The girl who would be Marilyn was a very conscientious model. She worked hard at posing. She took home proofs of the pictures of herself when the photographers would give them up, and she studied them to see where she had been caught in an unflattering position.

As a model Marilyn faced several serious if solvable problems. The first of these was poverty. She had literally nothing in which to model except her white dress with the bi-colored yoke. This problem was solved, slowly, by borrowing and by saving to buy the sweaters and skirts and bathing suits that a model was supposed to supply for herself. She saved until she could afford something she really wanted and then bought it: a red satin dress with black lace ruffles. It was not exactly what a girl from finishing school would wear to a party, but it did just what the girl model wanted. It showed off her figure and white skin against the red satin.

Marilyn's mouth was not a classic mouth. Her lower teeth were badly in need of dental work but she could not afford to have it done, and so nothing was said about it. The problem, however, was that when she smiled her lower teeth showed. When she relaxed her jaw, her mouth came open in the shape of an O, which gave her a look of incredulity, admiration, or stupidity, depending on the eye of the viewer.

This look, which stayed in Miss Snively's memory, was to become an important Marilyn Monroe property, but at the time it was not regarded as an asset.

Miss Snively's agency featured blonde girls. Blonde girls were preferred by the advertising agencies and photographers and movie studios and so all the girls who came to Miss Snively, except the obvious Spanish types, were advised to bleach. Marilyn did not want to bleach her hair. She was advised to have it straightened. She would not do that, either.

So Miss Snively shrugged and did the best she could for her recalcitrant model.

By the autumn of 1945 the girl who would be Marilyn was an accomplished photographer's model. She said she wanted to go into the movies and always had wanted to do so, but how many girls who modeled for Miss Snively did not? Every one of them, naturally enough, had the same ambition: to be "discovered" and to soar to stardom.

But a job in the movies—a screen test and contract—was more easily won by a beauty contest winner in Sioux City than by a photographer's model in Los Angeles. The way that any girl could win a screen test was to make herself noticed, and to make herself noticed she should win some kind of beauty contest. There was another way, which involved sleeping with someone in the motion picture industry. But this was not as easy as it sounded, because, even if it was the path a girl might choose, it meant meeting someone with influence, which was not simple, and any girl who came to a studio under such auspices was usually so labelled immediately and almost always dropped quickly into oblivion if her protector left the studio or lost interest in her.

The girl who would be Marilyn was not put to this particular test. She was not a prude or a sexual child. She was a married woman whose husband was overseas and who was only beginning to learn that his marriage ended on the day that the girl applied to Miss Snively for help and training. She did not know anyone of any importance. A handful of struggling photographers, the businessmen she met on her jobs, and the people who hired models comprised her acquaintances in the Hollywood area of Los Angeles. One of her dreams was to win a particular beauty contest and become Miss Western Fashion. Twice a year she entered this beauty contest. Twice a year she was eliminated in the early rounds. She had a pleasant little face and a good figure but so did a thousand

[25]

other girls. She was just Norma Jean Dougherty, née Baker, or Mortenson, and that was next to nothing at all.

The harsh goad of economic necessity created the second major change in this girl's life—the first change being the realization that in her looks she had a saleable commodity, the realization that brought her to Miss Snively's establishment. What Emmaline Snively could not accomplish with persuasion, a photographer named Raphael Wolff accomplished with a single short conversation. He offered Marilyn a job modelling for a series of advertisements for Lustre-Creme shampoo, if—but only if—she would bleach her hair. The amount of money was not large, perhaps sixty or a hundred dollars, less Miss Snively's percentage, but it was large enough to tempt a young model. She bleached. Not only that, she went the whole way. She was sent to Frank and Joseph, the Hollywood hair stylists (undoubtedly at Lustre-Creme's expense) and she was given the full treatment. Her hair was cut short, it was de-curled and then bleached a golden blonde. She then posed for the Lustre-Creme shampoo series of advertising photographs, the most notable of which shows a radiant blonde Marilyn nuzzling up to a boy with a proprietary air.

As the girl who would be Marilyn progressed in the modelling business, Miss Snively began to learn more about her, and when she became a dazzling blonde, Miss Snively evinced more interest than she had shown earlier. The girl was a hard worker. She had an unusual power of concentration for a pretty girl and a curiosity about the world that Miss Snively found engaging and revealing.

This girl, this Norma Jean, knew practically nothing about the world around her when she came to Blue Book Models. Perhaps that ignorance was responsible for the little-girl look that Emmaline Snively noticed on the first day. She had her troubles, including the measles, when she was beginning her work as a full-fledged model. But she persisted, and before the end of the year she was much in demand as a model for the girl pictures that photographers have glorified as "cheesecake." It had become apparent to her very quickly that sex was the key to her future. Once having abandoned her natural appearance as a brunette, she threw herself into the new role as a blonde.

She was living with her guardian at this time, Mrs. Grace Goddard, who was a friend of her mother. For a time the Goddards lived in Van Nuys, but during the period when Marilyn was modelling they moved to Santa Monica. Marilyn's mother had been confined to an institution for mental illness for some time, but in 1945 she was released and the two took up residence together. Sometime in 1946, however, Gladys Baker met a man who appealed to her and she left again. Marilyn then moved in with Mrs. Goddard again.

Alone or with others, she had really been living alone for a number of years, and she accepted loneliness as her normal way of life. Nor was she any lonelier than she wished to be, because, as she continued to model, she found many men who were eager for her company, day and night. She told stories of some of these men to Maurice Zolotow who recounted them in a series of magazine articles that were later published as a book. One was the story of the "talent scout," a tale so common as to be suspect as apocryphal. A man who claimed to be a talent scout for Metro-Goldwyn-Mayer pictures telephoned Marilyn one evening. He said MGM was casting for a musical and that he had heard much about her. He wanted to give her a screen test—that very evening.

Marilyn agreed. She was picked up by the stranger in a Cadillac and driven to the MGM studio in Culver City. There the talent scout took her into an office, handed her a script, and began in a few moments to make advances to her. She slapped him, she said, then kicked him in the shins, and ran out of the building.

Another story Marilyn told later involved a man who knew an old millionaire who wanted to marry her. He had high blood pressure and two million dollars. The promoter suggested that Marilyn marry the man, inherit, and split the fortune with him.

Far more prosaic (and probably true) was a story told by André de Dienes, a Hollywood photographer. He told the story to a reporter after Marilyn's death. In 1945, when Marilyn was nineteen years old, he said, she came one day to his apartment at Hollywood's Garden of Allah. She had been sent there by Emmaline Snively to model for some photographs and arrived wearing a pink sweater and checked slacks.

Photographs led to conversation and the conversation to an affair. Although Marilyn was married, she confessed that she did not love her husband. Perhaps she never had loved him. The marriage had been one of convenience for the lower-middle-class people who were responsible for Marilyn's conduct, and it had been arranged with all the care shown by a Yiddish marriage broker, but with less regard for the wishes of the girl. The marriage was arranged because Marilyn's guardian saw that it was time. The strict moral code of the middle class demanded close supervision of the girl until marriage. If supervision was inconvenient, as it was in Marilyn's case, then an early marriage was the solution. Marilyn had married when she was sixteen and James Dougherty was twenty-one. The principal reason for the marriage, she said later, had been to get her out of the way because the Goddards were moving. Once married, Marilyn was a dutiful wife, but when Dougherty left to go into the merchant marine, and she moved out of the world of middle-class morality into Hollywood, she had no qualms about seeing other men.

De Dienes and Marilyn decided they were in love. They went north on a tour of the West Coast for a month together, a trip that was to be a combination of business and pleasure. De Dienes said he was astonished at Marilyn's resilience and her willingness to work. She was always on time, always ready to take photographs, and usually she was ready earlier than he. And yet he found her frail in an odd way. As soon as she was finished with the model's task, she would curl up in the front seat of the car and fall asleep.

De Dienes wanted to marry her, he said, but he was called to the East Coast, and when he returned to Hollywood five or six months later, he discovered that she was involved with somebody else and was living in West Los Angeles.

Considering Marilyn's background, it might seem remarkable that she was involved with only one man at a time, but that was her pattern. She fell in love easily. She fell out hard.

The Marilyn who came to Miss Snively in 1945 learned a great deal about men and Hollywood. Attractive young women were the prey of various men in the motion picture industry then as they were to become later the prey of men in the television business. Emmaline Snively was not surprised at any story Marilyn did tell her or could have told about her experiences. In her years as model agency director she had heard hundreds of horror stories and had done what she could to protect the girls who worked for her.

But Marilyn did not prosper in this period as she might have if she had begun to peddle sex as a personal commodity. She did not wish to do so. It was understandable, because Marilyn, the real woman, was not a sexy creature. The still photographers who worked with her noticed this, just as others in Hollywood were to notice it later. The girl was able to turn sexiness on and off at will. Offstage, when she was not concentrating on playing the role of sexpot, she appeared almost aseptic to some. But facing a camera or an audience she wished to impress, she could become what one photographer called "a sex machine." The allure, the charm, the appeal, were turned on and off at will. In this sense, Marilyn possessed an excellent acting presence before she possessed her name.

[29]

She knew what appealed to men. She learned quickly from her photographer friends.

In 1945 and 1946 the call in Hollywood was heavy for photographs of attractive young women in bathing suits or other undress. This market was the photographic market in which Marilyn's wares were most appreciated. During the war and particularly just after it ended, what were called the "girlie" magazines flourished. Sometimes they carried articles or stories, but they depended for sales and readership on pictures of undressed girls. Marilyn, in 1946, was a cover-girl of a sort. Her picture appeared in next-to-nothing-at-all on the covers of several of these magazines. She was paid for the photos, although not very highly. But more important than pay was the attention these pictures brought her. Miss Snively began to believe that Marilyn might be one who could be helped into the world of motion pictures.

Emmaline Snively was a woman of resource. Having decided that the girl who would be Marilyn had what it took to crash Hollywood's doors, she set out to bring Marilyn to the attention of the movie-makers. When possible, she assisted Marilyn in getting modelling assignments where her picture would be widely displayed. She pushed Marilyn above others.

This was not altogether unselfish. Miss Snively had the reputation of her school as well as her agency in mind. The more girls she could place with studios, the more prestige her Blue Book Models school would gain in a fiercely competitive market. Further, Miss Snively had arrangements with several Hollywood agents. She would receive a fee or a percentage for anyone she sent to the agent, after money changed hands.

There was very little to be gained by calling agents without a reason. There was nothing to be gained by telephoning the casting director of a studio, or by appearing at the studio unannounced. The best Marilyn could hope for, thus, was to become one of a sea of faces in the extra department.

No, something special was needed.

It was now the summer of 1946 and Marilyn had done well, although financially she was not very well off. She was still driving the dilapidated Ford convertible coupe that had been hers and Jim Dougherty's before he went to sea. (It would soon be hers alone, for she was seeking a divorce from Dougherty.) Her wardrobe was not a great deal more extensive than it had been the year before, but she had added sweaters and a number of bathing costumes.

When her photograph appeared on the covers of two of the men's magazines simultaneously, Miss Snively decided the time had come for action. But what action?

Leafing through the newspapers, Miss Snively came upon a report about Howard Hughes, the owner of RKO-Radio Pictures. Hughes had been flying his private airplane over Beverly Hills one day, when he crashed on the green grass of the Hillcrest Country Club. His life was saved, but he was badly injured and was confined in a body cast to a bed in the Cedars of Lebanon Hospital, where his days were long and boring.

Miss Snively considered the sad condition of Mr. Hughes and was cheered. She had an idea. She wrote out a little tip for the gossip columnists and had it sent around to their various offices. Then she began to watch the newspapers with more than usual care.

It was not very long before Hedda Hopper reported in her column in the Los Angeles *Times* that Howard Hughes had been leafing through the girlie magazines on his hospital bed, and he had come across the face of a girl who seemed to him to have movie potential. He planned to give her a screen test. Her name? Norma Jean Dougherty.

Of course there was not a whit of truth in the story. Howard Hughes had never heard of anyone named Norma Jean Dougherty, and he did not make a practice of giving screen tests to unknowns, unless there was a good reason for it. Miss Snively smiled broadly, however, when she read the

Hedda Hopper column, and picked up the telephone. She called one of her agent acquaintances, Helen Ainsworth, and read the item to her. Perhaps, she said, Miss Ainsworth would be interested in representing this young girl with *other* motion picture production companies.

Miss Ainsworth telephoned to Ben Lyon, a talent scout at Twentieth Century Fox Film Corporation. The magic words "Howard Hughes is interested" produced their result. Lyon agreed to see Norma Jean Dougherty. He agreed to see her immediately, that very day, and an astonished, delighted young woman was whisked off to the Twentieth Century Fox Studio on Pico Boulevard in Beverly Hills and inside, past the careful guards who were so suspicious of attractive young women who appeared at their posts, along the hushed, heavily carpeted corridor, and into the office of Ben Lyon.

Lyon took a good look and apparently liked what he saw. He agreed to test her within two days. It would demand the approval of Darryl Zanuck, head of the Twentieth Century Fox Studios, and particularly so since Lyon wanted to test the girl in color.

Two days later Ben Lyon still did not have Darryl Zanuck's approval. Thus it was impossible for him to make a test of the usual variety. This would have called for a request to the central casting department to supply an actor or actress for a dramatic scene. It would have required Marilyn, who knew nothing about acting or motion pictures, to memorize a few lines and deliver them dramatically, in the small hushed voice that sometimes stuttered when she was under tension.

Possibly the failure of Ben Lyon to secure Darryl Zanuck's approval was the break Marilyn needed. She might well have failed an acting test. But Lyon wanted another kind of test; he wanted to see silent footage that would indicate this girl's ability to project a sex appeal he sensed.

The test was arranged for five-thirty one August morning on the set of the movie *Mother Wore Tights,* which starred

Twentieth Century Fox's leading female personality of the time: Betty Grable, the pin-up girl of World War II. Lyon found a tight-fitting, spangled evening gown in the wardrobe department and sneaked it out the day before without anyone noticing. Marilyn showed up at the studio early and dressed herself in the gown and spiked heels. She was very nervous and recalled that she stumbled over the tangle of cables as she approached the set. But once on set she recovered herself. The cameraman was ready. Lyon was ready, and Marilyn was as ready as she ever would be. She was to walk across the set, sit down, light a cigarette, extinguish it, and move around, then go offstage. She did so, and in a very few minutes the screen test was over.

The same day the print was ready. Lyon had it placed in with the rushes of the day's filming on the Fox lot. The verdict of the technicians was in already: they said that Marilyn had that luminescent quality that goes beyond what still photographers called "photogenic." In a two-dimensional medium she somehow appeared real and three-dimensional. Sometimes it was called "star quality." Sometimes it was called just "sex appeal." Sometimes it was called "oomph." One press agent tried out a handful of adjectives to describe the quality: alluring, incandescent, sizzling, alabaster, combustible, bonfire, sultry, pneumatic, curvaceous and pulchritudinous. All the terms seemed stale. Whatever the quality, it was the quality that all Hollywood producers are forever seeking in female players, the quality of projection of a personality and a presence.

Darryl Zanuck held an evening screening session on the Twentieth Century Fox lot at the end of nearly every day. He tried to see all the rushes of all the pictures that were being filmed on the lot. On this day he saw the rushes and, in the midst of them, the silent screen test of this young blonde girl. He recognized the ephemeral quality—or it was said that he did—and, although he had not authorized the screen test, it was said that he was executive enough not to complain about the violation of orders. He told Lyon to sign the girl to a contract.

The contract was drawn just before the end of August and was sent home to Grace Goddard for signature, since her ward was still under age. It was a typical Hollywood contract for a beginner. It paid her $125 a week. It ran for seven years, but only at the option of the studio, which must declare its intentions every six months to keep the performer. If the option was picked up, the player received an increase in weekly salary.

It was the bottom of the ladder, but it was at least a foothold there. The girl was delighted, was willing to take any and all advice. At Fox they advised her that the name Norma Jean Dougherty was wrong, suggested the name Marilyn, and left it up to her to find something suitable for a surname. The guardian suggested Monroe. And so a Hollywood bit player was born. The next problem was to find a bit to play.

Chapter Three

So, in the autumn of 1946, Marilyn Monroe was a starlet. Like most of the young contract actresses in the middle 1940's, she hoped that she would soon become rich and famous. The reason? Even such old hands on the motion picture merry-go-round as Hedda Hopper later declared that Marilyn had a special power. She "hypnotized the camera," Miss Hopper said, and she used every muscle in her body in her battle with the camera. Or she could. What was needed was an opportunity to do all that. For the moment Marilyn's qualities were undiscovered by Miss Hopper, or by anyone else in the moving picture industry save Ben Lyon and Darryl Zanuck.

Darryl Zanuck had very little time for concern about an unknown starlet. Had he seen the girl on the street he would not have known her, and had someone mentioned her to him by name, either the old name or the new one, there would have been no flicker of recognition. Mr. Zanuck was one of the half dozen most powerful figures in all Hollywood, in charge of production at one of the industry's half dozen largest studios.

Zanuck was a manager representing in Hollywood a cold, logical business which was owned in the East—at least the business was very cold if not always very logical. And it was a big business, by far the largest amusement business in the

United States. Movies represented about 70 per cent of the entertainment business in America. Some fifty-five million Americans went to the movies at least once every week. Box office receipts for the entire industry ran just under a billion dollars each year. And the key to success or failure in the business lay in the seventeen thousand movie theaters scattered around the country (more movie theaters than banks).

These seventeen thousand movie theaters were operated by the exhibitors. Many of these were managers, because many of the movie houses were owned by chains which were either owned or controlled by the same companies that produced the films. In Hollywood most pictures were made and most business done by the Big Eight movie studios which included Twentieth Century Fox. (Just before World War II the Big Eight accounted for 95 per cent of the rentals paid by theaters for the exhibition of films.) The Big Eight owned twenty-eight hundred of the seventeen thousand movie houses —the first-run houses in the important centers were largely under Big Eight ownership. The Big Eight and their affiliates controlled all movie exhibition in the cities of more than one million population.

The largest organization of all was Loew's, which held assets of $170,000,000 at the beginning of the war. Loew's owned 123 separate companies in the amusement business. Second to Loew's was Twentieth Century Fox.

It is apparent that the motion picture industry was a tight little community on the owning and operating end. The industry had plenty of money to spend. It was not unusual for Hollywood to spend two hundred million dollars a year in salaries and expenses on the making of movies. This represented product cost for a gross business of seven hundred fifty million dollars. Obviously, even with distribution costs and various cuts in profit, someone was earning a great deal of money. The problem was to keep the movie houses full, to guess what the people would go out of their homes to see, and to capitalize on the "trend" in the movie industry.

How did the corporate moguls discover the trend? They consulted with their exhibitors, who were supposed to have a feeling for public opinion at all times. The newspapers were of little use, because for amusement purposes the newspapers were the creatures of the industry, not the guardians of the public weal. The newspapers published the propaganda distilled in the movie production centers. They published the columns of Hollywood gossip reporters. Only a handful of the most powerful newspapers reviewed the movies with any pretense at judgment.

The movie industry controlled its market in every sense and could give the people anything it wanted to give them, except for one imponderable: the public will.

Since the public recognized mutely that there was little service in the newspaper comments on a film except to give general plot outline and the names of the players, movies succeeded or failed because of word of mouth. Hollywood produced good movies before, during, and after the war. It made bad movies, too. The bad far outnumbered the good and submerged them—as always happens. Hollywood had another problem: its competitors in Europe began denigrating Hollywood's product in the 1920's, when Hollywood invaded and captured much of the European market.

But the basic problem, and the reason for certain stereotypes in the motion picture business pattern, was the need to keep movie houses filled. The first-run movie theaters occupied expensive real estate with high tax and business overhead. The houses must be kept full.

During the depression exhibitors discovered certain ways of keeping the houses full. One was the giveaway. Frank H. Ricketson, Jr., a former *Denver Post* sportswriter, established the basis of a fortune by giving away merchandise and calling the evening's entertainment Bank Night. Another was the

[37]

double feature. For less than a dollar an adult could enjoy some four hours of entertainment: a major feature, a minor feature, a cartoon or two, a short feature, and a newsreel.

The movie-makers enjoyed a highly receptive audience which would go to see almost any motion picture. The intense competition in the industry tended to give much choice and yet tended to make movies very much alike. Movies like *Abe Lincoln in Illinois* brought prestige to the producers and lost money. Movies starring Errol Flynn or Shirley Temple sometimes brought little prestige to the producers, but they could almost always be counted on to produce a profit.

And why? Because the public knew when it heard the name Errol Flynn or Shirley Temple just what it was going to see. If the star was Flynn, the movie would have something to do with the French Foreign Legion or another military organization. It would be filled with action and pretty girls. A love affair would thread its way through the film. Flynn would outrage the sensibilities of society, but he would get the girl and salvage all, perhaps by dying a heroic death in a burst of gunfire or an explosion.

Thus was the star system born long before, to assure a market for the movies. The word "typecast" came into being to bedevil movie actors and actresses, but Hollywood's promise to the public in the star system was more subtle than that. Depending on ability, a star could move around with some latitude within his type. Clark Gable was the he-man of the movies, but he also played comedy roles.

As a star developed a following and could assure the exhibitors of large audiences, which assured the eastern owners of the movie companies of large profits, the actor or actress was sometimes rewarded accordingly. But not always immediately. Stars under contract could be traded off to other studios, sometimes at a profit to the studio; but, if the actor discovered that he was receiving one thousand dollars a week and his studio had lent him out for five thousand dollars a week, usually he was not pleased. Business being business, however, this was one of the practices of the industry. Such practices led to resentment, enmities, distrust, and the formation of a series of unions of actors, directors, and other "professionals" in the movie industry, and then the fine print in contracts became more important than ever.

Stars were commodities in the Hollywood world and valuable ones, although, like oil stocks, their values fluctuated according to production and recognized potential. Production could be measured. How much did the star's last picture gross? That was the first question asked by a producer who thought he might use that star in a similar vehicle. If the last gross had not been so high as to be profitable, the producer felt it necessary to rationalize: there had been bad direction, some event had thrown the picture into a bad light, the female co-star had been on her last legs. Whatever the reason, it was rationalization; but if this second picture did not produce a profit, the star's stock sank sharply. A third financial failure almost always meant an end to the star's career. As star Marie Dressler once said, three strikes meant out in the motion picture industry.

Such volatility produced a strange community, and that was not the only factor. First of all, Hollywood movie-making was a business, but it was not a business established by gentle men.

Hollywood was not the birthplace of the American movie industry; movie-making began in the East and flourished in studios and warehouses in New York and on Long Island for many years. But at about the end of the first decade of the twentieth century, a number of newcomers from the garment business, the circus business, and vaudeville saw the future of this new medium of entertainment and tried to get into the motion picture business. The industry had been founded on the basis of monopoly, a very common practice before the trustbusting days. The trust was the Motion Pictures Patent

Company, which held process patents and rights and released them only to its favored members. Independents need not apply.

Facing monopoly, the independent movie-makers turned west, to get as far away from their tormentors as possible. They chose Hollywood for several reasons. One of these was the accidental discovery by one movie producer that Hollywood lay close to snow-capped mountains, cactus desert, rolling plain, green forest, long, deserted beaches, and surf-tossed rocky cliffs. Nowhere else was there such diversity of scenery in the United States. Within two hundred miles of Hollywood existed scenery that would establish verisimilitude for a movie laid in almost any geographical scene in the world.

Another reason was the availability and low price of real estate. The climate was excellent for movie-making with preponderantly sunny days. Labor was cheap, and the climate and scenery helped attract specialists.

Also, Hollywood was close enough to the Mexican border so that a producer could reach sanctuary in a few hours, and thus escape process servers whose papers represented the monopoly back in New York.

The movie industry of 1910 was much like the steamboat industry of 1920, when Commodore Vanderbilt hid in a secret cabin aboard his steamboat when it docked at New York City to avoid law officers and process servers because he and his employer were breaking laws established in behalf of the steamboat monopoly.

Many of the original moguls of Hollywood were outlaws, just as were Vanderbilt and Thomas Gibbons, who ran the trust-busting Gibbons line.

Like the Vanderbilts of the steamboat business, the powerful men of Hollywood came from less than gentle backgrounds. Louis B. Mayer was to become the most important man in Hollywood, the control figure for Loew's. He was a Jew, which gave him feelings of inferiority when he discovered that no matter how much money he had, the gentiles of a sleepy Los Angeles society would have none of him or his kind. He was a dealer in human flesh, which gave him a contempt for people. He abused his male stars and seduced every female who would submit to him. Had there been no one else to help, he alone would have created the stereotype of the producer who demanded that the girl go to bed with him as price for a part or a raise in pay. Unfortunately, there were all too many in the movie industry who used their power in the same way. If it was lasciviousness or the lord's contempt for the slave, the result was the same: on the highest levels of Hollywood's own society the rules were established and they were followed down to the lowest levels.

This was the society into which Marilyn Monroe moved on the day that she signed her first contract with Twentieth Century Fox.

It was so very unusual as to be remarkable that a girl with Marilyn Monroe's background would receive a contract. Nearly 85 per cent of the actors and actresses in the movie industry had some experience before they came to Hollywood. She had absolutely none. Nearly half the actors and actresses in the movie industry had attended college and more than ninety per cent had completed high school. Marilyn had not completed a year of high school.

For her success she had Miss Snively, her first agent, Ben Lyon of Twentieth Century Fox, and the system to thank.

In the mid-1940's Hollywood studios found it useful to employ attractive young women as starlets, with the full knowledge that very few of them would succeed in the movie business. The initial investment for the studio was not large. It involved the cost of a screen test and a contract that gave the girl $75 to $125 a week, with six-month options. In the first six months the girl would be exploited for pin-up pictures and general publicity. She might be sent out to help publicize a film by appearing in cities where it was showing. The

[41]

fact that she had not appeared in the film was not necessarily important. She would be kept available for studio parties and walk-on parts.

During this first six-month period, if she came to the attention of one of the studio's producers, she might find a small speaking part in a movie. If not, her option would be picked up if she showed unusual aptitude at some associated task (if, for example, she drew much mail from pin-up fans). In addition to this, at all times, was the matter of "flesh." A girl could succeed up to a point by being a special friend to one or more officials. But this aspect of Hollywood life has been highly over-rated and never played a lasting role in the success of any major actress.

Marilyn claimed that sex did not play any such role in her career. As with many of Marilyn's statements, this was only partly truthful.

One of the young publicity men of Twentieth Century Fox, Roy Craft, was sent to interview Marilyn and write a brief biography of her pre-film career which would be made available to the press when there was some occasion to do so. Marilyn gave him a pack of whopping lies, including the declaration that she was an orphan. (Her mother, at that moment, was between institutions.) The lies were not effective, nor was the truthful part of her childhood story, because the studios had made so much, so often, of rags-to-riches stories that even the agreeable, patient movie editors of the newspapers shuddered to inflict another such tale on their readers. Marilyn's biography was filed quietly away.

In the autumn of 1946 Marilyn set out to become a movie star. She knew nothing about movie scripts, so she began to study them. When no one was looking, she visited sound stages. (Starlets were most unwelcome around the lot of Twentieth Century Fox unless they were asked to appear.) She missed no opportunity to visit the publicity department on the second floor of the administration building. She would wander in to talk to anyone who had time for her, and she would offer to pose for still pictures or do anything else that might enhance her movie career. She rode in parades, such as the pre-Rose Bowl Parade of the Pasadena Tournament of Roses. She attended the studio's newly organized new talent school, and there Charles Henderson taught her a dance routine. A few weeks later she presented it at the New Talent Show at which studio executives surveyed the accomplishments of the latest crop of young contract players. She telephoned her agent as often as she dared and was told that the studio was waiting for "the right part" to come along. She telephoned Ben Lyon, the only executive she knew outside the publicity department, and was told the same story. And she waited.

While she waited she tried to improve herself. Her best method seemed to be to read. Marilyn began to buy and read books. She had no education, no guidance, no standards. She had earlier purchased a few books, notably a copy of a modern edition of Vesalius' drawings on human anatomy. That might be considered a text, for she used it in practicing poses for photography, and in perfecting her projection of sensuality. Her other reading was haphazard, depending on the responses she received to the shy questions she dared ask about books.

For amusement Marilyn did what other young women did: she went to the movies and went out on dates when she was asked. She went out a few times with Lionel Newman, conductor of an orchestra. They would go to dinner and then often call on David Boutolph, a composer. Marilyn would sit quietly in a chair reading, while Newman and Boutolph played backgammon.

The first six months of her contract had nearly expired when Producer Walter Morosco began casting for a movie entitled *Scudda Hoo! Scudda Hay!* The movie had twenty-two acting parts, including players number twenty-one and twenty-two, who were, respectively, starlets Colleen Townsend and Marilyn Monroe. Marilyn's first option was picked up by the studio. Her salary was raised to $150 a week and she was assigned to the cast of the movie.

Marilyn and Colleen Townsend were to play roles designated in the picture's credit lines as "girl friends." They appeared in only one scene. They entered a canoe, paddled past Robert Karnes, who occupied sixth billing in the cast. He was fishing on a dock as they passed. They then paddled out into a lake. Upon sighting June Haver, the female star of the picture, they waved hello. It was one day's work for the two starlets, but no one knew when they would be needed so they reported daily during the filming on location. On the mornings that they were to go to location, they appeared at the Twentieth Century Fox studio on Pico Boulevard. There Marilyn was assigned to a car with Rose Steinberg, a script supervisor. Miss Steinberg noticed how young and shy Marilyn seemed to be, and began to talk to her. Marilyn asked how she could become a star. Miss Steinberg answered as best she could. She gave Marilyn a book called *As a Man Thinketh,* a philosophical study, and told Marilyn that the book ought to make her realize that she could do anything she set out to do.

"Do you really think so?" Marilyn replied, opening her big blue eyes wide and staring, open-mouthed, at Miss Steinberg.

Miss Steinberg noticed how intense Marilyn appeared to be when working on the set. The strongest quality she observed was the girl's intent to learn and to succeed—drive, Miss Steinberg called it.

Scudda Hoo! Scudda Hay! was not a spectacular although it was photographed in color, but it was a chance for Marilyn to be seen and remembered. The slender story concerned a farm boy who trained a pair of mules that hated everyone else, and the winning of the heroine, who was Miss Haver.

Miss Haver was the star, and Marilyn was little more than a fixture, so their paths did not cross during the making of the movie. This was not unusual—in years to come Marilyn would play in motion pictures with hundreds of other actors and actresses and would meet only a handful of them.

Three years later she would play sixth featured role in *Let's Make It Legal,* and a young actor named Jim Hayward would play eighth featured role, and they would never meet because they did not do any scenes together.

Marilyn met very few members of the cast of *Scudda Hoo! Scudda Hay!* and her performance was not demanding enough to impress director F. Hugh Herbert or any of the moviemakers. The close-up and medium shots of her scene were cut from the movie, leaving only a long shot in which the forms of two girls in a canoe can be seen, but the faces are not visible.

No one can remember a movie personality that they have not seen, and so Marilyn's chance for success was lost.

Later that spring Marilyn was lent to independent producer Sol Wurtzel for a small part in a melodrama called *Dangerous Years* which dealt with juvenile delinquency. The plot concerns a hoodlum who corrupts young people at a drive-in and plans a robbery. A well-meaning citizen attempts to foil the hoodlum, who kills him. There are other plot convolutions, but none of them important to Marilyn's role, which was that of smiling young waitress at the drive-in. It was a bit part, calling for only a few words of dialogue. A few years after the film was released practically no one in Hollywood remembered it. Marilyn thought so little of her own part in it that she failed to mention it in later years. Twentieth Century Fox was so unimpressed that the company dropped Marilyn's option in August, 1947, when the second six-month period ended and they had to decide whether to raise her pay or let her go.

This was a shock. Marilyn had followed Hollywood practice with the first exercise of her option and had gone into debt. She had been persuaded to buy some new clothes and had opened charge accounts at the expensive I. Magnin store, and elsewhere.

Twentieth Century Fox had given Marilyn one line of continuation in Hollywood, even though she had been fired. Before she left the studio, she and a member of other young contract players had been assigned to the Actor's Lab, a training program which was conducted by a number of professionals. Marilyn was a faithful attendant at the sessions of the school, and, after her contract lapsed with Twentieth Century Fox, she paid her own tuition there.

Through attendance at the Actor's Lab, Marilyn came often to eat at the original Schwab's drugstore on Sunset Boulevard. Here she met Sidney Skolsky, a Hollywood columnist, who made of Schwab's an informal headquarters for his rounds of the Hollywood community. Skolsky was for a time to be her friend and confidant. He did not drive an automobile, so she often took him home from Schwab's in the evenings in her old Ford. Sometimes they drove west to the ocean, Skolsky said, and Marilyn told him of her dreams of stardom and her troubles in attaining it.

Marilyn went through a difficult six months, sustained by modelling jobs she found with the still photographers she knew. They did not pay much, but they paid the rent on the apartment in which she lived. She collected her unemployment insurance, too. She borrowed money. She survived.

The Actor's Lab was to have an evil name in later years when the specter of communism frightened Hollywood half out of its collective wits, but it was valuable enough as an aid to the motion picture companies that they sent their youngsters there for a number of years. The Lab was founded in the late 1930's by J. Edward Bromberg, Roman Bohnen, and Morris Carnovsky, fugitives from Broadway, who had come from the same Group Theater where Lee Strasberg and Elia Kazan began to earn their reputations.

Many of the young actors and actresses who worked at the Actor's Lab were political creatures. There was much talk of socialism, communism, nihilism, and anarchy at after-hours parties. But Marilyn remained singularly untouched by the political nature of her companions. She read a few books that might be called "dangerous" literature in some quarters, but there is no indication that Marilyn was seriously concerned with the politics of revolution or anything else. She was a liberal with a strong feeling for the working man. Later she would become a Democrat and would even be elected an alternate delegate to the Connecticut State Democratic Convention in 1960, but at this time she was not politically minded. Marilyn, for her part, left little impression on the Actor's Lab. Mrs. Morris Carnovsky, who taught at the school under the name of Phoebe Brand, could not recall anything about the girl except that she had long blonde hair and was shy.

Marilyn was chosen for the second lead in a Columbia Pictures feature just about six months later. It seemed to come almost out of the blue. And there are two versions of the manner in which this first featured appearance originated.

One day early in 1948 Max Arnow, the head of the talent department at Columbia Pictures, was persuaded to run a screen test on Marilyn. Like Ben Lyon, he was impressed with the impact this girl made on the screen. Columbia signed her to another of Hollywood's long-term contracts with six month release clauses for the studio, and she began again in movies at $125 per week.

At the moment there seemed to be nothing for Marilyn to do at Columbia, but she was sent to see the studio acting coach, Natasha Lytess, who had been married to the German novelist, Bruno Frank, and who had been a member of the Max Reinhardt acting troupe in Germany in the pre-Nazi days.

Miss Lytess had influence at Columbia Pictures and she used it with the talent department in behalf of her new student. She persuaded the production department to give Marilyn the second lead in a second-rate picture called *Ladies of the Chorus*. The picture, as it turned out, was shot in eleven days, a timing reminiscent of the old Mack Sennett period in Hollywood. That alone stamped it as a bad picture.

That story may be true. Certainly, later when Marilyn achieved prominence she showed her gratitude and dependence by bringing Natasha Lytess into Twentieth Century Fox.

And yet, the jump from oblivion—worse, from discard—to second lead in a movie was enough to cause raised eyebrows in Hollywood, when anyone cared enough to consider the matter. In 1948 Marilyn became an intimate of old Joseph Schenck, then chairman of the board at Twentieth Century Fox. She was not employed then by the studio, but she was one of the many girls who was often picked up by Schenck's drivers and taken out to the Schenck house or to the Schenck hideaway in Palm Springs, and there wined and dined. To those of evil mind it appeared that Marilyn was Joe Schenck's girl, or one of them. She denied it flatly. The facts indicate that Marilyn was telling the truth. Joseph Schenck in 1948 was seventy years old and ill. His libido could not have been at its peak; even Charlie Chaplin had slowed down considerably by seventy. Some who knew Schenck well said that he liked to be surrounded by youth and beauty. He had so much money that the expenditure of a few thousand dollars a year in feeding hungry girls was a small price to pay for the companionship they brought him. Sometimes the girls came in large groups. Sometimes they came alone. Marilyn did both. People who knew could make what they wanted of it. Schenck, when questioned about it, said he supposed she liked the food. Marilyn said she did, and she denied flatly that she had "ever gone to bed" with Joseph Schenck.

Joseph Schenck was a power in Hollywood, and it might be that Harry Cohn, head of Columbia Pictures, would have accommodated him by placing "Schenck's girl" in a second lead in a cheap movie. The loss to Columbia would be negligible no matter how badly it turned out. The truth is clouded. But this opportunity opened a new period in Marilyn's life, a brief but very telling one.

Chapter Four

HAD it not been for Natasha Lytess, Joseph Schenck, or whoever exerted the influence on Columbia Pictures producer Harry Romm to use Marilyn Monroe in *Ladies of the Chorus*, her movie career might have ended in 1948. She was beautiful but she was getting nowhere.

She was learning to act, but she was not an accomplished actress. She needed experience and attention and, above all, confidence to help her on her way.

Some of this needed confidence was brought to Marilyn by a man she met through the part she was chosen to play in the movie. Marilyn played a young chorus girl who was suddenly thrust into a featured dancer's role in burlesque. She was required to dance and to sing two songs. She was sent to see Fred Karger, musical director of the studio. Karger asked her if she had any experience. She had none, although she said she had taken some singing lessons. Karger sat at the piano in his office, and she sang a song called "Love Me or Leave Me" for him. Karger noticed that her voice was very small but not unpleasant. He realized that by using a few mechanical devices to bring up the volume, she could do her own singing and it could be made quite presentable.

One reason for Marilyn's small voice and bad articulation, Karger saw, was that Marilyn had problems with her teeth. She needed the services of an orthodontist. Karger was friendly with Dr. Walter Taylor, a prominent Hollywood dentist. He sent Marilyn to Taylor with a private word to the dentist that she could not afford to spend very much money. Taylor found that he could straighten her teeth by use of a simple retainer brace. He made it without charge. There was something about the non-actress Marilyn Monroe that made people want to help her without thought of compensation. Even in *Ladies of the Chorus*, Marilyn's beauty was marred by a smile that showed only her upper teeth. Later she would learn the flashing smile that was to be another trademark.

Fred Karger began to teach Marilyn to sing. One song was "Every Baby Needs a Da-Da-Daddy," which she was to sing while in the chorus line hugging a rag doll. For several days they worked on the song. Karger played it for her. She sang it back to him. In the evening she would go home to her apartment and practice. In the morning she would return to the studio and show him the degree of her progress.

One day Marilyn failed to arrive at Karger's office for her music lesson. Karger looked up her address at the studio and stopped by that evening to see if she was sick. When he came into her one-room flat on one of Hollywood's bungalow-lined side streets, he was depressed by the dingy poverty in which she lived with a handful of possessions, a few books, and a pet chihuahua. Away from the lot and the false bravado of the studio, he was impressed with Marilyn's fragility and her apparent inability to cope with the world around her. She was not sick, he was certain. She was just hungry.

Fred Karger took Marilyn home to dinner with him that evening. It was the first of many evenings they spent together. He had been divorced and was living in a household of women: his mother, his sister and her daughter, and his own small daughter. Marilyn came into the household that night and charmed all the women with her naturalness. From that day forward the Karger women and Marilyn were always to be fast friends.

[51]

Karger did more than befriend Marilyn. He took her life in hand. He told her she must move from the slum in which she was living. He telephoned the Hollywood Studio Club, a residence hotel for career girls. A call from the musical director of one of the "Big Eight" studios was all the recommendation Marilyn needed. She might not have gotten into the Studio Club on her own, even if she had heard of it. With Fred Karger's help it was easy. There she would be surrounded by young women in her own general position in life, and she could make as many friends as she felt inclined to acquire. She was protected, too, by the rules of the YWCA about visitors and by its semi-charitable nature. The Hollywood Studio Club is operated by the YWCA, and, because it is subsidized, in 1948 it could offer residents room and board for about fifteen dollars a week.

The next few months were probably the happiest in Marilyn's entire life. Fred Karger was a handsome, cultured man. He was slim with slightly wavy hair. He spoke quietly. He was polite and attentive. His mother and his sister both liked Marilyn and made her feel at home at the Karger house. She liked them. She liked the children, and they doted on her. Marilyn rented another apartment near the Columbia studios. She and Fred Karger met there after the affair began. The affair continued for several months. Karger was in love with Marilyn, but he was afraid to marry her. The simple, brutal fact was that she was ambitious, and he did not believe she was the motherly type to whom he could entrust his child. When Fred Karger told her this, Marilyn froze. Things were never the same between them. The affair died a slow, lingering death, but at least it left no bitterness, for in the years thereafter Marilyn went on picnics and to dinner with Mrs. Karger and Fred's sister and went often to visit the Karger household. For the rest of her life, every two or three months she would telephone Fred Karger's mother or drop in to see her.

Probably no one has ever made an attempt to discover the worst film that was produced in Hollywood, and probably no one ever will, but if such an attempt were made, *Ladies of the Chorus* would certainly have to be placed in consideration. In this picture Marilyn sang two songs—the one with the rag doll, and "Anyone Can Tell I Love You," a duet with the male lead, an actor named Rand Brooks. Marilyn's performance, such as it was, was one of the few bright spots in thousands of dismal feet of film. The movie attracted almost no attention in the press, but in the trade journal *Motion Picture Herald* reviewer Tibor Krekes noted that Miss Monroe's singing was worthy of attention. Fred Karger had done a good job. Marilyn showed "promise," said Krekes. She had added another asset.

Surprising as her leap to temporary "stardom" seemed to the wise heads of Hollywood, Marilyn's immediate professional demise at Columbia Pictures seemed even less subject to reasonable explanation. Bad as the picture was, she was the best part of it.

Her only other claims to accomplishment at Columbia lay in two movies in which her pin-up pictures were used although she did not appear in person. One of these was a western, and it was, in a way, Marilyn's first venture into comedy. In this picture the hero from time to time pulled out a pin-up picture of Marilyn Monroe and showed it to his horse. The horse invariably snorted, either in jealousy or disgust.

When Marilyn's option came up in September, 1948, Columbia Pictures chose to let it drop. Marilyn was unemployed again.

Efforts were made by Marilyn's friends to have her reinstated at Columbia. One story has it that Sidney Skolsky heard about Marilyn's problem from his daughter, who was a student at the Actor's Lab with her. Skolsky called Joseph Schenck, the story goes, and Schenck called Harry Cohn at Columbia. Cohn then, supposedly, invited Marilyn to his office, showed her a picture of his yacht, and made a proposition to her concerning a weekend. She refused, and he told her that was her last chance at Columbia Pictures. She went out of the office, eyes clouded with tears, walked to a drugstore on Hollywood Boulevard, and, of her last thirty cents, spent twenty-five cents to eat a malted milk with a spoon amid the tears, and the final nickel for a call to her agent to see if a modelling job had come through. None had, so she went home, dejected, to bed.

That is probably Marilyn's story. Fred Karger was present at one meeting with Harry Cohn, at which he tried to influence Cohn to keep Marilyn on. He picked Marilyn up at the Studio Club and headed for the Columbia lot. Just before they arrived, Marilyn insisted on stopping for a moment in a drugstore. What did she want? She wanted to call her Christian Science Practitioner, she told Karger. She did telephone, and Karger heard her through the booth asking for advice and help before she went to the important meeting. Marilyn was a practicing Scientist for some time. During her affair with photographer Andre de Dienes she gave him a copy of Mary Baker Eddy's *Science and Health with a Key to the Scriptures,* and on the flyleaf she inscribed it with reference to certain passages that concerned everlasting love.

When Marilyn and Karger arrived at Harry Cohn's office, they were greeted warmly but not quite as warmly as the other story indicated. Marilyn was trying her best to convince Cohn that she should be kept on. She put her bag and a manila folder she had brought on the arm of the davenport in the office, so as to talk more freely. The folder fell off and onto the floor slipped a copy of the *Christian Science Monitor.* Harry Cohn relaxed his usual mask, for Marilyn, knowingly or not, had touched him on a tender spot. Cohn, through his wife, had been deeply impressed with Christian Science at one period in his life, and he had never lost his respect for that faith.

[54]

Harry Cohn was noted for inviting attractive young women for brief honeymoon cruises on his yacht, just as Louis Mayer and others of the powerful among the Big Eight of movieland were noted for their lechery. But Fred Karger said Cohn showed no lechery toward Marilyn Monroe that day. Perhaps Cohn's interest changed in Karger's absence.

Even Fred Karger's intervention in Marilyn's behalf really did not help. Once the Columbia authorities were given an indication that she had some ability and heard the testimony of Karger and Natasha Lytess, Marilyn might have been kept on the Columbia payroll save for one blatant problem of the times. Every Hollywood studio had its particular sex symbol. Columbia's was Rita Hayworth; Twentieth Century Fox had Betty Grable. The studios were not inclined to worry about the future, because the future was known to be entirely insecure and unpredictable. Marilyn Monroe was a sex symbol. There was no more place for her at Columbia than there had been at Twentieth Century Fox.

Marilyn went back to the Studio Club and to her double life of modelling and seeking work as an actress.

Marilyn's double life also existed on another plane, and this was becoming apparent to some acquaintances. Marilyn lived in two entirely different worlds. One was the workaday world in which she ate and drank and slept.

She went out on modelling assignments. She had many telephone calls, and she spent many evenings on dates with men. She later said that then she was trying to forget Fred Karger, who held such a hold on her memory. She spent many evenings with Joseph Schenck. Not all of her evenings with men were matters that she liked to discuss later in her career, but at twenty-two she was a grown woman and not a child. It meant very little to her to gratify men. It was, as Nunnally Johnson said, a way to say thank you.

She attended the Actor's Lab sessions, and she dropped in

at Schwab's drugstore for the companionship of the young actors and actresses there.

She lived at the Studio Club for a very short time—only until the spring of 1949. She came there with only two suitcases full of clothes but with the tools of her trade: a bathroom scale, a bicycle, an enormous beauty shop hair dryer—and a library.

The girls at the Studio Club noticed that Marilyn read a great deal and was very quiet almost all the time. She was quick to respond to gestures of friendship. She was ready to advise younger girls on hair style and makeup, and she was expert in these fields. She would sit in the common patio with its fountain and pool and listen to the others talk. But she contributed very little to the conversation.

One reason for her constant reading was that Marilyn was forever embarrassed by her own ignorance in many fields. She mispronounced words and failed to understand many of the lofty conversations in which she found herself. Instead of keeping quiet, as a dumb blonde should, Marilyn set out to remedy her ignorance. Her reading jumped from subject to subject, depending on what area she was remedying at the moment. And for people who took the time to know her and understand her, like the Kargers, Marilyn turned out to be more lovable than stupid. All she seemed to need at that time of life was attention, affection, and a real home.

But another Marilyn lived on another plane and had for a very large number of her twenty-two years. This was Marilyn the actress, who vowed to become the world's most important movie star. This Marilyn existed in the mirror of her room at the Studio Club. This was the dream-world Marilyn. This was the Marilyn with the driving ambition. This was the Marilyn who drove the body to an hour of exercise every day. This was the Marilyn who forced the body onto the scales. This was the Marilyn who pushed the body into a round of acting classes, dancing classes, singing classes. This was the Marilyn who spent the body's money for cosmetics and hair dryers instead of food. This was the Marilyn who let the body forget to eat. This was the Marilyn who forgot to bathe or to do the body's nails, who let the body's toenails grow long and unkempt. This was the Marilyn who could sit dreamy-eyed under the hair dryer for an hour without moving, staring into the mirror. This was the Marilyn who did not comb her hair.

This Marilyn was already tortured and contemptuous of the Marilyn who went out at night with men and allowed the body to be touched and caressed. When it cared. Sometimes it did not care. Sometimes it did not care about anything except success.

The existence of these two Marilyns began at a very early age. Marilyn's mother was a film technician in the movie industry, when she worked. She was unstable, and, because she was also attractive, she drifted from one affair of the heart to another. Marilyn had a half sister and a half brother; the brother died at an early age, and she seldom saw her half sister after childhood since they had little in common.

Marilyn was illegitimate, to begin with. Her mother kept the children long enough to inculcate Marilyn with the intense yearning to become a movie star, then deserted the children, and, finally, began her life in institutions. Marilyn was raised by her mother part of the time until then, and by her mother's friend, Grace McKee, who would become Grace Goddard. Both women worked in the movie industry, and there was very little talk about other matters during Marilyn's early years. The women talked to the child of the great stars. Their idea of a fine Sunday afternoon's entertainment was a walk in the expensive districts to peer at the lawns and houses of some of them.

Impressions are about all that Marilyn could have remembered, because, when she was five years old, she was placed in a foster home by Grace McKee; she said it was the first of eleven such homes. (Ezra Goodman, who investigated Marilyn's background for *Time* magazine, found fewer than eleven.) The foster parents were selected by Los Angeles County, which had taken over the mothering of the girl who would be Marilyn.

In the foster homes Marilyn encountered many kinds of people. There were Lutherans and fundamentalists, drinkers and prohibitionists. In one home, Marilyn said later, she was forced to take the pledge never to use liquor or tobacco, this before she was six years old. In another home she was given empty whiskey bottles as her playthings.

Sometimes Marilyn was happy, particularly with a family that sent her to the movies to stay all day on Saturdays. Usually she was miserable, for she came and went through all those foster homes in four short years. Then there was a brief interlude with Grace McKee Goddard and a stay at the Los Angeles Orphans Home.

In 1956, when Ezra Goodman was looking into Marilyn's youth, he encountered Jody Laurance, who was Grace McKee Goddard's step-daughter. Marilyn lived with them, and the two girls built a tree house where they hid out against an unfriendly world.

Miss Laurance characterized the Marilyn of the starlet years: she was looking for a father, mother, and family all rolled up into one person or one experience.

The years of childhood were so unhappy that Marilyn never escaped them. They produced basic feelings of insecurity and inferiority, and the dream world into which she could retreat at will.

Marilyn was a successful "orphan"; she did not cause trouble and earned good enough grades at school to cause no undue attention. She hated the orphanage worse than any of her previous trials, probably because she was older, and because she felt deserted by her mother and by the only other person she knew well, Grace McKee Goddard.

Marilyn lost any fondness she might have felt earlier for Grace McKee Goddard because of the orphanage stay. After two years Mrs. Goddard rescued her from the orphanage and sent her to live with Miss Ana Lower, who was Mrs. Goddard's aunt. Marilyn was then eleven, and the repairs that could be made to the ravages caused by inattention were to be made by Miss Lower in the next four years. The area in which she went to live was a slum called the Sawtelle district, which lay southeast of Santa Monica. Ana Lower was a Christian Science Practitioner, and she instructed Marilyn in this faith.

Marilyn attended Emerson Junior High School in Westwood Village. She was a girl from the wrong side of the tracks. She had very few clothes, and these were faded and worn. She did not distinguish herself at Emerson, except to play in two school plays. She had boys' parts in both of them, because she was tall and skinny. When she was thirteen, she ceased to be tall and skinny and became buxom enough to add several years to her age. She did so, too, and began to go on dates. She learned to use cosmetics, lipstick, eyebrow pencil, and blemish removers, and sweaters. By the time she was fifteen years old she was physically mature, although emotionally retarded and mentally ill-prepared for anything but further education. Further education was out of the question because Aunt Ana Lower was ill, and the Goddards were planning to move east. So the marriage to James Dougherty was arranged.

No one ever explained why Marilyn left Van Nuys high school in the middle of her first year there, which represented the second year of high school study. She suddenly dropped out of school, no reason given.

At that same time she began going steadily with Jim Dougherty, who had been picked to be her husband because he was "steady" and had a good job at Lockheed Aviation and was available. Dougherty claimed that she was head over heels in love with him. Marilyn said she had not loved Dougherty, that she had been faced with the choice of marriage or return to the orphanage, and she chose the lesser evil. She must have been a good actress, then, because she convinced Dougherty and his relatives that she loved him.

They were married on June 19, 1942, and the newlyweds celebrated in a typical lower-middle-class fashion: they adjourned with the wedding party to a Hollywood night club.

Marriage had been Marilyn's mode of escape from the prison of the orphanage, she said, but she found marriage equally confining. Dougherty objected to her interest in other men. He expected her to stay at home and cook and wash and sew for him. She hated such tasks. She told Dougherty once that she dreamed privately of being a Hollywood star. He did not understand what she was talking about.

Eventually the dream-world Marilyn came to Dougherty's attention. She darned socks well, he said, but she also tried once to bring a wet cow into the house during a rainstorm. She served him raw catfish, not understanding that he was not likely to appreciate raw fish served in what she thought was the Japanese style (she had just been reading about it). She served peas and carrots for dinner day after day. When her husband joined the merchant marine and was sent to Catalina Island as a physical training instructor, Marilyn joined him and embarrassed him by her provocative conduct with other men at dances. James Doughtery did not know that the world of movie stardom was Marilyn's real world. The other world, the one she inhabited with him for those few years, was the unreal world to her. From the very earliest days there was no question about what she wanted. The question was how she could get it.

In the autumn of 1948 Marilyn seemed to have lost the way to the land of success and glory. She was on the outskirts, outside the wall, and the gate had again been shut in her face.

Whatever else Marilyn had, she also had friends, and they

came to her assistance. Don Boutyette, a publicity man at Columbia, telephoned her one day about a musical comedy job. Boutyette had no interest in Marilyn except that he had seen her around the Columbia lot and felt sorry for her. He also helped her find a job for a few days as a magician's assistant.

Joe Kirkwood, Jr., who played Joe Palooka in the movies, was putting together an act and needed an assistant. Kirkwood was a trick-shot golfer and the act was built around this skill. The assistant's job was to stand on stage in a brief costume and hold a plastic golf ball at various positions on a string. Kirkwood would hit the ball.

Fred Karger heard of the Kirkwood plan and suggested that Marilyn be given the job. Kirkwood was agreeable. But on their maiden appearance, at a Veterans Hospital, Marilyn was so nervous that she could not hold her arm steady, and the string and golf ball danced around in the air. Kirkwood finally had to tee the ball on the stage, and they retired in confusion. That was the end of Marilyn in vaudeville.

The next few months of Marilyn's career were probably the most difficult in the launching of it. The help of friends could provide no more than sporadic employment. She had photographic assignments, but they were just enough to keep her head above water. She fell behind in her rent at the Studio Club, not far enough behind to be seriously concerned about eviction, but far enough to worry her. She might make forty dollars in one day, and then not a penny for two or three weeks. When she earned money in any amounts at all, she paid up the back rent and spent the rest of the money on dramatic lessons.

Marilyn persisted when there seemed to be very little hope. She fired her agent, or the agent dropped her, and she got another one. It did not help noticeably. Nothing seemed to help. She was very much in danger of total failure or of becoming a call girl in the forlorn hope that by making herself available she would appeal to someone important in the motion picture industry.

One day, however, Marilyn heard from a girl she knew that the Marx Brothers were finishing up a picture at the RKO studio. The producer, aside from Groucho and Harpo and Chico, was Lester Cowan. The film was nearly completed. At this time some zany business was added by the Marx brothers. They were in need of a sexy blonde for one bit.

Marilyn telephoned Cowan and indicated that she was a sexy blonde. She was invited to the RKO lot and waited there for some time until Groucho and Harpo returned from a long lunch to consider their problems of the moment. They considered Marilyn.

The part was singularly uncomplicated. It called for the blonde to walk across the set, projecting sex.

If there was ever a walk-on part made for Marilyn Monroe, this was it. She walked. She was hired.

The next morning, to the delight of all, Groucho wrote a little dialogue to try to bring Marilyn into some vague juxtaposition with what passed for the plot of this movie, *Love Happy*. The blonde, in a tight strapless gown, wriggles across the stage in this scene and accosts Sam Grunion, the private detective played by Groucho. The blonde says she needs a private detective. Grunion asks what he can do for her, and leers.

"Well," says the girl, "some men are following me." And she wriggles off stage, accompanied by (hopefully) catcalls and laughter from the movie audience.

It went off very well. When the Marx brothers and Cowan saw the rushes, Cowan said he was going to do something for Marilyn. What he did, apparently, was give her name to gossip columnist Louella Parsons, for in a day or so Marilyn learned from that column in the *Herald-Examiner* that Cowan planned to place her under contract and make her a star.

Marilyn hurried to find Cowan. He did not exactly have

a starring role for her at that moment, but he did have a job. A few days later he told her what it would be.

Being "put under contract to him personally," at that moment, meant that Marilyn would be sent on tour for a few weeks at $125 per week to promote *Love Happy*.

Marilyn said that she went because she still loved Fred Karger and hoped that by going away for a month or two she would make him jealous and he would ask her to marry him. She drew some money from the RKO cashier on Cowan's voucher and went out to buy some new clothes. With the simplicity that was to mark her forever, she deduced that, since it was hot in Los Angeles and New York was far to the north, it would be cold in New York that June. Marilyn's geographical knowledge, like so much else, was sadly deficient. She knew June was suit weather in San Francisco. New York was even further north than San Francisco. Ergo . . .

Thus began a starlet's publicity junket to the East, for in this instance Marilyn was functioning in the true starlet's role. She was escorted to Los Angeles' Union Station by a press agent in a limousine and decanted into a bedroom aboard the Santa Fe Chief. The press agent left her with a number of press releases relating to the movie and the information that she would be called the "Woo-Woo Girl" for the purposes of this triumphal tour.

Marilyn went east, but she did not memorize the facts about *Love Happy*. She looked out the window or read books of her own choosing instead. In Chicago the press agent used her as an excuse to have lunch at the Pump Room, and she was given another hypodermic of information about the movie she was supposed to plump. The following morning, outside New York, another press agent boarded the train, presented her with orchids, and made her ready to meet the New York press.

The New York aspect of the publicity tour was successful enough, although Marilyn roasted in her suits. Marilyn was installed at the Sherry Netherland, a hotel on Fifth Avenue across from Central Park. She was photographed, and her picture appeared in the newspapers. She was mentioned by columnists and reporters. André de Dienes was in New York, and he took pictures of her at Jones Beach on Long Island.

The junket moved on, to Detroit and across the Middle West. Marilyn became sick of it. Promises or no promises, $125 a week against nothing, she still was tired and refused to go on, so in central Illinois she deserted the promotion tour and returned to Hollywood.

Automatically this took her off the payroll. Cowan was undoubtedly annoyed, as he had a right to be, and he refused to return her calls. Another possible opening through the wall was suddenly sealed.

Marilyn had hired a new agent named Harry Lipton, and he managed to get her a bit part as a dancer in a Twentieth Century Fox picture called *A Ticket to Tomahawk*, almost as soon as she returned to Hollywood. Perhaps that is why she came back to Hollywood, for work on the picture began August 15, 1949, a few days after her return from the publicity odyssey. The pay was again the standard $125 a week for a bit player, and she was listed as nineteenth in a cast of twenty in the credit lines. It was not much of a movie, and Marilyn's part in it was so small that it aroused no comment at all among the reviewers of the press. She did not have a contract. Her employment was for this one motion picture only.

That she had the part at all was due to the good offices of Ben Lyon, who had originally signed her to the Twentieth Century Fox contract. Lyon did the casting for *A Ticket to Tomahawk*.

Immediately, Marilyn joined the others of the cast and crew to go on location to Durango, Colorado, where most of the movie was filmed. She shared a motel room with another girl. Richard Sale, director of the movie, found Marilyn to be something of a trial. She was depressed because she was still thinking about Freddy Karger. She was tense because she was hoping for a role in *The Asphalt Jungle*, and she kept calling Director John Huston by long distance telephone to be certain that she had a chance at the part.

Director Sale was a writer who was making his first picture in this new role. Marilyn flirted with him a little, hoping for a line or a close-up or something that would further her career. But Sale was a happily married man—married to Mary Loos, niece of playwright Anita Loos—and he sensed that she did not mean anything by her advances, that actually, while she was an obvious "sexpot" in tight blue jeans and a tight shirt, she disliked some aspects of her elemental appeal. Sex was a commodity. She turned it on. She turned it off.

Marilyn was so preoccupied with her career that she neglected herself. Sale came into her motel room once—only once—to awaken her when she was needed on call. He saw that the windows had not been opened since their arrival. Dirty underwear was hanging all around the room—Marilyn's and her roommate's. Both were in bed, sleeping in their underwear, their filthy blue jeans stacked beside the beds, and neither had taken off the makeup used the day before.

Her carelessness might have caused a filming problem. Marilyn's costume was a short frilly dress cut low at the neck, worn with long black net stockings. The costume became filthy, progressively soiled with everything from blueberry pie to wet handmarks. Since Sale was shooting film in sequence, the costume matched, day by day. Otherwise, it might have hurt the film or even caused the director to cut her out in some scenes.

Marilyn was miserable in Durango, and she caught cold in the mountain air. Then she took too much penicillin, which gave her a bad reaction, and when she returned to the studio, she was out of the film for a week while she recovered.

When the motion picture ended, Mary Sale told Marilyn

she was going to be a great star some day—because she had "all the *wrong* things that make a star." Marilyn burst into tears of gratitude, because another woman was for her—something quite unusual in Marilyn's existence. She told Mary Sale that very few women had ever treated her cordially.

Marilyn had a foothold in the motion picture business again, but only that. She was still very much involved in modelling.

Shortly before *A Ticket to Tomahawk* was released, there appeared in the Los Angeles *Times* a full-page advertisement for the reducing compound AYDS and decorating it was the life-size, scantily clad figure of reducing expert Marilyn Monroe.

That year Marilyn met Johnny Hyde, one of the most powerful men in Hollywood. They met at Palm Springs, where she had gone on a house party shortly after the release of *Love Happy*. Johnny Hyde fell in love with Marilyn, although she was twenty-three, five feet five and a half inches tall and aggressively healthy, and he was fifty-three years old, had a bad heart, and was scarcely five feet tall. (He was a millionaire, probably the one on whom Marilyn drew for her tale to Maurice Zolotow about the old millionaire who wanted to marry her.)

Johnny Hyde did want to marry Marilyn. He had enjoyed the favors of many other beautiful girls, no problem for an agent. But at fifty-three, friends said, Hyde seemed to feel that he was coming to the end of his life, and he wanted marriage and the security he hoped it would bring. It was a tribute in a way to Marilyn that Johnny Hyde should choose her among all the beautiful girls in Hollywood. Nunnally Johnson, the writer and producer, said that Hyde was more stirred by feminine beauty than nearly anyone he had ever known. Hyde was Johnson's agent—he was the agent of many of the most important people in the film colony. He had discovered Lana Turner, Betty Hutton, and Rita Hayworth, and he had brought Bob Hope to prominence. He was executive vice-president of the William Morris theatrical agency. Marilyn could not have picked a more important man to advance her career.

Marilyn became Johnny Hyde's mistress. There was no love in this, as far as she was concerned, but she was one to stick to her bargain. She refused to marry him, but she lived with him and by her own statement, except for one slip, she was faithful to him as long as she was his mistress.

Johnny Hyde made Marilyn successful. How he did it remains something of a mystery, although there are those in Hollywood who said they knew. It was true that as executive vice-president of an important agency, Johnny Hyde had access to the most important men in Hollywood, the executives who ran the Big Eight studios. But Johnny Hyde could not cram Marilyn down their throats. They had to be convinced.

He tried to convince many people that Marilyn had what it took to be a star. He began taking Marilyn to lunch with him at Romanoff's nearly every day. Clients and acquaintances would drop in and sit with Johnny and Marilyn—important men: writers, directors, and producers. Marilyn sat quietly and kept her eyes glued on the men she accompanied, while all others in the dining room played the celebrity game, looking up each time the door opened to see who came in and, as important, with whom. Nunnally Johnson could not remember Marilyn ever uttering a word at these lunches. He was convinced that she was another of what he termed the "eager young hustlers" of Hollywood, the girls who were call girls yesterday, are call girls today, or will be call girls tomorrow. No one disabused him; no one in the charmed circle knew any different. Marilyn was Johnny Hyde's girl, and she was not worth talking about outside his presence.

But Marilyn was not a rich man's whore; she was a courtesan of the old school. She traded her favors for Johnny Hyde's influence, knowing exactly what she was doing. Any

[67]

promises that he made to her were a matter between them. The story went around Hollywood that Johnny Hyde made her a star. The facts indicate otherwise. Johnny Hyde helped her. He protected her. He taught her something about dress. He taught her something about talking to people. But so did Fred Karger, and before him Joseph Schenck, and before him Emmaline Snively, and before her André de Dienes, and before him Aunt Ana Lower. Marilyn was not used. Marilyn was not pushed. Marilyn was the user and the pusher. She said it herself: when she was five years old and walking around Beverly Hills looking at the houses of the stars, she decided she was going to be a movie star. Everything she did from the day she escaped her drab youthful environment was directed to that end. Johnny Hyde was one of her helpers and she shared his bed. No more. Marilyn's preoccupation with Marilyn was complete.

Johnny Hyde's open efforts in Marilyn's behalf were not as productive as they might have been for someone not so clearly associated with him. He asked producers to give her parts, and he assured them that she had great promise. The producers listened, because Johnny Hyde had often been right before, but they saw how much in love he was with Marilyn, and they remembered that he was an agent first of all and that all the clients of all agents have "great talent" and show "great promise."

Marilyn's breaks came during her life with Johnny Hyde. They came in the form of six motion pictures produced within a year and a half. Marilyn's story was that somehow the old silent screen test made at Twentieth Century Fox in 1946 was sent over to Metro-Goldwyn-Mayer in the autumn of 1949, and that Lucille Ryman, a casting agent at Metro-Goldwyn-Mayer, was so impressed with this three-year-old screen test that she called Johnny Hyde and asked that Marilyn be brought in for talks.

Certainly Miss Ryman talked to Johnny Hyde about

Marilyn, because Hyde had purchased Marilyn's agency contract from Harry Lipton. But the *accidental* inclusion of an old Monroe screen test in a batch brought over to MGM from Twentieth Century Fox was so nearly miraculous that under the circumstances it might be disregarded as an unnecessary miracle.

Marilyn's calls to Director John Huston from Durango, reinforced by her relationship with Johnny Hyde, helped get her an audition for a part in *The Asphalt Jungle*.

It was to be a story of crime and punishment, of a gang of jewel thieves and a fence who fall out and into the hands of justice and the law. Marilyn was considered for a part in the picture, the part of the blonde mistress of the fence, who was played by Louis Calhern. That was Marilyn's chance, but a chance was not a key to success.

Marilyn appeared at a meeting with Huston at the MGM studio in Culver City. Johnny Hyde was with her, so she did not feel too nervous. Huston looked her over and said he thought she would do for the part, if she could act. He explained the plot to her, gave her a copy of the script with an injunction to read it all, and sent her home to learn. Marilyn did better than that; she studied the script for three days, aided by Natasha Lytess, an MGM dramatic coach, in whom Marilyn had immediate confidence. Natasha Lytess coached her on every one of her lines, and she practiced until she had the intonations as perfect as she could make them.

Marilyn appeared on this second day at the MGM studio with Johnny Hyde again. She insisted on reading her lines while lying down. This gave her a very fetching look but did not impress Huston. Still, she read the lines well enough. She insisted on a second reading, although the director as much as told her she had the part after the first one. The second reading, obviously, was to please Marilyn's sense of perfection.

Marilyn did well under Huston's direction. Well enough so that she could be recommended.

The Asphalt Jungle was scarcely finished when Marilyn was involved in another film, *All About Eve*, produced by Joseph Mankiewicz, for Twentieth Century Fox. This movie was to receive many awards and to be ranked among the finest produced by Hollywood in the post-war years. Marilyn plays the role of the mistress of George Sanders, a dumb blonde who cannot act, but who will do anything to become a star.

Johnny Hyde found parts for her in other films. Next was *The Fireball*, with Mickey Rooney and Pat O'Brien, a low-budget picture about roller racing produced by an independent who must have been a friend of Johnny Hyde's. Marilyn had a bit part. Then came *Right Cross*, another MGM production with June Allyson, Dick Powell, Ricardo Montalban, and Lionel Barrymore. Here Marilyn played another bit part, this time as a beautiful girl who is introduced to Dick Powell in a night club.

These movies were all made and released in late 1949 and 1950. In 1950 Marilyn secured another part with Metro-Goldwyn-Mayer. In the film *Hometown Story* she was cast to play the role of an office girl on a newspaper. It was not a good film, but, again, it was exposure, Marilyn's ninth exposure in the movies.

In this rush of movie-making, Marilyn's bit performance in *The Asphalt Jungle* stood out above her other acting. Her role in *All About Eve* also brought some comment, but not from the critics, as did the part in the Huston picture. The result of the helter-skelter six months was that Marilyn was signed to a new six months' contract with Twentieth Century Fox. It was not much but it was another chance.

Chapter Five

ALTHOUGH the MGM picture *Hometown Story* was Marilyn's ninth film, with the exception of the disastrous *Ladies of the Chorus* all of her parts were tiny supporting roles; still, by this time, Marilyn should have familiarized herself with sound stages and the requirements of an actress. Had she done so?

Only to a certain extent had Marilyn learned. Her ambition burned and she continued to study. She paid Natasha Lytess all she could afford for regular acting lessons. She went over her scripts with Miss Lytess and memorized the words and gestures. She concentrated desperately on making her own performance the finest. She concerned herself with nothing else in the process of making movies; nothing else counted with her. She was as single-minded as ever. She was going to become a great motion picture star.

When in 1950 Marilyn moved from one movie to the next, alternating between the MGM and Twentieth Century Fox lots, she had acquired friends, admirers, and helpers. Natasha Lytess disciplined her. She admired Miss Lytess extravagantly. Sidney Skolsky gave her confidence, as did Lucille Ryman. She went to live with Miss Ryman after she had moved out of the Studio Club and had stayed for a while in a slum bungalow.

Above all, Johnny Hyde gave Marilyn confidence. He loved her desperately, and he told her that she would become a star. She believed him. She never seemed to have any doubt about that, although she had doubts about nearly everything else. She had no confidence in her own abilities or judgments; she questioned every decision of her own after it was made, and she looked back constantly to remind herself that if she had done this or had not done that she would have been far better off. Later in life, much later, when she had achieved her goal, she remarked ruefully to an interviewer that, if she had her life to live over again, every decision would be exactly opposite to the ones she had made.

Marilyn protected herself by associating when possible with people she knew and trusted, and she trusted people she knew until they destroyed her faith in some way. It was as it had been with Grace McKee Goddard. "Aunt" Grace had made promises and had not kept them. Marilyn never forgot that.

Perhaps with Johnny Hyde Marilyn was able to forget her feelings of inadequacy. If worship could bring about such forgetfulness, she would have no further problems. Johnny Hyde kept asking her to marry him. He questioned her to discover the names of people she trusted, and then he went to them—he, one of the most powerful men in Hollywood—and asked them to put in a good word for him with Marilyn, to persuade her to marry him.

One reason that Marilyn would not marry Johnny Hyde was that she was strongly attracted to another man. He was Arthur Miller, the playwright. They had met during a brief interlude when Miller was in Hollywood. Their romance had been short and tempestuous. Miller had left Hollywood with plans to obtain a divorce and marry Marilyn. He must have had second thoughts then, because the months rolled by and there was no divorce and there was no marriage.

Had Marilyn been as immoral as her detractors in Hollywood believed, there was nothing to stop her from marrying Johnny Hyde and inheriting his money. She did not.

Johnny Hyde suffered a coronary occlusion not long after he and Marilyn became lovers, and he was advised by his doctors to slow down the pace of his life. His blood pressure was high and his heart was weakened. If he lived a quiet, semi-invalid existence he might live for many more years. But if he persisted at the current pace, courting a young woman, the doctors' view of his future was very dim. Rather than give up Marilyn, Johnny Hyde chose not to believe his doctors.

Marilyn was Johnny's girl, but he was not keeping her. For a time, she said, Miss Ryman gave her twenty-five dollars a week in spending money. That was before *The Asphalt Jungle*, when the motion picture roles began flowing in. When *The Asphalt Jungle* was released, Marilyn was already involved in the making of another movie. Could she act? John Huston said she could. The critics of *The Asphalt Jungle* said she could. Archer Winston in the New York *Post* praised *all* the performances of *all* the cast. Howard Barnes in the New York *Herald Tribune* mentioned Marilyn favorably. So did other reviewers across the land.

When she was selected for *All About Eve*, Marilyn saw that the part was basically the same as her part in *The Asphalt Jungle*, that of a sexy blonde. But she saw nuances and, instead of playing the same role, Marilyn played Miss Casswell in *All About Eve* as a more stupid, more designing blonde than the fence's mistress in *The Asphalt Jungle*. It was a fine point, and reviewers were not concerned with the shadings that one supporting actress might be able to give to the role of sexy blonde. If Marilyn knew that the scores of hours she spent in working over her part were largely wasted on the uncaring, she spent them anyhow. She was not playing the role for anyone else. She played it to suit herself.

Whether or not the effort Marilyn made was important, and whether or not it had anything to do with acting, is another matter. *All About Eve's* director, Joseph Mankiewicz, did not think that Marilyn's performance was good acting.

He did not believe she was either a good actress or potentially a good actress.

There is a school in Hollywood that says it is not necessary for film players to be able to act, that acting is a supernumerary talent. This school includes many of the writers, producers, directors, and executives of the motion picture producing companies. As any observer can see, the star system obviously does make it possible for personalities to thrive in an atmosphere denuded of acting talent.

Joseph Mankiewicz did not expect Marilyn to be a good actress. He expected her to project sex on the set, and under his direction she did so.

In the independent production *Fireball* that was filmed on the Twentieth Century Fox lot, Marilyn also played a sexy blonde. On this set she met hair stylist Agnes Flanagan, for whom she was to call time and again in future movies. Agnes Flanagan was hair stylist for the entire cast on this movie, and Marilyn was then an unknown bit player. Marilyn wanted to wear her hair in a certain way which called for a hairpiece, and she had no money to buy one. Miss Flanagan took pity on the wistful girl, loaned her a blonde hairpiece, and did her hair for her especially. As they finished the hair dressing, according to Miss Flanagan, Marilyn turned to the mirror.

"Oh gee, I wish I really looked like that," she said.

It was a remark that Marilyn was to repeat a score of times. No amount of reassurance ever seemed to convince Marilyn that she did look "like that." Forever the queen and her attendants were talking at cross purposes. They knew that she was as glamorous as any piece of tinsel that was called a star; she wanted the glamour to be constant and undiminished. She did not want makeup, she wanted glamorous immortality.

She was a long way from acquiring immortality. Except for *Love Happy* and *The Asphalt Jungle*, Marilyn's roles in movies during 1949 and 1950 aroused little comment. *Variety* noted with its usual acerbity that Marilyn was "up to script demands" in MGM's *Hometown Story*, but the reviewer also made it clear that the demands were extremely limited.

Having appeared in nine movies in three years, Marilyn's record was so far from scintillating that, although Twentieth Century Fox had signed her to a six-month contract, her future was still questionable.

With that contract Marilyn's biography was dusted off by the publicity department and brought up to date, and pictures and articles about her signing were sent out to the newspapers. The picture was a three-quarter photo of her in a low-cut strapless gown, wearing earrings, and her hair in a page boy bob, and the story was the biography with a "news peg" that she was now a contract actress at Twentieth Century Fox.

As those pictures appeared in the last few weeks of the year 1950, Marilyn was approaching a turning point of her career, and for a little while the course was most uncertain.

On December 17, 1950, Johnny Hyde was staying in Palm Springs when he suffered another heart attack. An ambulance took him to Cedars of Lebanon hospital in Hollywood. Marilyn was notified and she came to the bedside. Hyde asked her again to marry him and again she refused, although this time a wedding ceremony would have left her a widow and a wealthy woman, and she could not help but know that.

Three days later Johnny Hyde died. At the funeral Marilyn made a scene. She threw herself across the coffin, pounding on it and crying until she was led away by attendants. Few people at the ceremony took this seriously. More were pained by it than impressed, and the relatives of Johnny Hyde refused to allow Marilyn to join them in the mourners' pew. She was, after all, just his girl, not one of the family.

So Marilyn did not get Johnny Hyde's money, and she left the chapel that December day a poor, lonely girl without a friend to look after her.

Marilyn was in tears all that day. Richard and Mary Sale met her in the hall of the Twentieth Century Fox administration building and saw her crying. They came over to tell her how sorry they were, and she accepted their commiserations graciously between sobs. Then she headed straight for Darryl Zanuck's office to be sure that she had tied down a role she wanted in a picture—it must have been *Love Nest*.

Which was the real Marilyn?

The death of Johnny Hyde might have brought an untimely end to Marilyn's movie hopes. Her protector gone, her stock with a number of producers took a sharp turn downward. Marilyn Monroe, the voices whispered, that sexy blonde of Johnny Hyde's; and the eyebrows lifted and the faces were turned knowingly, because in Hollywood there is no greater respect than that occasioned by the fear of power, and no greater contempt than that occasioned when power disappears.

Johnny Hyde died on the day that Twentieth Century Fox began production of *As Young As You Feel*. Fortunately for Marilyn, the parts had been assigned. Marilyn was to play a sexy blonde secretary, appearing in more scenes than before.

Whatever she had been before, Marilyn was now Joe Schenck's girl. Like Johnny Hyde, Joe Schenck wanted to marry her, but for what were apparently the very same reasons, she refused. Schenck offered to establish trust funds for her, to make her into a very wealthy woman. She turned down his offers. She would share his bed but not his name. She would share his friends, but she would not share his money. Marilyn wanted fame and perhaps power to do what she wished in the motion picture industry, but she did not care for money. Again she showed it.

Through her friendship with Joseph Schenck, Marilyn made another important friend in Hollywood in 1950. One day at Schenck's house she met Spyros Skouras, president of Twentieth Century Fox. He was attracted to her immediately by three qualities: one was the aura of beauty and innocence; one was her native intelligence; the third was her driving ambition to make something of herself. Skouras was a self-made man and he respected ambition, particularly Marilyn's variety of ambition, which was not just to get somewhere but to become someone.

Thereafter, Skouras helped Marilyn in many ways. When possible he tried to persuade Twentieth Century Fox producers to use Marilyn in movies. He suggested her name to Nunnally Johnson when he was casting one motion picture, and one of his arguments was that Marilyn was costing the studio five hundred dollars a week, so her services ought to be used. Johnson did not believe Marilyn could act, and so he borrowed the services of Shelley Winters from another studio, at a cost of one hundred thousand dollars.

Skouras also tried to persuade George Jessel to use Marilyn in a movie he was producing for Twentieth Century Fox. Jessel paid no more attention than Johnson had.

Marilyn continued to work, to study, to read scripts and practice with Natasha Lytess. She spent most of her money on self-improvement—that part which she did not give away. One day Marilyn came to Joseph Schenck and Skouras and asked if they would lend her ten thousand dollars. She wanted to buy a house. Each of them put up five thousand dollars (which was later repaid in full) and Marilyn bought her house.

One evening not long afterward, when Skouras was again in Los Angeles and he and Schenck were on their way to dinner at Romanoff's, Skouras suggested that they stop by and see Marilyn and inspect the house they had helped finance. When they arrived at the house in Beverly Hills, they discovered that Natasha Lytess and her family were living in the house. Marilyn had taken up quarters in the garage.

Even with friends in such high places, Marilyn's career moved very slowly, it seemed, until some of the work she had done herself began to show results.

Before the end of 1950 the impact of the pictures of a scantily-clad Marilyn began to be felt—the pictures that had been taken in connection with *Love Happy* and pictures taken in connection with her other films and pictures taken just because Marilyn was always willing to pose and was always provocative in still pictures. Major markets for these pin-ups were the United States military installations everywhere. The Korean war was raging, and so was the pin-up fad, in a manner reminiscent of World War II. Marilyn became the Queen of the Pin-ups.

The indications began to arrive at Twentieth Century Fox around the end of 1950: fan mail. In the first week of 1951 Marilyn was chosen Miss Cheesecake by the editors of *Stars and Stripes* in Germany. This was strong recommendation, much more powerful than the comments of a hundred reviewers, for *Stars and Stripes* represented box office appeal, not ivory tower judgments.

Marilyn's fan mail began to grow (it was to reach two thousand letters a week within a year, and she was to receive five hundred proposals of marriage—a sure sign of box office power). In the beginning of the surge, not realizing that it had been prompted largely by Marilyn herself, the officials of Twentieth Century Fox were puzzled. It was even suggested by some that there was skulduggery. There was no sabotage. Marilyn had been working hard. For four years she had been posing for pin-up pictures, beginning with those covers for the girlie magazines. In *Love Happy* she had achieved a sophisticated "sexy" look. Later she had refined this to a look of innocent sex. Her popularity with the servicemen was real and was growing.

Harry Brand and the other publicists at Twentieth Century Fox now began to help it grow.

Miss Cheesecake of the soldiers was made Miss Cheesecake of the civilians. Marilyn was taken down to the Farmer's Market in Los Angeles and in a skimpy costume, wearing a frilly chef's hat, she was photographed cutting a monster cheesecake with an old sword.

Marilyn sometimes appeared at Schwab's drugstore and sat talking to Sidney Skolsky and others who came in. She showed humor and playfulness. One day a promoter came into Schwab's and sat down to talk to Skolsky and Ezra Goodman of the Los Angeles *News*. He noticed the attractive blonde with them and began to pay attention to her. He began talking "screen test" and Marilyn appeared to be very interested. Her name? It was Miss Barton, she said. Well, the promoter-producer gave Miss Barton a card and made a date for a "screen test." She did not bat an eye. She did not keep the date, but Skolsky and Goodman kept the producer guessing. Finally Goodman wrote an article about the joke for the *News*, using Marilyn's name. The publicity was wonderful for her, if not so for the producer.

For a time Sidney Skolsky occupied one position vacated by Johnny Hyde—not that of lover but that of father confessor. Marilyn's life was a constant search for the right direction, an endless leaning on people she considered to be strong. She was weak, and she knew she was weak—she believed she was far weaker than she was.

Marilyn was particularly conscious of her inferior education. The deficiency cropped up constantly, for the superior beings around her ventured day after day into realms where she could not follow them or understand them. They played backgammon, they played chess, they talked of socialism and communism and poetry. They argued about artists. What did Marilyn know of all these things?

The Marilyn of the mundane world who had been supplanted by the Marilyn of the movie dream wanted to understand the world around her. She enrolled in courses in the extension division of the University of California at Los Angeles in February, 1951. She took courses in art appreciation and literature. She attended classes faithfully for several months, and, of course, none of her classmates guessed for a long time that the quiet, shy blonde without makeup was an aspiring movie queen. Marilyn was not well enough known to make recognition inevitable until one day a fellow student discovered her pin-up picture in a movie magazine and brought it triumphantly into class. Shortly afterward Marilyn withdrew from the courses because the whole atmosphere had changed.

If this was a pose it was one that Marilyn affected all her adult life. She had more books than any other girl who lived at the Studio Club in her day. She read them. She came on the set of *All About Eve* with a copy of *Letters to a Young Poet* by Rainer Maria Rilke under her arm. When Joseph Mankiewicz asked her if she knew who Rilke was, she said she did not, but listened as he told her. He asked her where in the world she had picked up the book if she did not know anything about the author, and, opening her big gray-blue eyes wide, this was her answer to Mankiewicz:

"I was never told what to read, and nobody ever gave me anything to read. You know—the way there are certain books that everybody reads while they're growing up?

"So what I do is—nights when I've got nothing else to do I go to the Pickwick Bookstore on Hollywood Boulevard. And I just open books at random—and when I come to a page or a paragraph I like, I buy that book. So last night I bought this one. Is that wrong?"

Mankiewicz told her no, it was not wrong, there was no better way to choose books for reading.

Marilyn got under the skins of people in Hollywood because she did not pretend, or if she pretended, her pretensions were so carefully worked out that they exhibited the mark of supreme skill. Consider this: she had told her story about choosing books to Joseph Mankiewicz, but Natasha Lytess said that she, the student of Germanic literature, introduced Marilyn to the works of Rilke. Now, who did introduce her? Both of them? Or had Marilyn learned from Miss Lytess and allowed herself to be impressed and thus to impress Joseph

Mankiewicz in the way that she knew he would be impressed —by an honesty about her ignorance?

Marilyn resembled a dumb blonde, but in anything that concerned her career she was, as one of her physicians once remarked, "dumb-smart."

How "dumb-smart" she was became apparent early in the spring of 1951.

After her part in *As Young As You Feel* there was nothing for Marilyn on the Twentieth Century Fox schedule. She was certain that when her six-month contract expired in May it would not be renewed unless she brought about a situation in which the studio had little choice. There was no time or way to manage this through performance in a motion picture. *As Young As You Feel* would not be released until June, a month after the contract renewal date, and her part in it was that of the usual sexy blonde.

If Marilyn was to succeed she had to impress someone quickly with the materials at hand. She felt there was no use to try to impress Darryl Zanuck. He knew who she was now, and she was certain that he did not like her.

Cheesecake was Marilyn's weapon, but even in cheesecake she had to produce something spectacular. There was always a market for Monroe cheesecake, so she arranged with the publicity department for a series of pictures which would illustrate how a movie actress relaxes in the privacy of her apartment after a hard day on the lot with only the camera for company. The photographs were to be taken in the still-photograph gallery at the Twentieth Century Fox studio. She was to wear a wispy negligee. She was to pick up the costume at the wardrobe department, carry it the six blocks down the studio street to the photographic gallery, and change in a changing room there. Not Marilyn, not in this moment of desperation. She changed at the wardrobe department and walked, barefoot, six long blocks along the streets, slowly and gracefully in her negligee.

At first no one saw her, but then a few messenger boys on bicycles began to turn their heads and stare, and a few heads popped out of suddenly opened windows along the streets. The prop men and electricians and plumbers and stage hands and clerks and secretaries heard what was happening and deduced that she who goes to the photographic gallery in negligee must return to wardrobe by the same route. When Marilyn came back quite a crowd had collected along the streets. Public nakedness never bothered Marilyn. She glowed. The crowd was gallant enough to raise a cheer for her.

Within the next few days the story got around to the trade press and caused some stir. Marilyn had broken no rules, so officialdom could not complain. If anyone minded he could only grumble about Johnny Hyde's dumb blonde.

Marilyn had another bit of good luck a few weeks later. A group of exhibitors came to the studios, led by Spyros Skouras. All the starlets were ordered to appear at a cocktail party. Marilyn spent hours making up and arrived very late and very beautiful. She became a center of attraction. The exhibitors wanted to know who she was and what pictures she was going to be in. When Skouras told them that she was not scheduled to be in any pictures they were not very pleased.

The exhibitors were concerned about their economic problems. A few years earlier television had made its appearance on the entertainment scene. The movie moguls at first were inclined to shrug off television as a specialty and a problem of competition no more serious than radio. But by 1949 television had captured both coasts and was beginning to fill in the gaps. The Bell Telephone Company was working on coaxial cables which would make it possible to establish live network services. Play producers and a new crop of entertainment people were arising in the East.

Television executives came to the Hollywood studios early in the game and tried to work out various arrangements. The movie moguls rejected the overtures of the television people. They talked about new drive-in theaters, new wide screens and color techniques, and spectacular movies. The slogan, "movies are better than ever," came into being.

Television, however, did not dry up and blow away. Instead it began to capture much more of the movie market than anyone had expected. To be sure, the only movies that television could show at first were very old ones or foreign movies. So they showed very old movies and foreign movies, and people across the country stayed home in droves and watched them. They also watched special programs filmed for television and live programs on television.

By 1951 television had cut deep into the heart of the motion picture business. Along with other studio stockholders, those of Twentieth Century Fox were not pleased with the look of the financial statement. They could see worse days coming. The Federal Communications Commission was licensing television stations in the deep hinterland, and soon they would be built, operating, and connected to the national networks. First-run theaters and neighborhood theaters were suffering. The reaction of the exhibitors to television's inroads and the problem of competition of other entertainments had been to raise prices. This, theoretically, brought in the same amount of revenue from smaller audiences. This backward economic theory worked as well for the motion picture business as it did for the public transit business—and no better. Soon motion picture theaters began to go dark, to become warehouses, oddly-shaped office buildings, churches, and that worst of all insults: television studios.

Spyros Skouras at the party that day paid special attention to Marilyn Monroe, Miss Cheesecake of 1951. He took her by the arm and spoke to her in kindly accents, and the producers took note. Very soon a part was found for Marilyn in the production of *Love Nest,* which began on April 18,

1951, and a long-term contract, with the usual six-month options, was signed. It replaced her short-term contract.

A great many people in Hollywood believed Marilyn Monroe was stupid. This opinion was sometimes fortified by occurrences on the set, where she would blow her lines in take after take. It was not stupidity. It was nerves. Marilyn was acutely conscious, even in these early days, of the approval or disapproval of those around her. She could not bear disapproval. It upset her totally.

What could happen to Marilyn, given approval, was described by June Haver who played with Marilyn in *Love Nest*. (Miss Haver played the female lead in the picture, and William Lundigan played the male lead. Marilyn was fourth in the billing.)

"She was so young and pretty," Miss Haver said, "so shy and nervous on that picture, but I remember the scene where she was supposed to be sunning in the back yard of the apartment house we all lived in. When Marilyn walked on the set in her bathing suit and walked to the beach chair, the whole crew gasped, gaped, and seemed to turn to stone. They just stopped work and stared; Marilyn had that electric something—and mind you, movie crews are quite used to seeing us in brief costumes. They've worked on so many musicals and beach sequences. But they just gasped and gaped at Marilyn as though they were stunned. In all my years at the studio, I'd never seen that happen before. Sure, the crew give you the kidding wolf-whistle routine, but this was sheer shock.

"Anyway, Marilyn was aware of it and she just loved it. In her shy way, she smiled. But the crew's reaction gave her confidence because she was always nervous, always had trouble getting into a dialogue scene. Just on the first word or two, she had trouble getting them out, but once she did, once she got started, she was fine—always knew her lines, just was nervous about starting them.

"But the warmth of the crew's reaction to her relaxed her.

She suddenly seemed to be another person. She lost her shyness. I think it's the only time she felt confident—when she was in that bathing suit. It was strange, but just putting on a bathing suit and feeling that warmth, that approbation, that appreciation, not only lost her shyness but she seemed to undergo a complete metamorphosis; she became completely uninhibited in her movements, the way she sat in that chair—so gracefully, naturally graceful—and seductive at the same time. Suddenly, she seemed to shine like the sun."

Marilyn was again the sexy blonde in *Love Nest*, and still again in *Let's Make It Legal*, in which Claudette Colbert, Macdonald Carey, and Zachary Scott played the major roles. She was very much in danger of becoming typed, which would mean that she would get no further than other sexy blondes, such as Lana Turner of a decade earlier.

In *Let's Make It Legal* Claudette Colbert divorces her husband of twenty years because he is an inveterate gambler. Macdonald Carey plays the husband. Zachary Scott plays a millionaire who begins courting Claudette. Macdonald Carey makes love to Marilyn, who plays the role of a beautiful blonde who is staying at the hotel where Carey works as publicity director. In the end Miss Colbert and Carey are reconciled and remarry. Marilyn, all the while, has considerable interest in Zachary Scott's money.

Marilyn began running late. Even when she reached the studio on time, she was late to get on the set. Richard Sale, who also directed this movie, became very annoyed with her. He knew her trouble: it was fear of not being good enough. But he did not sympathize, particularly when she kept Claudette Colbert, Macdonald Carey, and Zachary Scott waiting for forty minutes one day while she made herself up properly. Finally, she rubbed saliva on her cheek to achieve an extra highlight and said she was ready.

Sale took direct action. He spoke harshly to her in front of the crew and demanded an apology for the other players.

She refused to apologize and threatened to call Joe Schenck.
Sale invited her to call Mr. Schenck.

Marilyn flounced off the set. A few minutes later she returned, in a completely different frame of mind. She apologized individually to the others and hugged Richard Sale and thanked him for "straightening her out."

The most important change in Marilyn's status at Twentieth Century Fox in the spring and summer of 1951 was the development of a strong publicity drive. This sprang full-blown from the studio publicity department. Marilyn's cheesecake pictures and stories about Marilyn began to appear in newspapers and movie magazines.

In June, when *As Young As You Feel* was released, Marilyn had her first tribute as an actress. It was the sexy blonde part again, but Bosley Crowther in the *New York Times* called her "superb" in the role of secretary. Later that year, when *Love Nest* was released, the comments were again about the sexy blonde. And so it was in November, when *Let's Make It Legal* began showing. By that time Marilyn was well launched. A long article about her had been written by Robert Cahn in a September issue of *Collier's*.

The publicity machine was effective. Marilyn quickly became "The Girl We Would Most Like to Go AWOL With," "The Woman Most Sailors Dream About," and service papers ran her picture almost every day. They should not have had much trouble in finding different pictures to run; Marilyn had been churning out cheesecake for five years.

The publicity stories leaned heavily on glamorous ideas and very lightly on facts. Marilyn was described as being under twenty years old, when she was, in fact, twenty-five years old. She was described as an orphan, and a Cinderella. The bad parts in bad pictures were forgotten.

In New York City Spyros Skouras added something else to the campaign for Marilyn. He encouraged the advertising department of Twentieth Century Fox to begin featuring Marilyn in the pictures in which she played. He was quick to recognize her extraordinary box office appeal. Soon Marilyn's name was in lights.

As far as the public was concerned, Marilyn's breakthrough came that year. As far as the critics were concerned, it came the following year, although the movie concerned was made in 1951. Marilyn had to move away from the Twentieth Century Fox lot to break away from the sexy blonde harlot stereotype. Sidney Skolsky arranged it. He spoke to the producers, Jerry Wald and Norman Krasna, who were producing Clifford Odets' *Clash by Night*. Marilyn met Wald and sold herself to him at lunch.

She was to play the part of a girl who worked in a Monterey fish cannery. Her costume for much of the movie was blue jeans, rubber boots, an old blouse, and a rubber apron. She still looked sexy.

Marilyn's insecurity showed itself vividly in the making of this movie. Director Fritz Lang frightened her, so she was late for performances. Barbara Stanwyck was the leading lady of this movie, and Paul Douglas played the role of the leading man. Robert Ryan played opposite Marilyn.

Marilyn kept them all waiting, and the longer the motion picture progressed, and the more strained she became before Fritz Lang's stares, the more she kept them waiting. The others resented it. They thought it was an act. No one knew that Marilyn was practicing every gesture and every motion, over and over.

Clash by Night represented a change, although not a very great change, from the parts that Marilyn had been playing. In another way it was a major change. For the first time since she had been in movies, she brought Natasha Lytess to the set with her.

All this time, since *The Asphalt Jungle*, Marilyn had been

taking acting lessons from Miss Lytess, and Miss Lytess was now living in her house, but the coach had not come to the studio. Marilyn was frightened of her directors and she felt that she needed someone on the set who represented her and could tell her whether or not her performance was the best possible in every take. Most actors and actresses contented themselves by looking at the rushes of the day's shooting. If they discovered something they did not like, they might protest to the director and perhaps reach agreement on reshooting the scene. But they did not bring in their own experts or personal directors.

Marilyn lost the first battle over the services of Natasha Lytess when Director Fritz Lang objected to reshooting takes that he had approved simply because Miss Lytess did not like them. Lang ordered Miss Lytess off the set. Marilyn refused to come to work as long as Miss Lytess was barred. The conflict was resolved when Miss Lytess was allowed to return to the set but was not allowed to signal to Marilyn or to contradict Lang.

When the movie was released, Marilyn's performance was hailed as *acting* by Alton Cook in the New York *World-Telegram and Sun*. John McCarten in the *New Yorker* disagreed. He never did come to believe that Marilyn could act, although he reviewed her movies faithfully over the years.

After *Clash by Night* Marilyn returned to Twentieth Century Fox to begin work in *We're Not Married*, a comedy written and produced by Nunnally Johnson. The cast was filled with players who were well known in Hollywood: Ginger Rogers, Fred Allen, Victor Moore, David Wayne, Eve Arden, Paul Douglas, Eddie Bracken, Mitzi Gaynor, Louis Calhern, Zsa Zsa Gabor. Marilyn received fourth billing.

The plot of this comedy concerns a justice of the peace who has illegally married a number of couples by mistake. They do not learn about it until two and a half years later.

[88]

In the interim Marilyn has borne a baby. She has just won the Mrs. Mississippi contest and is headed for the Mrs. America contest. But on learning that she is not married, she enters the Miss Mississippi contest and wins it. Then she and her "husband" are remarried.

Nunnally Johnson was not convinced that Marilyn had the physical attributes for the part. He asked an extra, a bathing beauty who had entered many beauty contests around Los Angeles, what would happen if Marilyn really entered such a contest. He expected an honest answer because he knew extras to be contemptuous of principal players in areas in which the extras are specialists. But this extra said that in any beauty contest Marilyn would win in a walk.

Johnson still was not favorably impressed by Marilyn. As far as he was concerned, she was still the dumb blonde he had encountered with Johnny Hyde. One day on the set she came running up to him and asked breathlessly, "Where's the men's room?" He pointed and she ran off. He never did discover what she was doing.

That was a minor irritation. Johnson's major irritation came from what he regarded as either unprofessional conduct or downright stupidity. In the important scene at the climax of the movie, Marilyn and David Wayne stand up at the altar of a church to be remarried. The groom carries the baby. During rehearsals for the scene the baby began to cry. Marilyn did not even look at the child, although, as the producer knew, a real mother would have taken the baby in her arms, frowned, or shown some emotion. Johnson stopped the action and spoke to her before the shot was made. She said it had never occurred to her to pay attention to the baby. Johnson could not understand it. Had he known her better at that time he might have understood. Marilyn was working under extreme tension, she was having difficulties in getting Natasha Lytess into the lot to protect her, and she felt that everyone in authority at the studio was her enemy. Marilyn was so much concerned with her own performance that she could pay no attention to anyone else, even a baby. It did not occur to her that the performances of others, outside the lines called for in the script, might affect her own work.

Chapter Six

MARILYN'S impact on the professionals in Hollywood continued to be slight. Her relationships with production officials of her studio would never be as good as with the exhibitors, and Marilyn would not forget the manner in which she was treated in the beginning. The leading production officials of Twentieth Century Fox still did not show the respect she felt was due her. The exhibitors loved her because she was becoming one of the most important box office stars in Hollywood without having yet played a major role, but the men and women who made the motion pictures yielded to the demands of the exhibitors reluctantly.

We're Not Married was completed in the first few weeks of 1952. Marilyn was earning $750 a week then, when she went to work on her new film as a "star," playing the female lead opposite Richard Widmark in a movie called *Don't Bother to Knock*. This movie was directed by an Englishman named Roy Baker, and there was no trouble with retakes, no trouble with Marilyn in the movie. She was behaving herself very well. She seemed pleased to have her first major role. Marilyn was then living in a small apartment in the Beverly Carlton hotel, but she moved in with Natasha Lytess to study, study, study.

The role called for real acting. Marilyn played the part of a psychotic blonde instead of a sexy one for a change—perhaps one should say a psychotic sexy blonde. Marilyn played the role of a girl who suffered from arrested emotional development. The critics were of two minds about the effectiveness of her performance. Some of them thought that *Marilyn* was a case of arrested emotional development; others thought she had exhibited fine potential as an actress. Natasha Lytess sniffed, said that Marilyn had not worked enough on the role. At least she had worked without hesitation. The film was shot quickly and on a low budget. There was no talk about excessive retakes.

During this filming two crises overtook Marilyn at Twentieth Century Fox, and in the studio's handling of them she was satisfied that the executives exhibited the contempt and dislike they held for her.

The first crisis concerned her health. She was finishing up scenes from *Don't Bother to Knock* and was beginning to work in another film, *Monkey Business*, when she suffered an appendicitis attack and was taken to the hospital by the studio physician, Dr. Eliot Corday. After a few days in the hospital for observation, Dr. Corday decided that she could return to the set and finish *Monkey Business*, a more important picture in which she had fourth billing, below Cary Grant, Ginger Rogers and Charles Coburn. It was the role of the dizzy blonde once again.

Marilyn went back to work. She was scarcely back on the set when a call came in from the publicity department. Aline Mosby, the Hollywood reporter of United Press Associations, wanted to interview Marilyn, the publicity department said.

Marilyn was not only willing, she was delighted. This interview represented far more than a cheesecake picture. It would be good publicity for Marilyn because Miss Mosby was one of the most important reporters—as opposed to columnists— in Hollywood. United Press served newspapers all over the world, thousands of them, plus radio stations, television stations, and news magazines. A major Hollywood interview by

Aline Mosby went almost everywhere and was sure to be widely used by the newspapers.

Marilyn appeared at the office of Sonia Wolfson, one of the publicity writers of the studio. Miss Mosby asked one question after another, and Marilyn, shy and appealing, answered them.

"And what about the nude calendar?" Miss Mosby said, out of the blue. "Why did you pose for that?"

"Because I needed the money," Marilyn said, without batting an eyelash.

Sonia Wolfson was in a fog. She did not understand the question and she did not understand the answer. But the questioner and respondent soon enlightened her.

The story spread around the office very quickly and created a considerable amount of concern lest Marilyn and Twentieth Century Fox be attacked in press and pulpit. It had happened before, over matters seemingly as innocent as this one. A nude calendar did not represent a very high degree of sinfulness, and yet women's associations the nation over sometimes found strange reasons to attack Hollywood. It was a universal custom that if a motion picture personality came under attack and embarrassed the studio, the studio had no recourse but to get rid of him or her. It was simple economics. The studio must survive. Any Hollywood personality could be expended in this process. If this seemed cruel, it was only business: the Hollywood actor ruined his own career by being subject to complaint on grounds of immorality. If the women's groups and church groups lined up against him, it wrecked his draw at the box office, and there was no place for him in Hollywood. The famous "morals clauses" of the Hollywood contracts were not often invoked, but when they were invoked there was no argument.

The nude calendar picture to which Miss Mosby and Marilyn had referred adorned thousands of walls in America that year. It had been widely circulated in 1951 and 1952 in barbershops, bars, service stations, and other places where lusty men were likely to congregate. The year 1952 in the motion picture business was far different from ten years before; the Hays office which imposed the sanitary code was nearly out of business and motion picture producers were turning more and more to sex to lure paying customers into the movie houses, and yet motion picture producers were still leery of incipient threats.

Marilyn had told part of the truth to Aline Mosby. She said that she posed for the nude calendar because she needed the money. That much was true, but it was not quite true, as she told Aline Mosby, that Marilyn had been out of work and half-starved at the time. She had needed the money because she was buying a new Ford convertible. That fact was to be concealed for a number of years, but it was unimportant, because the story Marilyn gave Aline Mosby was the most spectacular piece of news to come from Hollywood in weeks. It was placed on the front pages of newspapers from one end of the continent to the other, and not only on this continent but in Europe and elsewhere.

Back in the days before Johnny Hyde had entered her life, Marilyn had been approached by a photographer named Tom Kelley to pose for some nude pictures for calendars. She had refused at first, but, when she needed fifty dollars in a hurry, she had agreed, and one night she had gone to the pink stucco studio and had posed on a red velvet drape. Kelley's wife was in the room at the time, and for amusement they all listened to the phonograph on which Photographer Kelley was playing an Artie Shaw version of "Begin the Beguine" because it was sexy music.

Marilyn knew that this was not a very wise move for aspiring young actresses when she did it, in the dead of night. She had sworn Kelley to secrecy, and she had attempted to disguise her name when she signed the photographic release form. She had believed Kelley when he told her that her face would not be recognizable on the calendar.

There were no recriminations from Marilyn when this came to light. Once the question was asked, she capitalized on it. She was worried for a time as to the course she should pursue. Some told her she ought to deny the story, but others, including Spyros Skouras, advised her to tell the truth. So she did, and she stuck with it. Aline Mosby's story, when it appeared, was not contradicted.

"The beautiful blonde now gets a fat pay check every week from an excited Twentieth Century Fox Studio. . . ." wrote Miss Mosby. Excited was an understatement until the results of the story began to become known. Did it hurt Marilyn Monroe? Darryl Zanuck could have fired her if he had wanted to, if he had hated her as Marilyn said, and no one would object, least of all her agents, because suddenly Marilyn Monroe was the hottest property in Hollywood.

Her story, the sad tale of the poor hungry girl with the big blue eyes, brought strong protective emotion to the throats of millions of red-blooded American men, and tears of sympathy to millions of red-blooded American women who knew that Marilyn just could not have done anything wrong. Her performance was a complete success. And somebody said she was not an actress! Marilyn had appeared in fifteen films, but she had never given a performance to compare with this one.

Marilyn kept the story alive. A reporter asked her if she had anything on at all.

"The radio," said Marilyn shyly.

She thought that was so funny a remark that she telephoned friends, among them Fred Karger, to report on her quip. It *was* funny and the world laughed with her. The funny part was that Marilyn was laughing at her own sexiness; her attitude was that she knew and her audience knew that this was all just good clean fun.

Studio officials showed a low opinion of Marilyn a few

weeks later when she suffered another appendicitis attack and was forced to go into the hospital. She had not paid her bill for the previous stay, and the hospital would not readmit her unless someone would guarantee the bill. Darryl Zanuck was approached by friends of Marilyn's, but he issued orders that the studio was not to guarantee the bill. Finally, Marilyn was admitted when a group of friends guaranteed the bill for her.

Earning $750 a week and unable to pay a hospital bill? This was typical of Marilyn, typical of movie actresses and actors. She was in debt and was paying old debts. She was paying agents, high rent, and a healthy sum every week to Natasha Lytess for her coaching services. At this point, however, Marilyn was too sick to be resentful. She did not complain or mention this lack of generosity to many people, and she never mentioned it to the press.

After the filming of *Don't Bother to Knock*, Marilyn moved back into the Beverly Carlton Hotel. She lived in a one-room apartment with an exercise board, a phonograph, and her books. She also had barbells and a pair of roller skates, because she had to learn to skate for scenes in *Monkey Business*. A friend who called on her said her apartment looked more like the dormitory room of a college girl than the apartment of a movie actress.

Marilyn did not have very many friends in the motion picture business, and those she cultivated were the musicians, hairdressers, makeup men and designers—people who served the personalities, who were not competitive, who had nothing to gain by flattering her or by cruelty behind her back.

One night Marilyn went to dinner with Billy Travilla, the designer, who was a good friend. She thought it would be exciting to go pub-crawling in the Central Avenue district, which was the Harlem of Los Angeles. Travilla arrived at the Beverly Carlton early in the evening and knocked on the door. Marilyn shouted, "Just a minute," and he could hear her inside, rattling papers and moving about. While Travilla waited, another man came to the door carrying two dozen red roses, stepped past him and knocked. A bellboy came, carrying a telegram. Another bellboy came, carrying another telegram. Each rang the bell, and each time Marilyn said, "Just a minute," and went back to her rattling.

The four, designer, man with roses, bellboy, and bellboy, stood outside the door, listening and looking awkwardly at one another. They waited fully half an hour. Then the door opened and a dazzling Marilyn greeted them all with a winsome smile. She took one wire, and then the other. The bellboys were dismissed with special smiles and went off happily. The man with the roses was greeted warmly but reminded that he had made a mistake in the evening of their date. It was for the next night, said Marilyn. The man handed her the roses and bowed out, and she smiled at him, too. Travilla went inside for a moment, while Marilyn looked for some place to put the roses. She had a vase, she said, but she could not find it. Finally she took them into the bathroom and thrust them into the toilet bowl to await her return.

They went to a club on Eighth Street where Billie Holliday was singing. They walked past the manager's office, and Travilla happened to notice a copy of the famous nude calendar hanging on the wall inside. Marilyn had never seen it and she wanted to. Travilla took her back there, but the door was now shut. He knocked. When there was no answer, they walked in. Behind a screen at the other end of the room Billie Holliday was dressing. They apologized and said they had only wanted to see the calendar. Billie Holliday ripped it off the wall and threw it in Marilyn's face.

"Here," she said, "have a good look, honey."

They walked out, but Marilyn seemed hardly upset. Another woman might have gone home to cry, but in a few minutes Marilyn was dancing and laughing in a place on Central Avenue whose floor show featured Dinah Washington.

Marilyn went out nearly every evening during this period.

(The next night it was the man with the red roses.) She moved frequently, from the hotel to a house, to a larger apartment, to the Bel-Air hotel where she paid a week's salary each month for a suite of rooms.

In 1952 Marilyn met Joe DiMaggio, the Yankee baseball player who had retired the previous year. She knew nothing about baseball or baseball players, and their first evening together ended miserably. But there were other evenings, and soon the couple declared themselves to be in love. The romance might have been manufactured in the Twentieth Century Fox publicity offices, for it was just what the newspapers would have ordered if someone had asked them what they wanted. Marilyn, the new glamour queen of Hollywood, to be paired with Joltin' Joe, the greatest baseball slugger since Babe Ruth. It warmed the hearts of grizzled picture editors everywhere.

The romance was real, not manufactured. Joe DiMaggio came to the studio and watched Marilyn perform. They went out, but not often because they were almost certain to be surrounded by their fans. They visited friends. They spent evenings at Marilyn's apartment, where DiMaggio watched television.

The romance began before the appendectomy and survived it; DiMaggio went East, but he wired flowers to the hospital room. It continued by long distance telephone.

In the spring of 1952 Marilyn began to earn a thousand dollars a week and at that price was as great a bargain as Twentieth Century Fox had ever enjoyed. Her name was everywhere movies were shown. Her appearance in *Clash by Night* made that picture a success. It was released just after the huge publicity storm that revolved around Marilyn's calendar.

There was another storm, although a very minor one, when Marilyn's mother finally turned up—alive. Marilyn's fame was so widespread that the name had penetrated the walls of the

California state hospitals for the insane, and in one of them there was a patient who said she was Marilyn Monroe's mother. She talked about this to anyone who would listen. One day the talk was heard by Erskine Johnson, Hollywood correspondent of the NEA feature service, who then harried Twentieth Century Fox and Marilyn until she made her second confession. It could not hold a candle to the first one, but it provided more material for front pages of newspapers. Marilyn had been deserted by her mother, but Marilyn did not desert her mother again, after the lady's presence was announced in such clear tones. From that moment on she supported her mother.

It must have been painful for some of the producers to listen to the pleas of exhibitors for more Marilyn Monroe pictures. She really was not a very well-trained actress, when compared to other established players under contract to Twentieth Century Fox. But business was business, and the exhibitors showed how it worked. *Clash by Night*, *We're Not Married*, and *Monkey Business* featured some excellent, established players. And how were the movies billed on the theater marquees? Marilyn Monroe in this, and Marilyn Monroe in that. The diminishing crowd of movie-goers could be counted on to respond to a Marilyn Monroe movie, and the theater owners wanted more.

They got *O. Henry's Full House*, a series of five short movies stuck together because they were based on O. Henry short stories. Marilyn appeared in a Hollywoodized version of *The Cop and the Anthem*, which bore little relation to the short story. She played a harlot to Charles Laughton's tramp. Part of this concentration on harlotry for Marilyn's career was occasioned by the ease with which she played sleazy blonde parts as opposed to anything else. Part of it was the rapid breaking down of the old Hollywood moral code, which had demanded that in *The Asphalt Jungle*, just two years before, Marilyn be called Louis Calhern's "niece," although everyone who saw even publicity still photographs of the two could tell that if she was a niece, incest was rife in Hollywood.

Business being business, when higher box office prices did not solve the motion picture theater problem, the exhibitors demanded films that would bring their public back, and Marilyn's kind of films seemed to be the answer. Consequently, three big Marilyn Monroe pictures were scheduled for production after the calendar exposé, and Marilyn was to have top billing in all of them. As far as the exhibitors were concerned, Marilyn now could have anything, including an option on the studio.

At the same time that Hollywood had come to unhappy days because of competition, the federal government, in the late 1940's, had forced the breakup of the old producer-to-movie-goer control. The motion picture production companies were forced to divest themselves of their motion picture houses by threat of prosecution under the anti-trust laws. Thus arose regional groupings, such as Fox West Coast Theaters and Fox Inter-Mountain Theaters, which were no longer owned and controlled from New York, but were independent and sovereign in their own regions. This new importance of the exhibitors was the factor that made the stars blaze forth to dazzle the heavens. Hedda Hopper, who worked as a movie actress before she became a movie columnist, credits the bankers with bringing about revolution in the motion picture business. The bankers knew nothing about movie-making but they did know stars, and they took the position that stars were the drawing cards for movies. Motion picture companies needed bank money because they were suffering badly, and so the wishes of the bankers became the law of the industry. So bankers and exhibitors produced a new trend. Then, discovering that they were the props of a sick industry, the motion picture stars began to use the strength that had suddenly been given them. First came demands for huge sums of money. In 1938 only thirty-one persons in Hollywood earned more than two hundred thousand dollars, but in 1952 when Twentieth Century Fox began production of *Gentlemen Prefer Blondes*, Jane Russell, who played with Marilyn, received two hundred thousand dollars for that picture alone. The demands rose, and then the stars began asking for percentages of the profits in addition to six-figure salaries. Stories, direction, production, camera work—all these were forgotten in the concentration on big names to put in big letters above the box offices.

The stars began to make other demands. They formed their own production companies. Contracts had formerly been simple documents with the options and advantages nearly all on the side of the producers. Suddenly they became complex, multi-page affairs in which the artists stipulated the conditions under which they would work and the names, sometimes, of directors and other players they would accept. The Big Eight bent their heads, the executive producers bit their lips, the heads of studios muffled their gasps after quick looks at the beady stares of the bankers and stockholders, and the star system rose to a new brilliance. The bright lights of the handful of stars shone down on Hollywood, blinding everyone else.

In this atmosphere, beginning to feel the power that was becoming hers, Marilyn prepared to make the film *Niagara*, which would be shot on location at Niagara Falls.

Producer Charles Brackett worked out the story to fit Marilyn's qualifications. The girl was to be a beautiful creature with the "clear eyes and untroubled expression of a girl with no moral restraints whatever." Never was a more casual or telling description of Marilyn Monroe offered without insult in the motion picture colony. This was the real Marilyn, the honest, natural Marilyn. She was a lovely animal, who slept in the nude, who almost never wore any form of underwear on the set. She had the morals of an animal, giving her favors where she pleased. Marilyn was not immoral, she was amoral. She did not violate the conventions of a normal society, she did not even bother to discover them. She was not then, before, or later, the sleazy blonde that she had played in her earliest parts; she was what is called in some circles a *natural*, a person ruled by instinct and emotions that are honed far sharper than those of most of us, a person in whom the ponderosity of cerebration is missing. Marilyn was never stupid. She read more widely than many of her peers, but she never thought to connect what she read to life itself, for life was a different game. She was so extremely sensitive to people that she stuttered. Walking into a room, she could tell immediately if the atmosphere was charged against her, and she responded accordingly. She froze, or she melted into warmth and dazzling beauty. Marilyn had learned that she would have enemies, many enemies of many different kinds. She learned first on the set of *All About Eve*, when Zsa Zsa Gabor looked her up and down, gave her a tiger stare, and refused to speak to her. Zsa Zsa Gabor was then married to George Sanders, who played opposite Marilyn. Zsa Zsa knew competition when she saw it, and perhaps even then she knew that Marilyn would overwhelm her in any even match. At the studio Marilyn, with her simple directness, sometimes lunched in the commissary with George Sanders, with whom she played all her scenes. Sometimes—until Zsa Zsa heard of it, and then one day during lunch Sanders received a telephone call, and thereafter he moved warily away when Marilyn approached.

In the filming of *Clash by Night*, Marilyn had learned the dangers of being too popular. She was an unknown player, but the photographers and reporters came to talk to Marilyn, not to Barbara Stanwyck, Paul Douglas, or Robert Ryan. The other players resented it and showed it.

And so, now that she had the power, Marilyn determined that she would protect herself. For *Niagara* there would be no argument, as there had been on *Clash by Night*. Natasha

[102]

Lytess was to be on the set, she was to be able to communi-
cate with Marilyn, and if Marilyn wanted retakes, there were
to be retakes. All this was granted, naturally, for the movie
was to present the talents of Marilyn Monroe. Had she
wanted to play the entire part standing on her head it probably would have been granted too. The producers and writers
and directors were caught in the trap of exhibitor demands.
Stardom in 1952 granted royal powers to a twenty-six-year-
old girl who had neither the education nor the background
to assume such powers. It was apparent from that moment
that there would be excesses and difficulties.

Marilyn could work well without her own dramatic coach
on the set, but only if she felt that she had the complete confidence of the director. This had not always been her luck.
She liked some directors—Edmund Goulding, for example, in
We're Not Married had taught her a trick that enhanced her
glamour. He showed her how to take a quick little breath
before speaking her lines, giving her normal, husky voice a
breathlessness that was most appealing. In *Niagara* Henry
Hathaway managed her so satisfactorily that many who
worked with Marilyn quite forgot that Natasha Lytess was
on the set.

Niagara was a story of lust and murder. Marilyn plays a
faithless wife, and Joseph Cotten plays the husband who mur-
ders her. When the movie was released, it was to earn six
million dollars for a cost of $1,250,000. That was the kind of
return the bankers and exhibitors could understand.

Marilyn was not very happy about the small amount of
money she received in those days. The cost of her services,
which brought in the profits, was one of the lesser expenses
of the movie. She began to show her resentments. The resentments were not aimed at the working members of the crews
of the motion pictures. Almost uniformly the stage hands,
wardrobe mistresses, and other specialists loved Marilyn. One
reason was to be found in a little scene played off camera in

the hall of the General Brock Hotel in Niagara Falls during the filming of *Niagara*. Frank Neal, the Twentieth Century Fox unit publicity man on this movie, was getting up early one morning and groggily pulling himself together for the day when he heard an argument outside his door. He opened the door a little and saw Marilyn standing in the hall talking to Allie Hughes, the wardrobe mistress of Twentieth Century Fox, and Abe Steinberg, the unit production manager. Rather, Allie Hughes was talking and Marilyn was listening. Abe Steinberg was standing by with an embarrassed look on his face, trying to pretend that he was an innocent bystander.

As he opened the door Neal caught these words:

"Where yo' pants?" asked Allie Hughes. "Don't you know it's windy out? Why ain't you got no pants on?"

Marilyn giggled. "Because they gag me," she said.

"That don't make no difference," Allie said, shaking her head. "You's a lady. Ladies wear pants. You gonna wear pants."

Whereupon, as soon as the stores were opened, Abe Steinberg was sent to the J. C. Penney Company store to buy several pairs of nylon panties for the star of *Niagara*. And when Allie was in her presence, Marilyn meekly wore pants.

But not otherwise. In *Niagara* Marilyn began to establish her reputation for movie nudity. She was supposed to be naked in one bed scene, although covered by a sheet. And so she played it nude. She called it realism. She repeated realism in a shower scene.

Now that she was a leading lady, Marilyn could choose the people she would have around her. She could not yet tell Twentieth Century Fox who was going to play opposite her, choose her own roles, her directors, and her stories, but she could determine her personal staff. She had worked with Allan Snyder, the makeup man, since the earliest days at Twentieth Century Fox, and she now insisted that he be assigned to all her pictures. It was not that she distrusted the judgment of Ben Nye, Twentieth Century Fox's chief of makeup, but she was nervous around strangers, and the more movies she made, and the more conflicts in which she was involved, the more nervous she became.

When *Niagara* was completed Marilyn went down to New York City to see Joe DiMaggio, who was conducting a television show there. The studio wanted her to go to Atlantic City for the highly ballyhooed world premiere of *Monkey Business* and to be Grand Marshal of the Miss America Parade. Marilyn did not want to go because it would make her nervous. But she did go, after a few days in New York, where DiMaggio took her to meet his friends at Toots Shor's old-fashioned saloon, and the gossip columnists went after her like dogs after a very meaty bone. She added to a reputation as a quip mistress in an interview with Earl Wilson. When he inquired about the quality of her chest—"true or falsie" as he put it—she replied "everything I have is my own."

Cynics were inclined to believe that these bons mots were manufactured for Marilyn by the studio publicity department, but if so, the publicists continued to deny it long after her death, and her friends said she had a nice sense of humor if she could be kept calm and away from the consideration of the enormity of her problems as an actress and international personality.

Marilyn's tardiness on the set seemed to increase about this time. She had been tardy for Travilla, her designer, on their date in Hollywood, but that was the normal tardiness of a woman dressing. Now she began to keep people waiting for one, two, three hours at a time. In New York she was over an hour late for a press conference.

Because she was late, she missed the train to Atlantic City for the big parade. It was vital that she reach the station in time, and so the press agent with her chartered an air liner, and they flew, the two of them, in style to the home of the bathing beauty contest.

In Atlantic City she posed, as usual, for cheesecake pictures. She was wearing a red dress that had been made for her part in *Niagara*, a low-cut gown which exposed most of her chest. She posed with a WAC, a WAVE, a SPAR, and a WAF to do her bit for the armed services. The photographer stood on a balcony and shot down on her, thus making the most of the cleavage. The picture was released by United Press. A military man saw it and was horrified at the indecent exposure. What would American mothers think of sending their innocent little girls into the service if they saw pictures like this? So an order was put out to kill the picture, and picture editors everywhere reached into the wastebasket, pulled out the very ordinary, very routine cheesecake shot, and ran it on the front pages of their newspapers with explanatory articles and captions. No matter what Marilyn did these days, it seeemed to turn to gold for her and for Twentieth Century Fox.

When Joe DiMaggio saw the picture and was teased about it by his friends, he became proprietary and possessive, Marilyn said. DiMaggio was a San Francisco Italian boy, brought up in a good, solid Roman Catholic family which came from a land where the ladies wore black and lots of it. His sense of decency was offended. Just because she was having an affair with DiMaggio, Marilyn saw no occasion for him to lecture her on morality. She went back to California to ponder the troubles of being the most celebrated woman in the world.

Power now began to oppress her. The studio scenes in *Niagara* were completed in July, and Marilyn had nothing to do until the middle of November when she would begin work on *Gentlemen Prefer Blondes*. She went back to her studies with Natasha Lytess, who was now on the Twentieth Century Fox payroll at Marilyn's insistence. But now that she was so powerful, Marilyn began to study acting with Michael Chekhov, nephew of the Russian writer and a teacher of the "Stanislavsky Method" of acting, in which players work on their instincts and attempt to channel their real emotions into acting.

Marilyn had tasted the Stanislavsky Method in the Actors' Lab days, and she liked it. It did not demand intellectual exercise. Miss Lytess took the position that Marilyn needed to learn to control herself. Marilyn had no intention of controlling herself. In the gentle arguments between them seeds of doubt were planted in Marilyn's mind, and she began to turn from Natasha Lytess.

Chekhov was an honest soul. He suggested that Marilyn had everything she needed to be successful. Why tamper with nature? Marilyn said she wanted to be an actress and an actress she would become. So the lessons went on, lessons one day with Natasha Lytess telling her to control herself, and lessons the next day with Chekhov, telling her to express her emotions.

The Hollywood executives of Twentieth Century Fox were still fighting the losing battle of Monroe. They could not gainsay their eastern masters but they could ignore Monroe in Hollywood except when she was to be in a motion picture, and they did so. She said she telephoned Darryl Zanuck's office every day, seeking interviews and reassurances about her future. No responsible executive at Twentieth Century Fox in Beverly Hills would see her.

In this cold war Marilyn became desperately afraid. She was sure that her employers were waiting, like so many wolves, for her to make a slip. What should she do? Whatever she did, she was not going to trust them. She needed strength. She did not have it, and the strongest character she knew, Joe DiMaggio, had no interest in the motion picture business.

In Joe's absence Marilyn became involved with Hal Schaefer, an arranger who also helped her as a voice coach. She worried about her future. She was certain that Darryl Zanuck was her enemy.

In November Marilyn finally went back to work on *Gen-*

tlemen Prefer Blondes, but now she began to exhibit temperament that she had never shown before. She was desperately unsure of herself, but she was not inclined to trust anyone else either. Now the retakes began. Marilyn stayed in her dressing room most of the time with Natasha Lytess, going over her lines. She would emerge, trailed by Lytess, and a scene would begin. The cameras would turn, director Howard Hawks would signal that the take was fine. Marilyn would look at Miss Lytess, who would shake her head. Marilyn would demand a retake.

The arguments began. Marilyn and Miss Lytess argued with Hawks over angles, over lines in Charles Lederer's script. Marilyn wanted sympathy and coddling and Howard Hawks wanted a professional performance. Neither desire was gratified. The one bright spot in the motion picture, from Marilyn's point of view, was the friendship she made with Jane Russell, the brunette glamour girl.

The two studied dancing with choreographer Jack Cole, who taught them enough to put on a reasonable performance. They both studied singing with Ken Darby and Hal Schaefer. Miss Russell would work until five or five-thirty in the evening and then quit and go home. Marilyn would stay an extra hour or so, with Schaefer or Cole, and work out song and dance routines. It was worth it, if only for one song: "Diamonds Are a Girl's Best Friend," which Marilyn sang in the movie. Some critics said it was the best moment in the film.

DiMaggio came to Hollywood while the movie was being made and spent Christmas with Marilyn. He agreed to pose for pictures on the set with her. She retired to her dressing room that day to prepare and kept DiMaggio and the photographer waiting. Joe suddenly grew angry, told the photographer to forget it for that day, and strode into Marilyn's dressing room. Harsh words were heard inside, and then they came out, DiMaggio leading, Marilyn pale and subdued behind him.

[108]

According to Sidney Skolsky, Joe DiMaggio had a very simple idea about Hollywood: ignore the publicity and get the money while it lasted. That was as far as he would consider the nuances of the movie business. He had no use for most of the Hollywood people he knew, and he came to Hollywood to see Marilyn. She moved into a large apartment, and he spent most of his time there; she cooked for him and he watched television.

It was almost as if they were married, but they still were not married.

When Joe DiMaggio was not in town, Marilyn amused herself by seeing other men, which annoyed him. One day she went to a party given by Ray Anthony, the orchestra leader. She wore the red dress from *Niagara*, which DiMaggio hated, and she ended up the evening playing the drums with Mickey Rooney. It was not the kind of performance that DiMaggio liked. But Marilyn had changed. Four years earlier, when she was in love with Fred Karger, if he had asked her to stay home every night for a month she would have stayed at home. If he had asked her to wear nothing but Mother Hubbards, she would have done so, albeit reluctantly. But by 1953 Marilyn was powerful and concerned with her power.

Jane Russell recalled that Marilyn was always sweet and friendly with the stagehands and the crew on the set. She said that Marilyn seemed to be striving to be a well-rounded individual, trying to educate herself. "She seemed to me a thoughtful person, a searching person," Miss Russell said.

In December, 1952, Marilyn went one day to the Roy Goldenburg galleries to attend an auction of books. On sale was a collection of the annotated manuscripts of Max Reinhardt, the well-known theatrical director and producer under whom Natasha Lytess had worked in her youth.

Marilyn obviously had considerable knowledge of Reinhardt's work from Miss Lytess, but the general public and the press did not understand this. Reinhardt was an intellectual, a producer's producer, an artist. A representative of the University of Southern California was in the crowd that day, hoping to buy the collection to add to the considerable body of Reinhardt material in the university library.

It was a considerable surprise to him when the bidding began to discover that he was up against a slight blonde girl. Marilyn bid for the collection. She wanted it. The bidding reached a thousand dollars, and continued. Finally Marilyn bought it for $1335.

The auctioneers and the university officials did not know Marilyn and they jumped to conclusions. So did the press, sneering that this was a publicity stunt by a young blonde sexpot who wanted to get her name and picture in the newspapers.

The bad press upset Marilyn. She was insulted by many, including representatives of other universities who asked that she donate the manuscripts to them. Why should she donate them to anyone? Did she not have as much right to own the writings of her teacher's teacher as anyone else in the world?

She did not have the right, she discovered. The press would not grant it to her. So, wisely, Marilyn put an end to the matter as quickly as she could. She arranged to have Max Reinhardt's son purchase the manuscripts from her at the price she had paid for them. The hubbub died.

Marilyn learned something from this experience. She learned that the press and public did not believe that she had a brain. The press would never believe it, and so the public would not learn until after she was dead that she was a bright girl as well as a beautiful and sensuous one.

It was a shock to Marilyn that the world would not accept her as a thoughtful person or an artist.

Marilyn *was* thoughtful. During the filming of *Gentlemen Prefer Blondes* she sensed somehow that her big moment was in the production number, "Diamonds Are a Girl's Best Friend," and she created quite a stir. The singing and dancing occupied about five minutes of very active work for a number of people, including a full orchestra led by Lionel Newman. At the end of the first take the producer, director, Newman, the choreographer, and the sound engineers all said it was excellent. Even Natasha Lytess did not protest. But Marilyn protested. She said she did not think she had done her best. Newman, who was her friend, gave in. She was the star, after all.

They did ten more takes of that sequence—fifty minutes of gymnastic activity with the most difficult part of all of it carried by Marilyn, who sang and danced. And at the end, she admitted that the first take was best, and that Newman had been right.

She did not just admit it. Marilyn climbed up on the podium where Newman was standing to conduct, and apologized to the orchestra and the entire assemblage. Her only excuse, she said, was that she had hoped to be able to do it better, and she should have listened to Newman. The orchestra members, who had grown tense and moody during this torture, sat up and applauded her. The tension evaporated from the set in a moment.

That was one Marilyn. That was the Marilyn who was conscious of the needs and desires of others, the Marilyn who employed interior decorator Thomas Lane to do her new apartment in impeccable taste and then took Jane Russell to approve it. It was not the same Marilyn who promised Joe DiMaggio she would dress conservatively except for professional purposes and then appeared at Ray Anthony's housewarming in her revealing red dress from *Niagara*, surrounded herself with admiring men all evening, and finished off the occasion with a wild drum session with Mickey Rooney. That was Marilyn Monroe, the big movie star.

Chapter Seven

THE seventh year of Marilyn's career in show business was the year in which she rose to the top of her profession as a motion picture personality—and it was also the year in which she learned that success is a heady drink which one must drink alone.

All that Marilyn did created sensation and wealth. She made people whom she did not even know rich, without even knowing it. She became, in 1953, the leading box office attraction of Twentieth Century Fox. Other players could command high pay for appearing with her, stockholders and exhibitors welcomed every Marilyn Monroe picture, knowing it would succeed. Calendar manufacturer John Baumgarth was to earn a half million dollars in profits on the famous nude calendar. Only Marilyn was not profiting heavily from the immense wave of popularity in which she found herself immersed. At the beginning of 1953, under the terms of her seven-year contract with Twentieth Century Fox, which had nearly five and a half years to run, Marilyn was receiving $1250 per week. In May she would be raised to $1500, and in November to $1750.

Normally, with such a drawing card on their hands, the motion picture producers might be expected to see beyond the next few months and keep their "property" as happy as might be. Motion picture producers can be venal, but they are not usually so venal as to kill the goose that lays the golden eggs. They can be stupid, but are not usually so stupid as to close down the producing gold mine. Darryl Zanuck was not stupid, and Darryl Zanuck was not noted for venality as much as for overbearing authority.

A number of reasons suggest themselves to account for the strange treatment accorded Twentieth Century Fox's most brilliant success at the box office. First was the general contempt in which Marilyn was held because of the manner in which she had come to the studio. Studio chiefs traditionally detested pressure and nearly always managed to squirm out from under it. When Elizabeth Taylor came to Hollywood as a child, her mother secured the support of J. Cheaver Cowden, an important stockholder in Universal Pictures. Elizabeth was given a one-year contract. The studio then put her in the deep freeze and fired her when the year was ended. The same general story was repeated dozens of times in Hollywood.

The second reason for Marilyn's continued unpopularity at Twentieth Century Fox was her conduct. Nunnally Johnson was chosen to deal with Marilyn in her first picture of 1953, *How to Marry a Millionaire*. When she came on the set, he said, it was like talking to a girl under water. "She was either too fey for me to understand, or too stupid, and certainly too unprofessional for me," he said.

Johnson had written the script for *How to Marry a Millionaire*, so he had two relationships with Marilyn in a sense, as producer and as author. In both senses she offended him.

As producer, Johnson was annoyed by the headache Marilyn gave to Jean Negulesco, his director. Before the picture was begun a plan of attack had been worked out by the studio. The picture represented the studio's second use of the Cinemascope process, a French invention which allowed motion pictures to be displayed on a wide screen. This lent itself nicely to cavalry charges and scenes of Roman legions squaring off for battle, but no one quite knew how it would work in a comedy. It had to work, because Twentieth Century Fox was in serious financial straits and needed something that television could not deliver. So the picture was begun under all the usual tensions plus the unknown quantity of the new process and the problem of working with Marilyn.

The producers at Twentieth Century still did not believe Marilyn could perform. What they hoped to achieve was a maximum exposure of her torso with a minimum of trouble. At the highest levels of the studio on Pico Boulevard there was conviction that Marilyn Monroe was a temporary aberration that would soon disappear into the smog. Nunnally Johnson did not believe she had any talent for acting, or any charm, or delicacy, or taste. He called her a phenomenon of nature and compared her to the Grand Canyon, to which the only reaction could be one of voiceless awe.

Marilyn began by arguing about the script—picking on the key to her part in the movie, which was that of a blonde myopic beauty who decides to attract men by keeping her spectacles off. She did not like the idea of wearing horn-rimmed spectacles, she said. It would ruin her image.

Marilyn and Johnson did not get on well. But Jean Negulesco, the Rumanian-born director, had more of a way with women, and Marilyn could feel that he was sympathetic to her. So she brightened. And she allowed herself to be convinced during a long siege in which Negulesco took her to dinner a number of times.

It was obvious to all concerned that there would be tensions on the set, because *How to Marry a Millionaire* was a showcase for three of Hollywood's best-known women, Marilyn, Betty Grable, and Lauren Bacall. Temperament was the order of the day.

Betty Grable had top billing in the movie, which was proper, because she was, to that moment, Twentieth Century Fox's leading female property. Marilyn began by being resentful: she thought that she ought to have the part of Loco, which was Grable's, and she wondered why the studio always favored Grable over her. (Had she stopped to think about it, she might have realized that Grable had been an asset to Twentieth Century Fox for a far longer time than Monroe.)

Miss Grable was amused by Marilyn Monroe. Miss Bacall was not. The fireworks began on the very first morning of production. The call, on the set, was for eight thirty, and the three stars were to be there in full dress and makeup. Miss Bacall and Miss Grable were there on time. Miss Monroe arrived at ten thirty, with Natasha Lytess and no excuse.

Marilyn was similarly late the next day and the next. Director Negulesco tried to protect himself by making her call for seven o'clock, in the hope that she would be there by nine and ready to work at ten.

Betty Grable treated Marilyn very gently, which she had no need to do. In one scene, when the three girls are sitting on the terrace of their apartment discussing the means of meeting a millionaire, Miss Grable noticed that while she and Miss Bacall were both wearing polish on their toenails, Marilyn was not. So Miss Grable asked Director Negulesco to stop the action while she put polish on Marilyn's toes.

There were reports, nonetheless, that the set of *How to Marry a Millionaire* was an armed camp. Miss Bacall made no pretense of her feelings toward Marilyn: she had no use for Twentieth Century Fox's new sexpot.

Nunnally Johnson saw hope for a moment. One day when Marilyn was in a bathing suit and was preparing for a scene in which she was to be in a fashion show, he suggested that she wear a very short beach coat.

Marilyn stared at him for a moment with her big blue eyes. "You mean so they'll think I haven't got anything else on?"

"I'd like something so startling you'd get immediate whistles," Johnson said. "You don't mind whistles, do you?"

Marilyn grinned.

"Where do you think I'd be if I hadn't got whistles?"

Johnson said this was the first inkling of humor or even humanness that he had ever seen in Marilyn. It was human, but it was also Marilyn's uttering of the great truism of her career. She was the creature of the masses, the star created by the people who went to the movie theaters and paid their money. More than most others, she was the *people's* motion picture discovery.

Johnson failed to understand her as had so many others, and this moment of promise was not repeated.

The filming of *How to Marry a Millionaire* reached a crisis one afternoon about six o'clock in a long scene in which all three female actresses played. The cast and the crew were tired and everyone was growing edgy. Marilyn was blowing one take after another, fluffing her lines, or forgetting them.

Neither Miss Bacall nor Miss Grable said anything, but the tension grew with each successive shout of "cut" from Director Negulesco.

Johnson said he could feel waves of dislike and even of hatred on the set. Six fifteen came, and then six thirty. Marilyn still could not master the scene. Johnson began to feel sorry for her for being so inept, so embarrassingly at fault in public.

Marilyn fluffed it again and walked to her mirror to touch up her makeup—quite an unnecessary move for she had done it a dozen times in the last few minutes. Johnson could feel the loathing emanating from everyone, including Marilyn's old friends the stagehands. He thought it only right to go over and say something to encourage her, so he crossed the set to the mirror and spoke.

"Don't worry, darling," he said, in the words of Hollywood. "That last one looked very good."

Marilyn looked up, puzzled.

"Worry?" she said. "Worry about what?"

Marilyn did not worry. She let Johnson and Negulesco

do the worrying about the picture. All she could be concerned about was her own part. The concern was so overwhelming it left no room for any other emotion. Natasha Lytess stood at the side of the set, just in the shadow of the klieg lights, and nodded her head, one way or another at the end of each take. No matter what Negulesco said, if Natasha Lytess said no, Marilyn demanded that the take be filmed again.

Each day the lateness and the repeats and the fluffs grew more wearing. The picture was going far over budget, which was Johnson's prime responsibility. He barred Natasha Lytess from the set. Marilyn retaliated in her usual way: she did not show up for work the next day.

This time she would not compromise—and lose—as she had in *Clash by Night*. She refused to come back until Natasha Lytess was reinstated.

"There are times," said Nunnally Johnson, "when a producer has no choice but to give in to the actress."

Marilyn was so important to Twentieth Century Fox that such a time had arrived. Lytess and Monroe went back to the set together, and the additional takes were endured, almost without wincing, for the remainder of the picture.

Marilyn received an award early in 1953. Its careful phrasing was an indication of her place in the screen world. The award was from *Redbook* magazine, and while Julie Harris received the accolade as "best actress," Marilyn was acclaimed "best young box office personality." The harried officials of Twentieth Century Fox's Hollywood studio had no choice but to keep Marilyn moving in the public eye.

One of the problems of Hollywood with a new personality is timing. Particularly when an actress is on a weekly payroll there is a compulsion to keep her employed. More than that, the exhibitors wanted guarantees of a steady flow of Marilyn Monroe pictures. So, although *How to Marry A Millionaire* was not to be released until November, in the summer of 1953 Marilyn was given a part in a souped-up Western movie called *River of No Return*. The experiment, if one might call it that, was in throwing together the beautiful scenery of northwest Canada, the hothouse talents of Marilyn Monroe, and the head-them-off-at-the-pass excitement of a Western. Robert Mitchum was cast in the male lead, and he suffered along with everyone else.

Marilyn and Marilyn's friends and everyone Marilyn knew combined to say that this was her worst moving picture. It certainly was one of the worst. It was also one of Director Otto Preminger's worst efforts. But for that Preminger must share his load of blame. A performance could be coaxed from Marilyn, with the connivance of Natasha Lytess. But it had to be coaxed. It could not be ordered. Preminger was not a coaxer by nature, and while his strong character made him a good director, it frightened Marilyn into stupid silence.

Nunnally Johnson had misread Marilyn a few months before. He said she was lazy and did not bother to learn her lines. He said her diction was terrible. He said many other unpleasant words about her. Preminger repeated them all. Marilyn fought the Natasha Lytess fight again, and won. He tried the same tenderness that Johnson had tried, and Marilyn responded in the same manner, blinking her big eyes and asking if something was the matter.

She wrecked his best scenes, destroying even the impact of Cinemascope with which he hoped to soften the blow. Then, on location at Banff, she slipped in the Athabasca River during a scene in which she and Mitchum are boarding a raft to escape pursuing Indians, and she tore a ligament in her leg.

Marilyn and Joe DiMaggio had been arguing like an old married couple over the subject of marriage and Marilyn's pursuit of her career. When she was hurt, DiMaggio swallowed his dislike of the movie world and came to Banff to be with her. They went back to San Francisco, where Marilyn saw the DiMaggio family. (She had been taken up to San Francisco to meet them the year before.)

During this visit one of Joe DiMaggio's brothers was drowned in a fishing accident, and DiMaggio's emotional reserve crumbled. Marilyn was prone to cry at the sight of helpless animals, and not a few Hollywood men had penetrated her defenses with displays of weakness, not strength. DiMaggio's temporary weakness served him where his strength had not, and Marilyn agreed to marry him at the end of the year.

Marilyn's press was getting better. Columnist Henry McLemore met her and discovered her to be "a lady from way back." He said she was "quiet, gentle, gracious, and the sort of girl you'd like to bring home and say, 'Mamma, this is Marilyn.'" She met Milton H. Greene that year, a young photographer from New York who was working then for *Look* under contract, and he penetrated her defenses. Their meeting was the key to it. They met at Twentieth Century Fox studios. He was to take pictures of Marilyn for a cover for *Look*.

Marilyn looked him over as she came in the room, commented on his youth. "You're just a boy," she said.

"You're just a girl," he said, putting her in perspective.

It was the perspective that Marilyn sometimes liked. She did not demand hero-worship or subservience, except in the most important matters, such as control over directors and producers. The minor amenities of Hollywood prominence, such as toadyism, never appealed to her. And so she and Milton H. Greene understood one another. That is what she called him: Miltonhgreene, running it all together. His interest was professional. Marilyn's interest was never solely professional in anyone; she tried to make friends with all. And so they became friends.

No matter what she did, Marilyn's actions seemed to annoy someone at Twentieth Century Fox. Jack Benny asked her to appear on his television program. Marilyn did not want to do it, but she knew the publicity was important to her career, so she agreed reluctantly. She might have commanded ten thousand dollars for the performance had she been willing to have her agent talk money to Benny. She did not want money. She wanted a new black Cadillac, an El Dorado, with special glass and special tires.

She and Joe DiMaggio had talked it over, she said, and that was what she wanted.

Studio officials shrugged. They explained to Marilyn that if she took a Cadillac, she would have to pay income tax on the value of it. Why did she not take the money and then buy her own Cadillac?

No, she said. She wanted a Cadillac that was given to her by Jack Benny.

And so it was. And she had to pay the income tax of three thousand dollars. Besides that, when the Cadillac came it was white, not black, and did not have the right kind of upholstery. Joe DiMaggio took over the negotiations with Twentieth Century and the Benny program on that score and made himself as unpopular with the studio as Marilyn.

Perhaps anyone would have been annoyed by such idiocies, but Twentieth Century Fox studio seemed to annoy very easily as far as Marilyn and her affairs were concerned.

Joe and Marilyn continued to be together until just before the premiere of *How to Marry a Millionaire*. Johnson, Negulesco, and Marilyn knew that in this motion picture they had a hit. The retakes and the lateness and the unpleasantnesses were behind them, not forgotten, but looming as much less important since the overall effect of the film was so satisfactory. The story of *How to Marry a Millionaire* concerns the pooling of resources by three models who want to capture rich husbands. They rent an expensive penthouse apartment. Lauren Bacall meets the first one but thinks he is poor and spurns him. Betty Grable gets mixed up with a man with evil intentions but is rescued by a forest ranger. Marilyn is pursued by a playboy who wants her to meet "his mother" at Atlantic

City but gets on the wrong plane because she does not have her glasses on and meets her landlord instead. In the end Marilyn marries the landlord, who is rich, and Lauren Bacall marries the first man she met, who is rich, and Betty Grable marries her forest ranger. All three actresses played their parts with flair. Marilyn's performance was all the more surprising because it showed elements other than what was described as her "arrogant tailswitching."

DiMaggio refused to attend the premiere of *How to Marry a Millionaire*, which was to be held at the Fox Wilshire Theater in Hollywood. He flew off to New York. He wondered why Marilyn wanted to go. She told him that she did not like Hollywood and its ballyhoo, and that she hated premieres. It was true, but this was *her* premiere, and she had the definite feeling that she had scored a triumph.

If DiMaggio would not take her to the premiere, what should she do? She had been escorted to other Hollywood doings by Sidney Skolsky, but not this night. She called Harry Brand, head of publicity at the studio and asked him what to do. He called Nunnally Johnson and asked Johnson to include Marilyn in his party. How could Johnson refuse, even if he wanted to? But Johnson, too, had put the hard days of spring well behind him.

Just after noon on November 4, 1953, Marilyn drove to the studio and went into one of the dressing rooms. One of her favorite hairdressers, Gladys Rasmussen, was there. So was her favorite makeup man, Allan Snyder. They set to work.

Marilyn was now a platinum blonde and she would stay so. She had a permanent to straighten her hair. She had platinum polish put on her fingernails. Two women from the wardrobe department came in with her slippers, gloves, and evening dress. Diamond earrings were delivered. She had her own white fox stole and muff.

Telephone calls and telegrams began to arrive. Joe DiMaggio called and said he was sorry he was not with her. She was not very pleasant to him because she was disappointed.

Marilyn remained in the makeup room all afternoon. She was literally sewed into the dress, which was a long white lace body lined with flesh crepe de Chine and embroidered with Marilyn's favorite: sequins. It had a long train, which she had to carry as she walked slowly (she could not walk quickly) to the limousine which would take her to Nunnally Johnson's house.

At the Nunnally Johnson house there was a certain amount of tension, as the Johnsons and Humphrey Bogart and Betty Bogart (Lauren Bacall) awaited the coming of their studio-invited guest. The Bogarts and the Johnsons were friends, and Lauren Bacall's attitude toward Marilyn was well known to Dorris and Nunnally Johnson.

But Nunnally Johnson was inclined to forgive much on this night. He had what he was sure was a success on his hands. Further, he felt that Marilyn had reached a turning point in her career. He said that for the first time she had played without either the arrogance or the complacency of a high-grade whore.

Marilyn got out of her limousine and came into the house. Her first request, after a servant had taken her coat, was for a stiff drink, bourbon and soda.

Johnson got it for her.

Then she wanted another.

He got that.

He knew nothing about Marilyn's drinking habits, but these were very stiff drinks and he was beginning to admire her capacity.

Naturally, he said, he and Bogart were gentlemen and would not allow a lady to drink alone.

At dinner no one in the upper echelons of Twentieth Century Fox would have known Marilyn. She was vivacious. Her eyes sparkled. She laughed and she joked and she was friendly, even to Miss Bacall. Miss Bacall began to melt a little. Everyone melted. The dinner was thrown into a turmoil as the Johnson children climbed around Marilyn and the servants abandoned any pretense of work to crowd around and see her. But the chaos was pleasant.

Marilyn was very much on edge and she was terrified, but Johnson did not know it. She seemed to be gay and happy. One would have thought that attending premieres was what she had been brought up to do.

It soon came time to go out and get into the car, a limousine with driver hired for the occasion. Marilyn asked for one more drink. Johnson got the stiffest he had yet poured and then matched it with two others for himself and Bogart. They drank all the way to the theater.

The streets were blockaded around La Cienega and Wilshire for five blocks around the theater. Truck-borne searchlights played on the sky and on the entrance. On both sides and across the street bleachers had been put up and thousands of people sat in them; other thousands stood on the sidewalks behind sawhorses and ropes. In front of the theater under the marquee, reporters and cameramen crowded around the celebrities as they were assisted from their limousines and made their way inside.

As the Johnson party drew up and the ladies got out of the car, the crowd saw Marilyn and began to yell. Her name was on thousands of lips and the shrieking rose to the sky.

Around her the noise and the shrill spun on. She scarcely noticed the microphones that were thrust before her and the television cameras focused on her as she made her way, slowly, fetchingly, into the theater. She was caught up in a whirl of delight and excitement—and she was tight.

She giggled and smiled and enjoyed herself as she accompanied the Johnsons and the Bogarts to find their seats. Then, before the picture began, she discovered that she needed to go to the ladies' room. She was very tight.

Mrs. Johnson, who was not tight, accompanied Marilyn into the ladies' room, because Marilyn needed much moral support at that moment. And Marilyn was not only tight, Dorris Johnson discovered to her horror, but she was tightly wedged in the dress with the long train, sewn in.

Marilyn's long white gloves were so tight that she could neither bend her elbows nor get the gloves off.

What a contretemps! Dorris Johnson somehow got Marilyn first out of, and then back into her costume, and then down to her theater seat. And Marilyn, happy, tight Marilyn, was of very little assistance.

"Women who have been sewn into their clothes," Nunnally Johnson later said sagely, "should never drink to excess."

After the premiere Marilyn could have gone with the Johnsons to a supper party. She could have gone to a dozen others, because she was the hit of the evening, and suddenly she had been discovered by a handful to be human, too. But Marilyn had a hangover, and Marilyn did not feel well, and Marilyn started home.

She went outside and into a studio limousine, which took her back to the wardrobe department. The wardrobe attendant waited in the dressing room, although it was almost midnight. Marilyn doffed the gloves, and the earrings, and the shoes and crawled out of the sequined gown. She put on slacks, and a sport shirt and loafers. She walked out alone into the deserted parking lot and got into her car. And then Cinderella went home to her apartment.

The next day Marilyn called the Johnsons to thank Dorris Johnson for a pleasant time.

"But I'm afraid I got a little tight," she said. Johnson dismissed this with the gallantry of a southern gentleman.

"It's the first time I ever tried alcohol," she said.

And apparently it was.

Marilyn's idyll lasted but a few days. *How to Marry a Millionaire* was adjudged a critical success. It cost Twentieth

Century Fox $2,500,000 to make (including Marilyn's re-takes) but it grossed $12,000,000, meaning that it was a success with the movie-goers, too. Marilyn's notices were the best she had ever received. She was given credit for having developed into a comedienne. She had passed one barrier. She felt it and so did others.

But passing one barrier was not enough. At this time Twentieth Century Fox was casting the important picture *The Egyptian*. Marilyn wanted the role of Nefer-Nefer, an important dramatic part. Darryl Zanuck refused to consider her for it. Marilyn pleaded. She said at least let them test her for the role. If the test proved that she could not carry it, she would accept Zanuck's judgment and would not argue further. Zanuck refused to test her.

Marilyn was now beginning a struggle with the studio that would last for several years and would end unfortunately for all concerned. Money was a consideration in this struggle, but money was not the most important aspect of it. Most important was Marilyn's yearning to be recognized as an actress and to be treated with the respect that her abilities deserved.

In the motion picture world she was never to achieve that respect.

The struggle began in earnest toward the end of the year.

The studio had picked out another picture for her and wanted her to begin work on it on December 15. It was to be *The Girl in Pink Tights*, a remake of an old, very successful Betty Grable picture. Frank Sinatra was signed up to play the male lead, and he was to receive five thousand dollars a week beginning on December 15.

Fresh from her success, Marilyn demanded the right to read the script before she decided. The studio refused her the right. It was not in her contract. Oh, yes, the contract. That called for her to get fifteen hundred dollars a week. She would receive top billing in the movie, but Frank Sinatra would get three and a third times as much money as she did.

Marilyn had read her reviews and decided that she had become an actress—that was how it seemed to the studio. She told her agent that she would not appear on December 15 unless she was allowed to read the script. She wanted to be treated as a human being, she said, not a chattel.

Then Marilyn disappeared. No one could find her. Her agent did not know where she was. Natasha Lytess did not know where she was. No one else except Joe DiMaggio had ever cared enough where she was to be consulted, except Sidney Skolsky, and he did not know.

December 15 came and Marilyn did not show up on the Twentieth Century Fox lot, although Sinatra and others did. She was suspended by the studio, but nobody could tell her that because she did not appear to hear about it.

A few days later Marilyn telephoned. She announced that she was never coming back until the studio let her read the script. They sent it to her in San Francisco, where she was enjoying life with Joe DiMaggio. She read it, and replied in tones of outraged virtue. The plot concerned a schoolteacher who becomes a dancer in a low saloon on the Bowery in New York City. Marilyn seemed infected by her evening with the Nunnally Johnsons. She described herself as embarrassed to think of "rear-waggling."

Marilyn was rebelling, and for several reasons. In the spring of 1953 after the *Redbook* awards, Marilyn had also been selected by *Photoplay* as the most important new star of the year, and she was to receive the award at a dinner. Marilyn had wanted to wear the revealing gold lamé gown she had worn in *Gentlemen Prefer Blondes*. She came to see Travilla, the Twentieth Century Fox designer, about using it. He advised her against it. He said it was made for a musical number, not for an evening in public. She would have to be sewn into it, it was so tight. He told her it would be very bad taste to wear it.

Marilyn grew annoyed. She wanted to wear that gown. It was one of the dresses which had brought her fame. What was wrong with appearing in public as she appeared on the screen? She did not see the difference.

Travilla did not want to argue. He said she would have to have an order from the front office before he would release the gown to her.

Marilyn left and in an hour the order arrived.

Travilla made one more effort. If she was going to wear the revealing gold gown, let her be sure not to wear any jewelry and to have her hair done simply and to walk daintily, without wiggling her hips. She promised. She did not wear jewels. She had her hair done simply.

Joe DiMaggio refused to take Marilyn to the dinner, so she persuaded Sidney Skolsky to substitute for him. Jerry Lewis was the master of ceremonies.

All went well until it came time for Marilyn to accept her award. She got up, wriggled around the table, and started for the rostrum. In her wriggling she aroused Jerry Lewis to action. He jumped up on the table and began to whinny like a stallion. And there was cold silence from the crowd.

A few days later Hollywood columnist Bob Thomas interviewed Joan Crawford, and she attacked Marilyn's brazen display of vulgarity. Marilyn also began to receive negative mail from women's clubs and other groups. She was shocked that she should be attacked. It upset her and worried her.

While Marilyn was slow to learn the ways and many standards of mankind, she did learn. All summer and all autumn Marilyn had been quarreling with Joe DiMaggio, off and on, about the roles she played in movies and the publicity pictures she allowed. Natasha Lytess had been speaking up loudly against crudity and was encouraging Marilyn to seek roles with more dramatic potential than those she had played.

In defending herself against the attack by Joan Crawford, Marilyn had played a role she often adopted when driven into a corner: she fell back on her "orphan" background and pleaded innocence. But Marilyn had used that device several times: to quell complaints about her nude photograph, to quell complaints about her mother's unfortunate reappearance, and then to hush her critics in the Joan Crawford outburst. On the last occasion, even she must have noticed, the effectiveness of the plea was gravely diminished.

The worst aspect of the *Photoplay* fiasco, as far as Marilyn was concerned, was that Darryl Zanuck had been in attendance and had seen all. Marilyn did not ever realize that she had acted in atrocious taste in appearing in that costume at the dinner. What was the difference? If Mr. Zanuck and the others wanted her to appear in thousands of theaters before millions of people in such a dress, why should they object if she appeared before them in it?

Given a mind that does not accept multiple standards of behavior, that is a difficult question to answer. Nobody ever answered the question of the *Photoplay* dinner very satisfactorily for Marilyn Monroe. And now, months later, in the script they offered, her studio was asking her to behave again in a manner for which she had been so severely criticized.

Marilyn did not know whom to believe. Should she believe Natasha Lytess and Joe DiMaggio and stay away from sexy roles? She began to think so. She returned the script to the studio and refused to play the role. She talked about serious drama. Perhaps she would do Dostoevsky. The studio was unimpressed. Marilyn was suspended again, and again was taken off salary.

So, Marilyn decided that she would marry Joe DiMaggio, as he had been pressing her to do, not realizing that marriage could mean the end of a beautiful friendship. Perhaps she did realize it, for she was quite willing to go to Japan with DiMaggio without marrying him. He said it would be indecent. Marilyn never did understand these niceties and duplicities, but she grew to accept them because they were thrown at her so often.

Marilyn married Joe on the fourteenth of January, 1954, in San Francisco.

Marilyn lied a little bit about her age (just two years) when they were married, by a Municipal Court judge at San Francisco City Hall, while the manager of Joe DiMaggio's restaurant and Lefty O'Doul, a baseball crony of DiMaggio's, stood up in attendance with their wives. Marilyn wore a tailored blue suit with a high ermine collar and looked the epitome of tastefulness. Not a curve was more than suggested.

Just before the ceremony, Marilyn stopped in a telephone booth and called Harry Brand at the studio. She informed him that she was getting married; she had promised him she would if she ever did. Then she hung up the telephone. Quite overcome by the harvest of favorable publicity anent the marriage, Twentieth Century Fox relented and took Marilyn off suspension, which was really a generous gesture considering the fact that she had done nothing for them except earn more money than any other star on the payroll in 1953.

Chapter Eight

THE marriage of America's All-American girl to America's All-American boy created a powerful euphoria among publicists everywhere. Consequently the honeymooning couple found it difficult to stay out of the eye of the press.

Their bridal night was typically American: it was spent in the Clifton Motel in Pasa Robles, California, where they managed to stay incognito. They went to the Pasa Robles Hot Springs Hotel and ate steak. Marilyn wore slacks, a blouse, tan wraparound coat, and a kerchief over her head. To be sure that it was recognized that she did not want to be recognized, she wore dark glasses. They escaped the news hunt all that day and made their way to a lodge in the mountains above Palm Springs. Marilyn's attorney, Loyd Wright, owned the lodge and let them borrow it, which meant two weeks of real quiet, without television or telephone. Then it was back to the grind: Joe DiMaggio flying to New York, while Marilyn hid out in Los Angeles and stayed away from her apartment.

She had to talk to some people, and she had to get ready because she and DiMaggio were going to Japan, and so it was known that she was in the city. But she did not want to be found, and so no one found her.

In a few days they were back in San Francisco, and then they were suddenly in Honolulu where a huge crowd met them at the airport, mobbing them and actually tearing hair from the head of the most popular actress of the movie world. Marilyn did not like this at all. The prospect of being dismembered by her fans caused her to cry out for the relative anonymity of Los Angeles. But Joe DiMaggio said they must continue. Tokyo was a huge city, growing to be the largest in the world. They would be undisturbed there.

So they flew on. At Tokyo airport the plane was surrounded by a crowd estimated at ten thousand, more than twice as large as the crowd in Hawaii. Marilyn took one look outside, escaped through the baggage hatch, and took refuge in the customs office whence she refused to emerge for an hour.

Then, to preserve their anonymity, they entered a long black convertible with the top down and were driven the eight miles to the Imperial Hotel, past an almost solid line of Japanese movie fans who just happened to be in the area, waving banners, screaming, grinning, and singing out the magic name *mon chan*, which means sweet little girl in Japanese, and which was the Japanese cognomen for Marilyn Monroe. Somebody, it seems, had let the bird escape from the cage, as they say in Japan. The route was known, which was not very difficult, and the hotel was known, which was not very difficult either, since most important foreigners put up at the Imperial. All ten entrances to the Imperial were blockaded, but the Japanese police are used to blockaders, and they ran interference, letting Marilyn and her husband enter the hotel without broken bones and with their clothing intact.

Joe DiMaggio had his first taste, then, of what it meant to be the husband of the world's movie darling. How did he like it? Not very much, it seemed, because when Marilyn went to Korea two weeks later, Joe DiMaggio did not go along. He had commitments in Japan, but that did not seem to be the only reason. It was not particularly easy for a shy man who had little use for huge crowds of humanity to stand up on a platform, if he knew that all the cheers and whistles were for his wife, and that the whistlers and cheerers were privately voting her "the-girl-they-would-most-like-to-go-to-bed-with" right at that moment.

DiMaggio and Lefty O'Doul remained in Tokyo, concerned with the more important matters of baseball, while Marilyn was whisked away by the military, fitted out in cold weather clothing and combat boots, and taken to points as near the front lines as possible. In two days she did ten shows, entertaining a hundred thousand servicemen. There were no dressing rooms or makeup men or hair stylists for these performances. She dressed in makeshift rooms or out in the open protected by burlap sacking. She had four numbers planned, but one of them, "Do It Again," was removed from the repertory after the first rendition, as too suggestive for soldiers in the mass. She sang "Diamonds Are a Girl's Best Friend," "Bye Bye Baby," and "Somebody Loves Me," songs on which she had spent hundreds of hours of rehearsal in the past. She sang well, or well enough at any rate to please her loyal fans. They shouted and cheered her all the way. She caught cold and developed laryngitis, which turned into influenza. When she returned to Tokyo to be met by her husband at the airport, she was running a fever, but that did not entirely account for the brightness of her eyes. Marilyn had appeared a few times at marine and army camps in the West but she had never before seen adulation like this.

Marilyn returned on February 21. Her plane was early, and so she waited for fifty minutes in the base coffee shop for her husband to come and pick her up.

When DiMaggio found her they kissed briefly.

"Well, how are you?" Marilyn asked.

"I've found a place in Osaka that has very good pizza," said Joe DiMaggio.

Marilyn told the press that she felt like a movie star for the first time on this trip to Japan and Korea. She tried to tell her husband about it, but he did not seem to be very interested.

And that was the end of the triumphal tour.

Marilyn and Joe DiMaggio remained in Japan until April. DiMaggio went to the ball park to coach his Japanese players. Marilyn was ill. Really ill. She developed pneumonia. She recovered. Then she either went out to watch baseball, which bored her as much as movie-making bored DiMaggio, or she shopped or remained in the hotel.

When the DiMaggios returned to San Francisco, there was some talk about the time when they would settle down and begin to raise a family. DiMaggio had talked about raising half a dozen children. Marilyn had talked about quitting Hollywood in another two or three years and becoming a full-time housewife.

The chances of this coming about were very dim, especially after Korea. Marilyn liked to cook, but only as a lark. She detested housework. She could be intensely domestic, but only for brief periods of time. If there was a time when Marilyn might have been willing to give up her career as movie actress in favor of a career as Joe DiMaggio's wife, this might have been it. It might have worked, had it not been for that three-day trip to Korea.

DiMaggio owned a house in San Francisco, a restaurant on Fisherman's Wharf, and a boat in which he sometimes went fishing, although he did not work at the old family trade in the old way. He had saved his money as a baseball player. Since he earned about a hundred thousand dollars a year at his top and was in the high brackets for a number of years, he could live comfortably and support a wife very well, perhaps even one with the champagne tastes that Marilyn was developing.

Marilyn spent several weeks in San Francisco, but in May the lure of Hollywood was too great. She had gone fishing with Joe DiMaggio outside the Golden Gate. She had played golf with him. She had gone to his restaurant and waited while he played host. She had tried housewifely tasks, and she found herself bored. She liked the DiMaggio family and got along well with the women, but she had gone too far on the road to film success to cut herself away. Instead of Marilyn coming to make her home in San Francisco and becoming the wife of Joe DiMaggio, they rented a house in Beverly Hills and DiMaggio went south for a time to become the husband of Marilyn Monroe.

This problem had been foreseen by some students of life and Hollywood during the long courtship. There was a conflict in careers.

"If marriage is their ultimate goal," wrote Joe Franklin and Laurie Palmer, "they must resign themselves to the fact that it can't ever be a completely normal union. Marilyn will remain in show business and Joe won't like it."

There was more to it than that. Although both were native Californians, DiMaggio and Marilyn could not have come from more different backgrounds. DiMaggio was the product of a close-knit religious family. Marilyn was the product of no home at all. DiMaggio came from San Francisco, once the cultural center of the West, a city where the sea meant fish and ships and the smell of Oriental climes. Marilyn came from Los Angeles where the sea meant surf boards, bikinis, and beach bums. San Francisco is a conservative city whose men favor neat blue suits and white shirts. Los Angeles is the fad capital of the United States, where men wear bright blue shirts and red trousers and sandals, and the women delight in appearing in public in slacks and high-heeled shoes. San Franciscans shudder when they contemplate Los Angeles, and Angelinos, particularly those of Hollywood, have a built-in inferiority complex which they exercise by calling San Francisco dull. In spite of all, Los Angeles had become the cultural center of the West, exporting a brand of culture that was abhorred up north.

At that time a serious problem, the most serious, was that

Joe DiMaggio had nothing to do in Los Angeles save amuse himself, and Marilyn had everything to do, everything that brought her into constant touch with other men outside the home.

Marilyn talked in glorious terms of working at the studio, rushing to the Beverly Hills house and preparing dinner for her husband and spending quiet evenings in their patio or in the living room. It was a dream. No motion picture actress can long burn the candle at both ends, and those who work at their trade hire servants to take over household responsibilities. Motion picture acting is a serious business. The actress might arise at five in the morning and work a day that lasts until six in the evening and be expected to arise at five the next morning without signs of weariness. Marilyn worked longer hours, with rehearsals and study at the knee of Natasha Lytess. So the plans for domesticity never materialized.

Marilyn and DiMaggio began to quarrel almost from the beginning of the new life in Beverly Hills. She insisted on going to Hollywood parties as a matter of business as well as pleasure. Joe DiMaggio refused to attend. He would deliver her and pick her up at the end of a party and take her home.

The movie vehicle for which Marilyn came south was *No Business like Show Business*, a musical. She did not want to play in this particular movie, but was persuaded to do so by a promise of the feminine lead in *Seven Year Itch*, a comedy which was to be directed by Billy Wilder.

Filming of *No Business like Show Business* began in June on the Twentieth Century Fox lot in Beverly Hills. Marilyn proved difficult for producer Sol Siegel from the very first moment. She refused to accept the assignment of designer Miles White and insisted that Travilla be brought in to make her costumes. He was, although Miles White made the others. She would not accept choreographer Robert Alton, but insisted that Jack Cole be brought in, because she knew and trusted him from their work on *Gentlemen Prefer Blondes*.

[135]

He was, although Alton supervised everyone else. Alfred Newman was assigned to supervise and conduct the music, but Marilyn insisted that his brother, Lionel, be brought in, because she had worked with him before. He was.

She complained because Donald O'Connor, the male lead, looked younger than she and was three inches shorter than she. She was upset about airing her voice in juxtaposition to that of the old professional, Ethel Merman. She did not trust the director or the producer, or herself. She looked at the rushes at the end of a day's shooting and said she felt sick.

Marilyn often ate lunch with Travilla during the making of this movie. Sometimes they would go to the studio commissary, walking by the entrance to the Gold Room, where the stars and important officials ate, and avoiding the front of the room where others sat when they wanted to be seen. Marilyn and Travilla would walk down to the far end where the extras and bit players and technicians ate.

Sometimes Marilyn would tie an old bandanna over her head, remove her makeup, and they would go to a lunch counter called The Apple Pan on Pico Boulevard, which drew its major business from a neighborhood shopping center. Here Marilyn could eat without concern. No one ever recognized her. At the commissary, no matter how far back she went, or how bedraggled she looked without makeup, the lunchers stopped their forks in mid-air or let the smoke from their cigarettes rise in thin plume as they stared at the studio's largest money-maker.

Marilyn hated the staring, but she loved it too, and could no longer do without it. It was a barometer of her success and it gave her a momentary feeling of confidence.

Every day Marilyn made judgments, about her performance in an individual scene, about people, about her surroundings. They were not simple judgments, but most complicated, dredging up the past and involving her every day in a merry-go-round of emotion.

Here, midway in her career, Marilyn was already cursed with the habit of worry. Rose Steinberg, the script supervisor, watched Marilyn on the set with concern. She liked Marilyn, and had liked her since the days of *Scudda Hoo! Scudda Hay!* She believed that Marilyn's reliance on others was tearing her apart.

Natasha Lytess was on the set, of course. She had become a fixture in any Monroe picture. And now Marilyn wanted the opinion of Miss Lytess on every move.

Rose Steinberg had the feeling that too many people were catering to Marilyn's weaknesses rather than to her strength. And her strengths? She was the hardest-working actress on the Twentieth Century lot. No time was too long to spend to get a gesture correct and to learn her part, whether it be a dance or a song or a speech. Marilyn had more drive than any other actress Miss Steinberg had observed, although her energy apparently could not match that drive, and under the stress of emotion she often fell ill. Three times in the production of *There's No Business like Show Business* the filming had to be shut down or moved around her because Marilyn fell ill.

Marilyn's illness was almost all emotional. It was growing to be a real problem in her life. She was caught between too many people—not just two or three. Joe DiMaggio wanted her to be a wife. Natasha Lytess wanted her to be a great actress. Director Walter Lang wanted her to follow his direction. All these conflicts occurred every day. She sensed that her co-stars disliked her, and this made her more nervous and apparently less concerned with the convenience of anyone but herself.

But she worked. She worked harder than anyone else in the picture.

One of Marilyn's songs in the movie was "Heat Wave," which called for Marilyn to appear in a revealing adaptation of a Brazilian dancer's costume and to dance and sing in a very provocative manner. Marilyn put on head phones the first day and made twenty-five recordings of the song. One of her singing coaches, Ken Darby, then took the twenty-five pieces of tape home with him and cut them up and put them together so that she had the proper phrasing in each part of the song. The next day Marilyn listened to the paste-up and tried to recreate it—tried until she succeeded. This involved the complicated matter of keeping the orchestration and vocal records on separate tracks, but this is the kind of technology in which Hollywood always led the rest of the world. Marilyn was not a real singer, and yet she was always able to handle her singing parts without dubbing because of the expertness of the technical crews, which could make the most of her voice.

After a day of this work, Marilyn was scarcely up to creating dinners with candlelight and wine. She and Joe would either go out to dinner, or, if it was in a period when they had a housekeeper or cook, they would eat quietly at home. Then DiMaggio would turn to the television set. There was even a television set in the bedroom.

Relations grew strained. DiMaggio tried his best to solve the problem in one way, by seeking outside advice. He went often to see a friend of Marilyn's who was a doctor, and talked to him about their problems. But the problems were not solved. DiMaggio wanted to stay apart from Marilyn's world, hoping that he could bring her into his world. Marilyn had no real intention of settling down and moving out of the theatrical world, and slowly this became clear to DiMaggio. One of Marilyn's major lapses, unwitting, had been to mislead him by flights into fancy and discussion of the days when she would put on neat little aprons and play housewife.

DiMaggio made the mistake of withdrawing and rejecting Marilyn—and this was the one mistake that no one could ever make with Marilyn without bringing on disaster. She responded to rejection by counter-rejection, and then there was no hope.

Soon, during the filming of *There's No Business like Show Business*, Marilyn was depending on other men to do for her the homely, friendly tasks that normal husbands did for normal wives. Ken Darby went with her one day while she went down to Jax, an expensive women's clothing shop, to try on clothes. She staged an impromptu fashion show for nearly two hours, asking Darby what he thought of each ensemble.

On another day she was concerned because she had to buy a refrigerator. She did not know how to go about it. She did not want to go to one of the department stores because she was sure to be recognized and she thought people were laughing at her. ("Everyone makes jokes," she said.) Darby knew a wholesale distributor and telephoned to ask him to remain open after his normal closing hour. They went together to the store to look at the gleaming array of dozens of refrigerators.

Marilyn "oohed" and "aahed," and asked Darby's advice on the purchase. On his recommendation she selected a refrigerator.

Darby was pleased and proud. He analyzed her emotions thus: "Here is somebody who doesn't think of me as a big star; we are just two human beings who work together."

But Darby did not know his Marilyn. She did have such comradely feeling toward those in an inferior position, but she asked his opinion because she was in desperate need of it. She had no firm opinion of her own, and she found it painful to develop one, even about a refrigerator. She was slowly sinking into a morass of helplessness in every department of her life.

Marilyn also spent many hours with Hal Schaefer, her other singing coach and arranger on the movie, and sometimes she went out with him in the evenings. DiMaggio did not like this at all, but by this time Marilyn was following her own path. Earlier, before they were married, DiMaggio had once dated another woman in Hollywood while Marilyn was busy working on a movie. When Marilyn discovered his waywardness she "attempted suicide," or some might say that she did. Her action in her resentment was to take an overdose of sleeping tablets, but when DiMaggio was there, and she told him about it. He called the doctor who came and pumped out her stomach.

Was this really a suicide attempt or an act in a drama? Whatever this early attempt was, Marilyn did not repeat it when the bloom wore off the marriage. Outwardly there seemed nothing wrong. She was considerate of others. One day during *There's No Business like Show Business* Marilyn learned that Virginia Westmore was ill and in the hospital. Marilyn got flowers. She did not just send flowers; she went to a florist, bought flowers, and took them to the Hollywood hospital personally. A furor was created at the hospital when bedridden patients ignored doctors' orders and got up to see Marilyn Monroe, but Miss Westmore was a very happy woman.

Marilyn was capable of such gestures when there was no thought of publicity. Dr. Walter Taylor, the dentist who had made the retainer for her lower jaw all those years before, fell on evil days and was eventually confined to a Veterans Hospital. Marilyn heard that he was dying and went to see him, sat beside his bed, and held his hand. No one in the world of publicity ever heard of that visit.

Marilyn kept in touch with the Karger family, too. The affair with Fred Karger was over long before, but Marilyn maintained contact with Mrs. Karger and Fred's sister, Mary. These were among the few people in Hollywood, of all the ones Marilyn knew, that Joe DiMaggio liked.

Marilyn's relations with the cast of *There's No Business like Show Business* improved, but her relations with Joe DiMaggio did not. Donald O'Connor told Hedda Hopper that he was quite pleasantly surprised by Marilyn on the set. "She doesn't throw herself around," he said. "She's subtle." But, when DiMaggio was finally inveigled into coming on the set to quiet rumors of family discord, he refused to pose with Marilyn, and posed, instead, with Ethel Merman, whom he knew well from the days in New York. He did not have to volunteer the cutting remark, but he did, that Merman was his "favorite" movie star.

Soon Marilyn was making no pretense of coming home for dinner. It was often ten o'clock before she got to the house. Sometimes she did not come home at all.

And Joe DiMaggio, a man's man, sat and waited.

DiMaggio played golf in the daytime. He bought clubs for Marilyn, but she would not play golf with him, even when she found the time. She was totally unathletic, except for the exercises that she needed for her figure, and ballroom dancing, which she enjoyed.

Any similarity between Joe DiMaggio's world and Marilyn Monroe's world seemed to grow more unrecognizable every day. Joe DiMaggio hated invasion of his private life by the press. Marilyn lived in a bath of publicity, particularly when she was in the middle of a movie.

On the first day of shooting of *There's No Business like Show Business*, when she showed up for work on the set, the newspapers were given this word picture by the publicity department:

"The nation's Number One Box Office star was simply dressed in a matching sleeveless shirtmaker blouse and skin-tight black toreador pants ending in a deep point below each knee. Only accents to her costume were a matching black handbag with an ornate scroll of gold, and the hot pink sandals with four inch heels."

Marilyn got wolf whistles, and any couturiers who read the description (east of the Mississippi) got sick.

When her "Heat Wave" number was scheduled, publicity reported it. When the number was finished, publicity reported it. When she worked on dialogue sequences with Donald O'Connor, it was reported to the press. On the set, a still photographer named Emmett Schoenbaum, employed by Twentieth Century Fox, tried to get a "different" angle on Marilyn for publicity pictures, and sprained his sacroiliac. This became a story for the newspapers, and it was reported "that Miss Monroe was wearing black skin-hugging jax-slax, which inspired Schoenbaum to attempt the angled shot which led to his self-inflicted injury."

A dance was named for Marilyn, the Marilyn Monroe Mamba, by Arthur Murray, and the world was promised that some day one of his instructors would teach her how to do it. (There is no apparent record that the lesson was ever delivered.)

Influenza struck the set, attacking Marilyn and all the other principals except Ethel Merman, and it was so reported.

It was revealed that Marilyn had the old dressing room occupied by Betty Grable in days gone by, but that it had been repainted, and so had her portable dressing room.

When she sang a song called "After You've Got What You Want You Don't Want It," publicity reported that she sang it in an outfit "composed of several strategically-placed white and silver sequins on illusion net over flesh crepe."

A young man teaching at UCLA told a newspaperman that he once bet a tailor in Kansas a new suit that he would meet Marilyn Monroe. So the newspaperman told the publicity department and, sure enough, the young man was brought to the set and photographed with Marilyn, and the picture was sent out to the world.

"I don't care about the suit," said the young man, whose name was Keith MacIver and who taught geology at UCLA, "but meeting Marilyn and finding her as sweet and friendly as she is beautifully stacked, made me glad I made that bet."

Marilyn dressed for one scene in an ordinary—well, almost ordinary, woman's costume. It was "white mousseline de soie, a short formal, with bodice entirely of appliquéd fuchsias, with pale pink narrow shoulder straps tying under the bust, slim waistline, and flaring fuchsia-appliquéd skirt over pink taffeta." It had an irregular hemline, short in front and long in back, built for the scene of young innocent love in which Marilyn was to play. But, said designer Travilla, hastily, "though it's made to stress the romantic rather than the sexy, it's impossible to disguise the latter quality in Marilyn."

Old friends visited Marilyn on the set, and the visits were duly recorded. Jane Russell came. Emmaline Snively came and said she was glad that Cinderella (Marilyn) had found her Prince Charming (Joe). Marilyn's "Number One Fan" Jane Lawrence came to the set. She was fourteen and a half years old and daughter of the head of RKO's legal department. She had collected four thousand pictures of Marilyn, using a clipping service (which gives some idea of the number of pictures outstanding). She had seen *River of No Return* eight times, *How to Marry a Millionaire* five times, and *Gentlemen Prefer Blondes* and *Don't Bother to Knock* each ten times.

Everything Marilyn did was recorded for publicity—or almost everything. She collapsed on the set three times during the filming for one reason or another. Not all the reasons were reported. The virus, or the grippe, or whatever it was, was reported, and it was reported that Dr. Robert Rosenfeld came to the set to give her penicillin shots. But it was not reported the night that she was found in a condition so disgraceful that a major Hollywood scandal was narrowly avoided. It was not reported that she was addicted to sleeping pills, or that she was drinking heavily, or that she was desperately unhappy in her marriage and so was her husband.

It was reported that she wore a fifteen-thousand-dollar Blue Sapphire mink coat in a scene (rented from a Los Angeles furrier), but it was not reported that she went out with other men at night.

It was reported that she had great humility. On the set one

day actress Robin Raymond and Donald O'Connor were sitting at a table. The action called for them to be talking until Marilyn reached a certain point. But Marilyn was off balance or out of synchronization, and she was late in reaching the marked point. So the pair at the table did what actors and actresses have done for generations—they ad-libbed a little conversation.

Marilyn expressed great wonderment. Robin Raymond expressed great surprise and pleasure at Marilyn's humility.

It was now reported that she was growing testy and that one of her doctors had resigned her case because she refused to see a psychiatrist. That shock did send her to a psychiatrist. For the first time Marilyn realized that there was something seriously wrong, and that it was wrong with her.

For five years Marilyn had worried, off and on, about the possibility that she might one day become insane. Her family history planted the idea in her mind. Marilyn looked the part of a grown-up little girl, that is, a woman with the figure of a goddess but the face of an innocent child. Her face was still rounded and unlined and seemed not quite finished. And she was matching her face in her actions. She was becoming more willful every day, and there was no one to control her. DiMaggio had little influence on her as summer wore into autumn. Natasha Lytess had influence, as a dramatic coach, but she did not resolve Marilyn's personal problems. She said that Marilyn resented interference with her personal life. Then and until the day of her death, people in Hollywood talked about Marilyn's Svengali. One of Marilyn's troubles was that she had no Svengali. Had she taken the advice of Joe DiMaggio, she might have been a happier woman—or, had she taken any advice and even allowed herself to be manipulated, she might have been happier. She did not take DiMaggio's advice. Marilyn took advice from one person for a time, then rejected it and took advice from another. She had no standards of behavior nor any capacity for personal judgment. And the pat-

[144]

tern was a crazy quilt, a life of formlessness, an excursion on a stationary bicycle.

Marilyn moved from *There's No Business like Show Business* directly into work on *The Seven Year Itch*. The "Heat Wave" sequence was the last filmed. Then she began fittings for costumes for the new picture.

DiMaggio began to stay away from home, too, and soon there was very little left of the marriage but cohabitation of a rented house. When the dialogue and interior scenes were completed early in September, the cast of *The Seven Year Itch* moved to New York City for shooting of exteriors, since this was the setting of the movie. Marilyn announced to DiMaggio that she was bringing Natasha Lytess on the plane with them, when she and DiMaggio went to New York. DiMaggio did not like Natasha Lytess, and he did not like her interference in his life. He said that if Marilyn was taking Miss Lytess he would not go with her. In a sense he threw down the gauntlet then, and told Marilyn it was either her career or their marriage. Marilyn picked it up. Natasha Lytess accompanied her to New York and Joe DiMaggio did not. The two women went to the St. Regis Hotel.

Joe DiMaggio was considerate, however, until the last. He drove Marilyn to the airport, and waited outside the house of Hedda Hopper while Marilyn went in to tell her the non-secret secrets that are the homage paid by Hollywood personalities to the powerful columnists. He appeared in New York City and stayed with her at the hotel while the exterior scenes for *The Seven Year Itch* were filmed. The most sensational of these called for Marilyn and Tom Ewell, the male lead, to stroll along Lexington Avenue. It is a hot summer evening, and they have just returned from a movie. Marilyn is dressed in a revealing dress, of course, and she stops to cool herself by standing on a subway grating while a train shoots by underneath, sending a current of air up through the grate. This sends Marilyn's dress up about her shoulders, and, since the dress was designed for such treatment, the effect is very impressive.

The scene was shot after two o'clock in the morning, when life is relatively tranquil along Lexington Avenue as a rule. But, of course, somebody let the news get out, and there were four thousand people to watch Marilyn's skirts blow about her ears. Joe DiMaggio was there, an unhappy Joe DiMaggio.

Marilyn captured New York in her short stay. Every newspaper but the conservative *Times* plastered her picture over its front pages nearly every day for a week. Marilyn held press conferences and appeared to be gay and happy. She denied that there was any difficulty between herself and DiMaggio. She seemed to be the happiest young woman in the world.

Secretly, while all this occurred, Marilyn was meeting with Milton H. Greene, the photographer, and his attorney. She was asserting that she was no longer bound by her contract with Twentieth Century Fox and wanted to join Greene in a production venture. They had talked about this earlier, but now the talks became very serious.

Marilyn was very resentful toward the studio for not giving her the parts she wanted. She was beginning to believe that she would never get them, that the only way to be treated as an actress was to break away from the studio and start anew. Milton H. Greene found Marilyn most receptive to his ideas. He proposed that they be partners, and she agreed gladly to give him half of their earnings. Again, Marilyn showed how little avarice there was in her soul. She wanted to become a great actress and to be recognized as one. Money meant nothing to her at all. Recognition as an artist meant everything.

The arrangement between Marilyn and Milton H. Greene was not settled when Marilyn returned to Hollywood with Joe DiMaggio. Anything might have happened; a single gesture favorable to her aspirations would have persuaded Marilyn to remain in Hollywood. She did not plan to leave; she did not plan to have her marriage explode. After the return

[146]

from the East, however, events moved quickly. Joe DiMaggio declared that he could not continue, that Marilyn would have to live a quiet, sensible life of monogamy, or he would have to get out of that life. Marilyn made her choice. When it came right down to the decision, there had really never been a question. All else was illusion—she was wedded to the motion picture business and the American people, perhaps even the people of the world. How could she trade the public acclaim for the role of San Francisco housewife? In five years no one would even know who she was. Joe DiMaggio would not compromise—or he had already compromised as much as he could. And so on October 1 she telephoned Jerry Giesler, Hollywood's best-known lawyer, and she telephoned Billy Wilder. Wilder called Harry Brand at the studio, and Brand called the world. It was not long before the press arrived at the house in Beverly Hills and waited. Mary Karger went in to see Marilyn. Jerry Giesler and Harry Brand went in to see Marilyn. The press waited.

That was Monday.

The press waited on Tuesday. The divorce papers were brought to the house, and Marilyn signed them and Joe DiMaggio signed them.

The press waited.

On Wednesday Joe DiMaggio came out of the house in mid-morning, accompanied by a friend with his golf clubs and two suitcases. That represented Hollywood's hold on Joe DiMaggio. He got in the car, told the newspapermen he was going home to San Francisco, and left, waving a little sadly. A few moments later Marilyn came out on the arm of Jerry Giesler and went to the studio, apparently to work on her comedy part. She was crying and unhappy. Her face was swollen, and the press could get nothing except many, many pictures. Billy Wilder sent Marilyn home that day as unfit to work. The next day she showed up, chipper as a young canary, knowing every line and fluffing nothing. She arrived at seven o'clock in the morning. No one would know that she had just played a tragedy.

Perhaps it was the realization that she had resolved a serious problem which had troubled her for months. Perhaps it was the euphoria of having made a decision, a commitment by someone unused to deciding and always fearful of the process. No matter, Marilyn seemed a changed woman. She was on time for everything, and she had never performed more brightly. If this was tragedy, it might be that she was born the tragedienne.

Chapter Nine

THE break with Joe DiMaggio coincided with the end of the Monroe-DiMaggio lease on the house in Beverly Hills, so Marilyn moved to an apartment near Sunset Boulevard and considered what she would do about her future.

She was, at that moment, of several minds. She had much affection for Joe DiMaggio, and, as many problems as they had, she could not help respecting him for his honesty and the strength of character that made him behave as he did. She considered reconciliation, but she also pursued the legal action that would bring about a final divorce in a little over a year.

Marilyn considered the business proposals of Milton H. Greene. There was much to attract her in those ideas. If she formed a company with Greene, she would be her own mistress. She would be able to choose her directors. She would be able to choose her screen plays. Less important to her, but attractive, were the possibilities of high income and capital gains. Marilyn did not care for the money, but she was frightened when she thought that she might not have any money. Hers was the fear of the absolutely insecure: that she might not have a place to sleep or anything to eat.

If she worked for herself, she would be able to prove that she was an actress and not simply a sex symbol. Marilyn had grown very tired of being known only as the Sex Goddess. The praise for her as a comedienne both stimulated and upset her. She was stimulated because it opened a new avenue for her talents, upset because so few in Hollywood believed that she had any talents other than a handsome body and an opalescent quality of displaying it on the screen.

The events of Marilyn's last three months in 1954 would have disturbed anyone. In Marilyn's case they were enough to make her flee to try to create a new life.

First, there was the divorce. At the end of October she took Mrs. Mary Short and Mrs. Inez Melson with her to appear as witnesses in her suit for divorce from Joe DiMaggio. They testified to DiMaggio's mental cruelty. A week later she was visiting a friend in an apartment in Hollywood when a private detective broke into another apartment in the building, apparently with the idea that there he would confront Marilyn with another man. It was all very fuzzy: Frank Sinatra was involved in it somehow, and through him Joe DiMaggio was indirectly involved. The story appeared in the newspapers briefly, but so much confusion was spread about that the newspapers abandoned the story in the belief that it was just another Sinatraism—which had become a synonym for wilder and woollier behavior than is usual even in Hollywood. A week after that Marilyn was in Cedars of Lebanon hospital undergoing a gynecological operation with the announced purpose of correcting a condition which made it impossible for her to have children. For a woman who was considering only her career, Marilyn had some odd mannerisms. Joe DiMaggio, back from San Francisco, was a daily visitor at her hospital bedside. For a woman who was divorcing her husband, Marilyn had some odd enthusiasms.

Just before her hospital stay, following the end of production of *The Seven Year Itch*, Twentieth Century Fox suddenly became more amenable to Marilyn. Darryl Zanuck appeared at a party given at Romanoff's for her by her agent, Charles Feldman, of the Famous Artists Agency, and Zanuck was charming, as he could be when he wished. Marilyn was at her best—as she nearly always was when the atmosphere was cordial. She had absorbed the lesson of the *Photoplay* dinner and appeared in a more conservative red dress. She talked to many notables, including Clark Gable, and they discussed the possibility of making a picture together some day. Why not? Gable was the leading male actor in Hollywood. Marilyn was the leading female. All that was needed was the opportunity.

Milton Greene came back to Hollywood in the middle of November to discuss plans for the independent production firm. It would be called Marilyn Monroe Productions.

Before any other action could be taken, however, they must settle the question of Marilyn's contract with Twentieth Century Fox. Greene and his attorney took the position that no contract existed. There were various complicated reasons for this contention, including a letter written by a studio official concerning contracts during the time of her suspension, and the claim that hers was a "slave contract" which bound her to serve for a small salary relative to the huge amounts of money she was earning for Twentieth Century Fox. During the course of the discussions that followed, Marilyn believed she had found the absolute clincher: somehow, she said, the studio failed to announce its intention of renewing its option on her services at the November renewal date, and thus no contract existed between them.

In the autumn of 1954 Darryl Zanuck and Twentieth Century Fox were prepared to be generous with the studio's most important asset. The studio was also talking about a new contract, or her agents were, and the studio was listening.

If attitudes, such as acceptance and friendliness and respect, could have been written into a contract, Twentieth Century Fox might have retained Marilyn's services. The odds were all against it. The studio thought in terms of money primarily (and so did the agents) but this was not Marilyn's major motivation. Seven years of intensive study had created in Marilyn the desire to become a fine actress, even if she had not achieved much as an actress at the end of those seven years. The studio indicated that it wanted her to continue to play the same type of role that she had played in previous movies, either the red-hot mamma or the spoof of the red-hot mamma, to phrase the idea in terms of an earlier epoch. Marilyn was ready to balk at the suggestion that she did not have what it took to become an actress. She was the more intractable on this point because she was sorely unsure of her own capabilities. She needed assurance. Suddenly the assurances of people she paid to give them to her, such as Natasha Lytess, did not mean what they had meant before.

Marilyn did not make a decision, she let one be forced upon her by the collision of the ideas of Milton H. Greene and those of Twentieth Century Fox.

The studio told Marilyn that Nunnally Johnson was writing a screen play just for her. This was true, absolutely true. The screen play was to be *How to Be Very, Very Popular*, and it was a comedy featuring a Marilyn Monroe-ish blonde. The idea for the movie had come to Nunnally Johnson following his experiences with Marilyn, "the girl who moved around under water," during the filming of *How to Marry a Millionaire*. Marilyn investigated. The girl became popular by being hypnotized. Marilyn did not like the idea. Thus, immediately the question of a veto right on scripts assumed a major importance in her mind.

The problem came to resolution in mid-December. Marilyn had remained in Hollywood, and Milton H. Greene had spent much of his time there, too, talking to Marilyn and taking her dancing and dining, until he was quite wrongly mentioned by the Hollywood press minstrels as her current beau.

The release of *There's No Business like Show Business* settled the matter of Marilyn's future. The reviews were terrible. They were particularly upsetting to Marilyn because she had not wanted to appear in the picture for just the reasons that the critics used to attack her. Once the decision was made to appear, she threw herself into the role with her usual thoroughness. If a sexy blonde was wanted, she was the sexiest blonde that ever walked across the threshold of a Hollywood set.

Bosley Crowther, of the *New York Times*, found the sexiness overdone to the point of embarrassment. Other critics praised the other members of the cast and brushed Marilyn aside, referring to her "trademarked sexy manner," as did Frank Quinn in the New York *Daily Mirror*. Ed Sullivan presented a Catholic point of view, attacking her for a "dirty" portrayal in the touted "Heat Wave" song-and-dance routine when there was a priest elsewhere in the script. Hedda Hopper turned on Marilyn to remark that her performance was hardly tasteful.

An experienced publicist could have told Marilyn that some of this was bound to come. During the stay in New York when the skirt-lifting scene from *The Seven Year Itch* had been photographed, Marilyn had aroused the irritation of many of the moralists of America. From press and pulpit then had come chiding remarks about the propriety of turning America's largest city into a sound stage. Marilyn, and not the producers of her pictures, was accused of eroding American morality. Marilyn, and not the crowds who came to watch her skirts shoot up, was accused of fomenting juvenile delinquency.

Suddenly, the success she had achieved seemed unimportant to Marilyn when equated with the manner in which she had achieved it. She had no real revulsion against what she had done, but a sickened feeling about the reaction it had caused. The reaction continued to be severe enough for her to take serious note of it and for it to worry her. Some of her fan mail became abusive. Most of this was from good, God-fearing, church-going women, that much was apparent. Relatively, there was not enough of such abuse to give Twentieth Century Fox much cause for alarm, but Marilyn was looking for reasons to be upset by the sex role and she managed to find them.

Experience had taught Marilyn that flight was an excellent tactical move. She had won her battle with the studio just a year before by the same method. So one dark night Marilyn and Milton H. Greene boarded an airplane and set off for New York City in secrecy. The secrecy was so important to Marilyn that she wore a dark wig and dark glasses and called herself Zelda Nonk for the benefit of the passenger list. When the plane arrived in New York, she and Mr. and Mrs. Milton H. Greene went to the Greene house in Weston, Connecticut, where Marilyn could remain in seclusion.

She so remained for about three weeks. During that period the papers of incorporation were drawn up, and Marilyn Monroe Productions came into existence. Marilyn held slightly more than fifty per cent of the stock, which gave her control of the company. Greene held the remainder. Marilyn contributed herself, which was the company's single greatest asset. Greene contributed his promise to support her in case of a protracted argument with Twentieth Century Fox, and his business abilities.

The new corporation took the position that there was no contract between Marilyn and Twentieth Century Fox because they had failed to notify her that the studio was picking up that November option. The studio took the position that it had a valid contract with Marilyn and that if she did not work for Twentieth Century Fox during the next three and a half years she would not make movies for anyone. Marilyn took the step, quite prepared to sit it out for three and a half years if that was necessary, so that she could make motion pictures in her own way.

Early in January Marilyn held a press conference at the home of Greene's attorney. She appeared an hour late, which convinced the newspapermen that she had not changed as much as some thought. Marilyn had talked with the press before about her desire to play serious roles in motion pictures, and the newspaper men and women had reported these statements to the public. No one took them very seriously, however, because Marilyn was so definitely typecast as the dumb sexy blonde. All she had managed to add to that illusion in seven years was the impression that she was capable of a certain type of light comedy—the dumb sexy blonde playing the innocent in a sophisticated world.

Marilyn told the press again that she wanted to play serious roles. She was tired of sexy parts, she said. She did not want to play that kind of role ever again.

A reporter asked her what made her believe she could play serious parts. She became solemn and adopted a broad A as she replied that she had more ability than most people seemed to think. And then came the notable exchange:

"Do you want to play *The Brothers Karamazov?*" said a reporter, knowing that she had said she did.

"I don't want to play the brothers. I want to play Grushenka. She's a girl."

This was probably the most instructive and revealing remark ever made by Marilyn. It put the reporters down. There was nothing more to be said. Marilyn was not "under water." She was simply on a different wave length.

It may have hurt Marilyn's feelings to learn of Billy Wilder's reactions to her announcement about playing the role of the girl in *The Brothers Karamazov*. Wilder suggested that they film an entire series, *The Brothers Karamazov*, *The Brothers Karamazov Meet Abbott and Costello*, and other epics of a similar nature. Billy Wilder liked Marilyn. He had a very simple view of her: that the day that she stepped before a movie camera she was a genius and that she could not improve on that—that she ought not to try. Michael Chekhov had really told Marilyn the same thing—to relax and be happy, but Marilyn could not relax, and it is doubtful if anyone ever taught her the basic ingredients of happiness. She never achieved any settlement with herself, or any diminution of ambition, in any event. Marilyn did not like ridicule, even when it came from people who had been kind to her, as Wilder had, and people she trusted, and she had trusted Wilder in the role of director. But, when Marilyn returned to Hollywood a few days after the press conference, she greeted Wilder without constraint. Later Wilder said, regarding Marilyn's acting lessons, that if she wanted to go to school she should go to railroad engineering school and learn to run on time. (She said she once carried a railroad conductor's watch for a week—but it did not help.)

Marilyn vacillated in her attitude toward Twentieth Century Fox. The studio announced that it had no intention of granting her request that she be allowed to play in Dostoevsky's *The Brothers Karamazov*. She said she really did not want to play in heavy dramas—or that is what she told Louella Parsons she meant, anyhow. She also said she would make more pictures for Twentieth Century Fox, and that she would not make more pictures for Twentieth Century Fox. Both statements were made within one week. Twentieth Century Fox said that she would not make any more pictures for anyone, unless she made them for Twentieth Century Fox.

This was cold war, and it continued for nearly a year. In the beginning, Marilyn's assets were Milton H. Greene, who could support her, and her box office position, which was very strong. Someone estimated that the name Marilyn Monroe made a difference of at least a million dollars in the gross income of any motion picture, and they were talking only about the first year's run. Marilyn's major liabilities in this struggle were her lack of cash, and the nervousness common to all in the theatrical business about suits and liabilities. The prospect of not working in films, of losing her appeal to her public, did not frighten Marilyn, although the fear of non-exposure for over a year might have driven a weaker character to capitulation.

During the next few months, Marilyn did not work in motion pictures, but that is not to say that she disappeared from the public eye. For one thing she was helped greatly by the lead time—the time that it takes for a director to cut and assemble and manipulate his film once the work of the players is completed, and then the time it takes for the prints to be made and the promotion campaign to be set in operation. *The Seven Year Itch* was released in June, 1955, halfway through Marilyn's self-imposed exile in the East.

In the meantime, she had been very busy in her own way. For several weeks Marilyn remained in the guest room of the Greenes' house in Connecticut. She walked in the woods and she read. She talked long and confidentially with Mrs. Greene. She helped care for the Greenes' child and helped with the cooking. She was undertaking another venture in domesticity.

Marilyn was a serious reader—that is, she acquired serious books, although apparently she did not read them from beginning to end the way other people do, but dipped in where she caught a phrase or a paragraph that appealed to her. She was a dilettante rather than a student of literature. At various times Marilyn mentioned reading Lincoln Steffens' *Autobiography*, *Look Homeward, Angel*, by Thomas Wolfe, *Swann's Way* by Proust, Freud's *Psychopathology of Everyday Life*, and *An Actor Prepares*, by Stanislavsky. Perhaps if she had started with something a little less taxing, such as *Treasure Island* or *Little Women*, Marilyn would have found the world a more pleasant place.

At the end of January Milton H. Greene was asked by a fatuous reporter for his assessment of the principal asset of his company. "She is fabulous, wonderful, very sincere and sensitive, and she has a great sense of humor," he said. A little over a month later Edward R. Murrow took his cameras and his electronic equipment to the Weston house for a "Person to Person" interview to discover the truths about Marilyn Monroe insofar as they were available. Marilyn did not produce the new Marilyn for him. She was at her worst, physically. Her hair was its usual platinum, but it hung down the sides of her head in ringlets, and she looked an overgrown child. Her hostess, Mrs. Greene, was prompted to answer questions directed to Marilyn and to indicate that Marilyn was thinking, which did not impress critical viewers with Marilyn's progress in the world.

In Hollywood, after the viewing of the "Person to Person" show, the bright of wit remarked that Darryl Zanuck ought to release Marilyn from her contract and sign up the dark-haired, chic Mrs. Greene. Hedda Hopper told Marilyn, the next time she saw her, that this new Monroe road led to disaster. She criticized Marilyn's clothes and compared Marilyn's public appearance unfavorably to Mrs. Greene's.

Marilyn was still learning.

Soon she left the bare winter woods of Connecticut for the inner warmth of Manhattan. She took over actress Leonora Corbett's apartment in the Waldorf Towers, the expensive residential portion of Park Avenue's Waldorf Astoria Hotel. She rode a pink elephant in a Mike Todd production of the circus at Madison Square Garden for the benefit of the Arthritis and Rheumatism Foundation.

Then she settled down to wait.

Marilyn had learned that for appearances before her public, she must maintain the artificial Monroe which had captured the public eye. She kept a personal hairdresser on salary at $125 per week. She had representatives of every specialty in beauty care at her beck and call. Milton H. Greene indicated that the upkeep of the Monroe symbol and the Monroe woman cost the company a thousand dollars a week, which he advanced because Marilyn was unable to earn money at her chosen profession. Marilyn used perfume with a lavish touch, and the perfumes she used were Chanels. She also needed a publicity man and a private secretary.

And still it was not the same. Marilyn was glamorous, but

without the resources of Twentieth Century Fox studios behind her, Marilyn's publicity began to suffer. The news magazines and the general interest magazines and the ladies' magazines took great interest in Marilyn in 1954. In 1955, articles and pictures about her activities appeared very seldom.

This neglect could be dangerous. By declaring herself bound to become a serious actress, Marilyn had assumed the responsibility to do just that or to back down and admit that the studio knew better than she where her real talents lay. Marilyn was also seriously interested in learning the Stanislavsky Method of acting. This decision marked the end of Marilyn's association with Natasha Lytess. The beginning of that end had come when Marilyn began taking acting lessons from Michael Chekhov.

The charge was made in later years that Marilyn changed people as she changed her clothing, that she used them and then discarded them. There was much exaggeration in this claim. She did change attorneys and agents with considerable frequency. But take the matter of her agents. She was delivered into the hands of one agent as a model-about-to-be-starlet. When she was abandoned by Twentieth Century Fox and then by Columbia Pictures, she changed agents. She did not abandon this second agent; Johnny Hyde bought the contract because he loved Marilyn and wanted to be close to every part of her life; besides, he could help Marilyn in 1949 far more than Harry Lipton. After Johnny Hyde died, Marilyn changed to Famous Artists Agency, where she was represented in the main by Hugh French. Milton H. Greene changed her over from Famous Artists to MCA, because this was now a package arrangement and demanded a fresh start. Certainly not all these changes were necessary, but it was stretching points to look for Machiavellian intent in them.

So it was with dramatic coaching. Marilyn had various dramatic lessons, which she paid for herself, as a model. Her first real exposure to drama technique came in the Stanislavsky school conducted at the Actors' Lab in Hollywood. She went on, then, to Natasha Lytess, whom she respected, who taught acting in the traditional manner, but she came to the conclusion during the summer of 1952 that the Stanislavsky Method was best for her. Paula Strasberg, wife of the leading advocate of Method Acting in America, said later that "the Method" was a godsend for Marilyn, and Marilyn agreed with that thesis down to the last day of her life.

Marilyn decided to enroll in the Actors' Studio, if they would have her, and to take lessons in acting from Lee Strasberg. At a dinner party she met Cheryl Crawford, one of the founders of the Studio, and an appointment was arranged with Strasberg. After an interview, Strasberg agreed to let Marilyn join a class of thirty members, because he saw in her a fine talent. In that first interview Marilyn began by stammering. Strasberg probed, to discover why she could not express herself cleanly and gracefully. People kept misinterpreting what she said, Marilyn told him, and they laughed at her or looked at her with queer expressions on their faces. She had now come to the point where she could not really say what she meant, because she must think carefully over every word lest she be ridiculed.

As Strasberg grew to know Marilyn better, he learned that this was indeed true. He had seldom seen anyone who had a better, more direct control of language. Marilyn was not erudite; her control was the control of a natural person who says exactly what she means and does not use language as a method of concealment or a weapon.

Later, this facet of Marilyn was to be emphasized for the Strasbergs by Arthur Miller, the playwright who became her husband.

"Don't ever ask Marilyn how she is in the morning," Miller told Paula Strasberg, "because she is sure to tell you."

On that first day, when he met Marilyn Monroe, Lee Strasberg was conscious of being in the presence of an unusual talent. As he talked to her, and decided that she might enter his class, he continued to probe.

He learned a great deal about Marilyn as a person, as well as about Marilyn as an actress. Marilyn stayed with the Strasbergs for a time. She moved into daughter Susan's room. She went to Fire Island to visit them in their seaside house. There, one day, Paula Strasberg picked up a brush and began to paint —all the Strasbergs painted.

"I wish I could do that," said Marilyn wistfully.

"What do you mean?" Paula Strasberg asked. "Marilyn, every human being can make a picture."

Marilyn looked up hopefully. Even her, Marilyn Monroe? she asked. Paula Strasberg assured her that, by all means, Marilyn Monroe, too, could make a picture, and invited her to select some medium of expression, from water colors, oils, and charcoal that were available.

Marilyn picked up a charcoal drawing pencil and a sketch pad and drew a picture of what was obviously a Negro girl with one long stocking up and the other down around her ankle. It was a powerful, primitive sketch.

"What do you call it?" Paula Strasberg asked, when it was complete.

"Lonely," said Marilyn.

So the Strasbergs grew to understand Marilyn, and she them. She wrote poetry, which she sometimes showed to them shyly. They paid her the supreme compliment. They did not laugh. They did not want to laugh, but she could not have known that at the beginning, for everyone had laughed.

Marilyn slipped naturally into a child-father relationship with Lee Strasberg. From the beginning he saw her as an actress who needed to be brought out of herself, and he began the process at their first meeting. Further, he gave her private lessons before she undertook class assignments. He was very much impressed with the results of his probing, and he declared that Marilyn had the potential to become a great actress.

It was apparent, by the trials she was now undergoing, that she also had the desire.

Strasberg learned that Marilyn was the most nervous actress he had ever known. He also learned that she had greater range as an actress than she had been called on to use in the parts of dumb sexy blonde or dumb-sexy-blonde "foot-in-the-mouth" comedienne. Strasberg sensed that Marilyn had the makings of one of the world's greats among dramatic actresses. He was not to change his opinion.

Marilyn now began a two-fold program of self-improvement. She undertook psychoanalysis, spending five sessions a week with a psychiatrist. She took three months of private lessons from Strasberg and then entered a class with other actors and actresses and attended meetings of the Actors' Studio.

The two disciplines were complementary. Both involved the unmasking of emotion, the psychoanalysis for the purpose of self-revelation and the Stanislavsky Method of acting for the purpose of using personal emotions and transferring them smoothly to the actor's role. If this was dangerous play for Marilyn, as some of her non-understanding friends believed, and if it was a waste of great natural talents, as many of those she knew in Hollywood believed, it was a system of life into which Marilyn could throw herself with the fervor others might bestow on a religion. She believed, and because she believed, she began to prosper emotionally.

June 1, Marilyn's birthday, was the date scheduled for the premiere of *The Seven Year Itch*, and it was to be held at Loew's State Theater in New York City. Marilyn was seeing Joe DiMaggio again, and he agreed to take her to the performance. He also took her to a party at Toots Shor's after the theater, and there became involved in an argument, after which Marilyn went home.

This was nearly the end of the Monroe-DiMaggio relationship. Joe, who had never liked Fred Karger because he knew of Marilyn's old relationship there, once encountered Karger in Central Park in this period and hailed him. "What did I do?" asked the anguished DiMaggio. Karger could not answer. It was nothing DiMaggio had done. It was who DiMaggio was and who Marilyn was. There was hope, perhaps, that they could come together again—if Marilyn Monroe Productions failed and if Marilyn's career faltered. But it was a forlorn hope.

The Seven Year Itch received good reviews, although Marilyn was complimented for all the reasons she now hated. In the picture she plays the role of a girl upstairs in an apartment. Below is a Casper Milquetoast variety of married man whose wife is out of town. Through incident and coincident, Marilyn and the man downstairs, played by Tom Ewell, are thrown together in unusual situations for strangers, and the movie audience watches Ewell struggling with lust and his conscience, while the young blonde from upstairs is as provocative as she can be without apparently meaning anything by it all. Double entendre cascades upon delicate situation, and the result is a constant temptation for the harried innocent male and constant suggestion to the movie-goer.

This latest of Marilyn's movies had an important bearing on the future of Marilyn's career because it was another box office success. That much became apparent within a month. As the exhibitors displayed the magic name Marilyn Monroe above their marquees and counted their revenues, little chills ran up and down their spines, because as far as anyone knew this would be the last of the Twentieth Century Fox pictures to be made starring Marilyn Monroe.

The brave financial venture known as Marilyn Monroe Productions, Incorporated did not prosper in the period of Marilyn's motion picture inactivity. By autumn Milton H. Greene discovered that he had pledged most of his own resources to maintain the expensive creation that was the public Marilyn Monroe. He had even mortgaged his house. There were thousands of dollars in debts and no cash to meet them. It was only a matter of time until the creditors began to get insistent, then nasty, then to put the accounts into the hands of collectors whose sole interest was in wringing as much blood from as many turnips as possible.

Given sixty days more, Marilyn Monroe Productions would have collapsed of its weight of debt. But sixty days were not necessary. For in the autumn of 1955, Buddy Adler took over as chief of production of Twentieth Century Fox. He had no experience, pleasant or otherwise, with Marilyn Monroe. He had the intense desire to resolve any outstanding problems and to strengthen his own position, naturally enough, by bringing back into the fold a wandering asset. Before the end of the year a new contract was negotiated between the corporate Marilyn Monroe and the studio. Marilyn was to receive a hundred thousand dollars for each film she made for Twentieth Century Fox within the seven years of the new contract. She was committed to only four films for the company during that period. She could, otherwise, make at least one film a year on her own and could appear on a half dozen television shows each year if she so desired. When she was working for Twentieth Century Fox, she also was to receive expenses, five hundred dollars a week for incidentals, and the services of a studio maid. (Considering the maid, it was more money for expenses alone than she had earned altogether five years earlier.) She had approval of the script of any film, in fact, and she had the right to approve the director of any Twentieth Century Fox movie in which she was to appear. She named sixteen directors who were acceptable to her. Marilyn had appeared in twenty-three films by the fall of 1955 and had worked with twenty different directors. Of these, she found only three to be acceptable in her new list, and not one of these was one of the directors with whom she had made more than one picture. Of her old directors only John Huston, Joseph Mankiewicz, and Billy

Wilder were on her acceptable list. The others she knew only by reputation and social contact.

Marilyn made no such stipulations about producers, or writers. She recognized that her natural enemy was the director, for the director was in control of the motion picture. She also recognized the special powers of cinematographers and named several who would be acceptable to her. The contract was eighty-five pages long and it gave her everything she ever wanted. Surely, then, Marilyn Monroe's professional problems were solved, if her personal problems continued to plague her. After all, as the Strasbergs said, there was no reason that a great actress should expect to be happy. It must be enough that she would be a great actress.

Chapter Ten

IN January, 1956, Louella Parsons told her eager world that Marilyn and Twentieth Century Fox had resolved their differences and that Marilyn had scored a victory and established the basis for a fortune. She was to receive eight million dollars in the course of the seven-year contract, said Miss Parsons.

How Miss Parsons arrived at the eight-million-dollar figure is a mystery, but it was at least certain that Marilyn Monroe Productions had become solvent. Hours before the end of 1955 (for tax reasons) Marilyn received checks for nearly $350,000. Of this, two hundred thousand dollars represented the sale of the screen rights to a novel which Twentieth Century Fox said it wanted. Marilyn purchased the rights earlier at a much lower figure and this represented capital gains. The remainder of the money came from compensation that arose out of a mix-up between Charles K. Feldman, co-producer of *The Seven Year Itch*, and Charles K. Feldman, agent.

The victory was total, and now the plans came tumbling forth. Milton Greene announced that Marilyn Monroe Productions would begin acquiring screen properties. The company would also acquire the services of other established stars. Greene had in mind an organization like the old United Artists Corporation, in which Charlie Chaplin, Mary Pickford, and Douglas Fairbanks worked together. Monroe Productions would also engage in television, and it might even dabble in real estate and other ventures. These were the years of diversification in business, and the new corporation was not going to miss any opportunities.

In all her reading and in the mention of the scores of significant books that Marilyn owned, there is no indication that she ever riffled the pages of the novels of François Rabelais. Had she, it might have given her some insight into her new relationship with the motion picture industry.

"How shall I be able to rule over others, that have not full power and command of myself?" wrote Rabelais.

How indeed should Marilyn be able to use this new power? For the fact was clear that Marilyn was slipping into a course of self-destruction and needed either a strong outside influence or the most militant self-control to stop the course of the slide. In the next few years she was to desert strength for weakness, as she already had done in the breakup with Joe DiMaggio, and she was to show fewer and fewer signs of self-control. Power, in her hands, would become the instrument of her ruin.

Marilyn had discovered the joys and release of alcohol since the days when she and Johnny Hyde lunched at Prince Romanoff's elegant restaurant, and she sat quietly listening to the conversation of the great of Hollywood and toying with a glass of Dubonnet which she never quite finished. For preference she now drank champagne, Dom Perignon, and others from the best French houses. She was capable of drinking a bottle or two of wine by herself in the course of a conversation. She also drank vodka, sometimes, and whiskey. And she sometimes used these beverages to wash down a handful of sleeping pills just before retiring. The sleeping pills gave her temporary relief from her chronic insomnia, but, like a number of her peers, she exercised no judgment in the use of them. While staying with the Greenes she used sleeping pills. On one occasion, when she was awake at four o'clock in the morning, she took sleeping pills, although she knew that she must arise at five to go in to New York City from the country with Greene to keep an early morning appointment. Fortunately, such excesses were not regular. Only when she was under stress did she behave so, and days and weeks went by in which she appeared to be unworried. Particularly during the halcyon period in which she was working at the Actors' Studio, Marilyn was relatively happy. She immersed herself in the parts assigned to her. The secret was that someone—the small, dark, understanding Lee Strasberg—was directing her efforts and taking from her the responsibility to make judgments. All she need do for him was perform, and in this she had genius. One day, when she had accustomed herself to working with others, she and another actress played a scene from *Anna Christie*. They did it very well, Strasberg reported. Marilyn *was* an actress.

Marilyn was at ease with the Actors' Studio group. No one paid her any special heed, because she dressed simply and did not turn on the special machine that controlled her sex appeal. She baby-sat for Eli Wallach and his wife. She was anything but imperious and anything but selfish. Unlike almost all the actors and actresses with whom she associated, she was truly concerned with the welfare of other people. Others might show such complete narcissism and egocentricity as to make them unbearable. Marilyn did not do this; forever she was loved by the people she could most readily have abused, those who served her personally. She never abused them. She gave them gifts: a gold money clip for Allan Snyder, her makeup man; a toy French poodle and an oil portrait of herself and a dozen other small gifts to Hazel Washington, her maid on several movie sets; a copy of the nude calendar to Billy Travilla, the designer, with the inscription, "Billy, Dear, Please Dress Me Forever—Marilyn"; a wristwatch to Bunny Gardel, her body-makeup girl, with the inscription, "Bunny, Remember UP is the only direction—Love, Marilyn."

[168]

This gift and the inscription were typical of Marilyn and her relationships with those close to her. Once Miss Gardel took the watch to a jeweller for repair, and he raised his eyes to the ceiling, murmuring: "What a lovely thought!" But UP did not mean Heaven, it was a private joke between Marilyn and Bunny Gardel. Marilyn insisted that her soft, white skin be massaged in an upward direction only. She gave Bunny Gardel a long, rambling dissertation on this subject one day, and then laughed at herself. The two never failed to joke about it on subsequent movie sets.

Marilyn's departure from Hollywood had not eliminated the interest of the newspaper columnists and newspaper reporters in her affairs. Earl Wilson and Walter Winchell and Leonard Lyons and Louis Sobol checked on Marilyn occasionally and wrote about her activities. But she had no more publicity, really, than she wanted in this period, and most of it was the result of the easy face-to-face conversational interview with a single reporter at a time. In such meetings Marilyn never failed to charm her companion and to win him over to her championship. Women reporters liked Marilyn, too, or most of them did when they came to know her, but Marilyn preferred, always, to deal with men, for she was a man's woman and was most sensitive to the enmity and dislike she sometimes aroused in other women for no reason other than the way she looked.

All this was true until Marilyn won her joust with Twentieth Century Fox. Suddenly the power went to her head, for a moment.

Humphrey Bogart had an odd way of dealing with the press. He snarled at publicity—all of it. The actor owed the public nothing but a good performance, Bogart always said. But he always said it, and he kept his share of the bargain: he did not seek publicity.

Marilyn, having risen to new heights, decided that she would now choose the timing of her publicity. There was considerable reason behind her argument and perhaps some pique. For immediately after her reconciliation with the studio, the publicists of America converged on Marilyn. The demand could not have become more universal had they held a meeting and taken a vote. Perhaps Marilyn began to realize that the popular magazines often followed one another. Marilyn was suddenly catapulted to greater fame than ever. In 1956 articles appeared twenty-two times in various magazines. *Time* wrote about her on six different occasions that year, including a cover story which gave the details of her life, or purported to do so, and her hard times in struggling to the top of the motion picture industry. Pete Martin, the casual biographer of the notorious for *The Saturday Evening Post*, wrote a series of articles about Marilyn that year which were later published as a book entitled *Will Acting Spoil Marilyn Monroe?* Maurice Zolotow went to work on his articles for *McCall's*. *Look*, *Life*, *Saturday Review*, *Collier's*, *Vogue*, *Theater Arts*, even the sententious *Reporter*, ran articles about her.

Suddenly it seemed, in January, 1956, that all the magazines were descending on her at once for exclusive interviews, exclusive photographs, exclusive revelations.

Marilyn was the creature of the press more than any other Hollywood personality in history. Jean Harlow, to whom she has often been compared, made no such publicity splash in her lifetime. Marilyn had always sought and received courteous and generous treatment from the press, and she had been grateful for it in the past. Marilyn had known four years before where she would be if the press had not made her into an international film personality, and she had told Nunnally Johnson quite frankly that she knew. Even during the year just past her press agents had sought all the publicity she could get to keep her name before the public. Now she chose to forget. She shunted aside the would-be interviewers and photographers and relegated them to a common press conference which Her Presidency would deign to hold on a day early in

February. It was to be a joint press conference held with Sir Laurence Olivier, and the purpose was to disclose details of the forthcoming collaboration between Marilyn Monroe Productions, Inc., and the knight. The corporation had just purchased the movie rights to Terence Rattigan's *The Sleeping Prince*. Sir Laurence would act in the motion picture opposite Miss Monroe. He would also direct it. But Marilyn was hiring Sir Laurence.

An autocratic Marilyn offended the sense of propriety of the newspapermen who remembered, only too well, that they had made this girl's career possible. A hostile atmosphere at a press conference could not help but create negative publicity, because the results of the press conference usually depend on the questions of the reporters. For the first time in her life, Marilyn faced a definitely hostile press.

The newspapermen had the stories about Marilyn's ambitions to play Grushenka. It was rumored that she was very close to playwright Arthur Miller, who was married and had children. A reporter asked her about Miller. She was all wide-eyed innocence. Another asked her how to spell Grushenka, and Marilyn did not know. She told her inquisitor testily to look it up. The photographers took pictures of her, and a strap of her low-cut sheath broke. One of the photographers asked her how it felt when the strap broke, and others in the room laughed, because there was general belief that it was part of the act. Marilyn grew angry, retorted hotly to the photographer, and rushed out of the room.

This, indeed, was a New Marilyn Monroe.

The new Marilyn and her entourage moved temporarily to Hollywood in February. Marilyn was to renew her relationship with Twentieth Century Fox with an appearance in *Bus Stop*, a movie whose script she had approved, and whose director, Josh Logan, was on her list. Ben Nye, head of the Twentieth Century makeup department, would make up her face. Bunny Gardel would make up her legs and other portions of the anatomy that were to be displayed. Agnes Flanagan would make up her hair. Travilla would do her gowns. Ken Darby would be her voice coach. Milton Krasner, one of her approved cinematographers, would be in charge of the camera work. Marilyn was queen, and everyone was ready to do her bidding.

Josh Logan was prepared for what he would find in the new Marilyn. He was a graduate of the Stanislavsky school himself—one of the most distinguished in America because he had actually worked with Stanislavsky in Moscow.

Logan had conferred with Strasberg, and Strasberg had told him that Marilyn was a *real* actress. Strasberg had to tell him several times, because in Hollywood nobody believed it, save Natasha Lytess, perhaps.

Poor Natasha Lytess. All these months she had sat in Hollywood, on the Twentieth Century Fox payroll, and had waited for Marilyn to come home. Marilyn did not answer her letters, but Marilyn seldom wrote to anyone. To Marilyn, departure from Hollywood had been a declaration of war, and she had, perhaps, parted company with Twentieth Century Fox forever when she left that night masquerading as Zelda Nonk. But to Twentieth Century Fox Marilyn was merely a wayward actress, and all these months she had been listed at the studio as "suspended." Natasha Lytess remained on the payroll, and like Twentieth Century Fox, she waited. Now that Marilyn was off suspension and was the holder of a new contract, Natasha Lytess hoped to pick up where she and Marilyn had left off. But Marilyn was now a "Method" actress, and she would not forgive the slighting remarks that Natasha Lytess had made about the Stanislavsky Method. Natasha finally received a letter—from a lawyer. The letter said that her services would no longer be required by Miss Monroe. Twentieth Century Fox received the word that it would be quite in order for them to drop Miss Lytess from the payroll, and the comptrollers of Twentieth Century Fox hastened to act. Miss Lytess could not reach anyone at the studio or at Marilyn Monroe Productions Incorporated to secure amplification of this sudden switch. She felt deserted and spoke up about Marilyn's ingratitude—not mentioning such matters as the Beverly Hills house Marilyn had bought for her.

The Queen of Hollywood moved with Milton H. Greene and Mrs. Greene into a rented house. There was no intention of remaining in Hollywood for long, for the headquarters of Marilyn Monroe Productions Incorporated was to be in New York City. Marilyn would fly to Hollywood for such brief stays as were necessary. And perhaps most movies would not even be made in Hollywood. The trend in the industry in the 1950's was to move far away. Production was cheaper in any number of places: Rome, London, Spain.

When Marilyn arrived in Los Angeles, Twentieth Century Fox went far out of its way to make her comfortable and welcome her home. The studio gave a cocktail party for her, inviting all the local press representatives. They, too, were introduced to the new Marilyn, who was now reserved, dressed decorously—and far later than ever before. The gamin had suddenly become a lady. Such change was regarded with friendly interest by the Hollywood reporters. There was no animosity. There was no suggestion of the girl who had wriggled her way to the lectern at the *Photoplay* awards dinner. No one could imagine this Marilyn behaving in such a fashion.

Marilyn had been very close to Sidney Skolsky in earlier days, but no more. Perhaps the publication of Skolsky's book *Marilyn* had caused the rift. She did not talk about it and neither did he.

Each break with an old friend or associate cost Marilyn dearly in emotional credit. She was desperately unsure of herself—even this beautiful, queenly new Marilyn. Lee Strasberg knew it and applauded this aspect of her character. He said that the most nervous, most unstrung actresses gave the best performances. He also suggested that eventually Marilyn

[173]

would wind up on the stage, and that here was the place she belonged. She was an actress. What made a good actress did not necessarily make a person who could live with the actress in her. The breaks with people came—people like friendly, generous Loyd Wright, her attorney, who had lent his mountain retreat for her use on the honeymoon with Joe DiMaggio. Marilyn suffered from the affliction of those to whom success and grandeur come too quickly. She found that her interests were no longer those of her old associates.

Marilyn did not understand the workings of success and the processes by which people grow apart, although it was easy for an outsider to see why Marilyn and Natasha Lytess must part. Marilyn was terrified after she broke with Miss Lytess; she talked as if she were afraid for her life, but what she was really saying was that she had committed a terrible crime against Miss Lytess and therefore ought to be afraid for her life. She could no more face Miss Lytess and tell her that the new Marilyn had a new way of dealing with the matter of acting, than she could work with her old teacher. She felt guilty and angry and ashamed, all at once.

Instead of explaining or trying to explain, Marilyn dropped Natasha Lytess cruelly in a way that injured the acting coach as a force in Hollywood. It would have been possible for Marilyn to make some place for Miss Lytess somewhere. The new Marilyn had every power to do so. But Marilyn, new or old, could not face such a problem and make a decision. She willed the problem to go away.

In Hollywood Marilyn prepared to play the role of Cherie in *Bus Stop*. She had studied the script carefully, and she told Josh Logan how she wanted to play the role. She would play it, of course, by making Cherie into Marilyn Monroe. Would this girl who wants respect ever get it?—that was the way she put the question. That question had very little to do with the plot of the motion picture, which concerns a young Montana cowboy who falls in love with a soiled dove of an entertainer

[174]

and determines to marry her. She wants to escape but eventually agrees to marry him, and it is apparent that she will.

Bus Stop was a comedy, but it was also a tender love story. This posed questions for the director and for the players. From the beginning Marilyn went about her business as if she knew it. She was to play the role of a tawdry dancehall girl, so, in the fashion of the theater, not of the motion pictures, she invented her tawdry dancehall girl. The usual practice would have been for Travilla to have created a series of costumes for her. Instead, Marilyn took Travilla into the Twentieth Century Fox wardrobe and together they searched to find cast-off shoes, a worn, cheap skirt and blouse, and cheap used jewelry. Marilyn was not trying to save money for the studio. Three sets of the costume were especially made and aged, and that was expensive, but Marilyn felt that she would play the role more realistically if she wore an old outfit.

Physically, Marilyn was not at her best for this picture. She was a little fat, and it showed in the bulge of her belly. When Marilyn put on weight it always showed, but for this part it seemed just right that she should be a little overweight; she still projected sex with every gesture.

There had been trouble with the casting for *Bus Stop*. Marilyn was consulted about her leading man, and, true to form, she agonized over a decision she was not competent to make. She wanted Rock Hudson, but she did not want him. She was afraid he might overshadow her. She wanted Albert Salmi, a Method actor, but she did not want him. In the end she got neither one, but an unknown actor named Don Murray.

On March 12 the company was to go on location to Phoenix, where a rodeo was to be held. Marilyn missed the plane, and those in charge of production began to tear their hair because they needed that rodeo for background. But Marilyn showed up on the very next plane, a TWA flight.

No one should have worried, she said innocently. She and Milton H. Greene had agreed that they would always fly

TWA, and so, naturally, she had to wait for the TWA flight instead of the one everyone else had taken.

But soon there were stories about Marilyn's misbehavior. She did not like the turn the story was taking in the movie; her part began to bother her. But this brought tensions that bothered others. At one point Marilyn, or someone in her entourage, insisted that actress Hope Lange's hair be darkened, because it was too much the color of Marilyn's and might detract from the attention given Marilyn. Logan refused. Marilyn walked off the set. Miss Lange's hair was darkened. Josh Logan wanted to film one particular scene at about twenty minutes past six in the evening. It was what is called "the magic hour," a moment when the light is good enough for motion picture photography, but when the film that is exposed seems to have been shot late at night. In this particular scene Marilyn has sneaked out of a rear window of the Blue Dragon Cafe to escape the attentions of Murray, the Montana cowboy. She is carrying her suitcase, and then she is seen running down the street to the bus depot where she will try to board a bus for Los Angeles.

Marilyn began to prepare for this scene at 2:30 in the afternoon. Her hair was done. Then her face was done. At 5:45 she was still not on the scene, so her stand-in traced the course of the action, and the cameras were put into position. At 6:05 Assistant Director Ben Kadish was sent to the Sahara Hotel to tell Marilyn that the time had come. He did not return. Logan sent a script girl to get the assistant director and Marilyn. None of them came back.

At 6:16 Logan ran from the scene to the Sahara, dashed into the penthouse suite and into Marilyn's bedroom, and found her sitting in front of the mirror looking at herself. He grasped her by the arm and yanked her down the stairs, and when they reached the scene he pushed her into action and shouted to the cameras to roll the film. Marilyn performed.

That was one way to get a performance out of the new Marilyn.

She proved that she could be almost thoroughly impossible on this film. She argued with Don Murray and once struck him viciously across the face with a piece of spangled cloth. Then she refused to apologize to him.

While Director Josh Logan managed to break through the Monroe guard and seize his leading lady to bring her to the set, others were not so fortunate. Frank Neal, of the Twentieth Century Fox publicity staff, brought a number of newspapermen and magazine correspondents to Phoenix to interview Marilyn. They were told by representatives of Marilyn Monroe Productions, Incorporated, that it would be impossible to see the president. A handful of reporters sat around the hotel for days, waiting. Most of them never did get to see Marilyn.

The complaint was that Milton H. Greene and Paula Strasberg were the corporal's guard who would not let the press or the press agents in. Yes, Paula Strasberg. Mrs. Lee Strasberg. She had replaced Natasha Lytess as Marilyn's acting coach. For Marilyn was still Marilyn, and even if Miss Lytess was no longer useful since Marilyn had shifted to the Stanislavsky Method of acting, Marilyn must still have a coach to make the decisions for her. Marilyn simply could not face decisions.

Roy Craft, the unit publicity man for Twentieth Century Fox, was running up a huge bar bill at the hotel trying to keep the newspapermen from realizing that they were not getting what they came to Phoenix for—interviews with Marilyn. Craft gave a party in his suite in the hotel and brought in a strip teaser named Stormy Lee Scott to take the minds of the reporters off their difficulties in getting to Marilyn. He was only partly successful.

Ezra Goodman of *Time* got to see Marilyn, although not immediately, but only because *Time* was planning a cover story on her, and even Marilyn's advisors agreed that this was important enough for an interview. Goodman finally interviewed Marilyn when the company moved from Phoenix to Sun Valley, Idaho, on location for the winter scenes. Marilyn sat in her room in a white terrycloth robe and sipped sherry during the interview. She was amenable and friendy and not at all haughty.

Goodman would probably not have had the interview, had not Frank Neal crashed the guard at Phoenix one day. He did so by simply forcing his way into Marilyn's suite, ignoring the sputtering that this occasioned, and finding Marilyn. Marilyn threw her arms around Frank Neal and asked him why he had deserted her—why he had not been to see her for so long. There was no time for Frank Neal to tell her that her entourage was making it impossible for anyone to see her. Besides, it would not have been useful to begin that argument since what Neal wanted was two interviews, one for Goodman and one for Cecil Smith, the influential movie-writer of the Los Angeles *Times*.

Buddy Adler, who was the chief of production and thus the head of Twentieth Century Fox in Hollywood, came to Phoenix one day. The newspapermen and press agents were offering three-to-one odds that Adler would not get in to see Marilyn, either, whether on the set or at the hotel. At the hotel she was barricaded by her staff. On the set they kept her locked up in an aluminum house trailer which was the portable dressing room.

No one could understand the secrecy, and Marilyn apparently did not know that it existed. She quickly consented to the interview with Cecil Smith and followed it with the interview with Goodman.

Smith wrote frankly about the Marilyn he saw.

"She's almost completely unapproachable these days," he said. "She surrounds herself with a wall of people, an impenetrable cordon." But, once Frank Neal had run interference through the wall, Marilyn talked freely.

She did not much care about money, she said. "I don't want

[178]

to be the highest paid movie star in the world. When I am old and in a rocking chair, I may need a roof over my head, but I want memories of having been a real actress." That was what all this study and use of the Stanislavsky Method was about.

Smith asked Marilyn if she would like to play Lady Macbeth.

She was quite honest. "I don't understand Shakespeare," she said. "I haven't been educated that way."

He probed for more information about the change that had come over her. Why did she want to get away from sexy parts in the movies?

"When I was a model, I wanted more than anything in the world for my picture to be on the cover of the *Ladies Home Journal*," she said. "Instead, I was always on magazines with names like *Peek* and *See* and *Whiz Bang*. Those were the kind of movies I made, too. You see what I mean?"

They spoke of Hollywood and her reasons for leaving it to live in the East.

"This [Hollywood] is my home," she said, "but I have to have more than they gave me. I just couldn't go along with what they wanted me to do."

The location work on *Bus Stop* had been dictated by the timing of the rodeo at the state fair grounds in Phoenix. Finally it was over and the established material had all been used. The company went to Sun Valley, then moved back to Beverly Hills to complete the filming in the studio.

Marilyn became virtually impossible. She behaved strangely, possibly due to a combination of liquor and sleeping tablets. The sleeping tablet habit was growing more serious. Allan Snyder, her makeup man, knew how to handle her and how to work with her. Sometimes Marilyn practiced her lines on him as he was working over her face. Sometimes she called him late at night, and he talked to her or came to see her.

Josh Logan began to worry about the cost of this film, and,

if he was worrying, Producer Buddy Adler was worrying twice as much. Every scene in which Marilyn appeared had to be filmed time and again—as many as fifteen times. She would blow her lines, or she would forget her lines, or she would make a mistake in the action.

This, again, was attributable to the sleeping pills. Marilyn was nervous and worried. She had romance on her mind. She had business on her mind. She had her future career as an actress on her mind.

In the morning Marilyn would appear late, perhaps an hour or so. It might take much longer than that to get her on the set. Some mornings it was not so bad, when she had slept well. This was not often. As Allan Snyder put it:

"She'd be keyed up by the day's work, get home at night keyed up, and start worrying about the next day's work. She just didn't get to sleep until all hours. She wanted to get everything right, so, instead of trying to relax and fall asleep, she would think out everything she could about the next day's scenes."

Marilyn tried to be on time. Sometimes she got to the dressing room in plenty of time to get on the set before her call. But she would be so full of sleeping pills and so woozy that Snyder would make her lie down for half an hour and would brew a pot of black coffee to try to bring her out of it. Then came the laborious job of making her up, and before anyone knew it an hour or two had gone by and she was later than ever.

Marilyn blacked out several times on the set of *Bus Stop*. She did not eat properly during the filming of the movie. Sometimes she did not eat at night. She gulped sleeping pills and then ate no breakfast, and brought a cooked New-York-cut steak from home which she hoped to eat for lunch. But often she could not eat that, and she would give it to someone to take home for the dog.

Logan tried to make Marilyn relax. He deserted Hollywood

[180]

technique and kept the cameras grinding through take after take so that Marilyn would not be disturbed by the stopping and starting. This involved processing about ten times as much film as normal, but Logan was using ten times as much film as normal anyhow, and film was the cheapest commodity at hand.

Bunny Gardel helped Marilyn create the part of the no-talent show girl. There was no choreographer on the set of *Bus Stop*, because a bad performance as a dancer was wanted. But Marilyn felt that even a bad performance had to have some structure, and Bunny, who had been a dancer on the Orpheum Circuit, took Marilyn behind the set and helped work out a little routine.

The most poignant scene in *Bus Stop* is one in which Marilyn is performing at the Blue Dragon. She sings the song "Old Black Magic," and she sings it so badly, tortures it so, that the movie audience wriggles in embarrassment as the performance continues. Marilyn did not know that song when she came on the set—it was not part of her very limited repertoire. Further, Josh Logan wanted the song worked into the action without prerecording, so an orchestra was seated on the set out of sight of the cameras, and it accompanied Marilyn during the filming.

Marilyn practiced a bit, and then when the time came, she did the scene in two takes. She could do it when she really put her mind to it, but it surprised even her.

During the filming of *Bus Stop* Marilyn sometimes seemed to be her old self, but sometimes she seemed even further removed from reality than in the past. Yet she was still capable of the shy gesture. One night, after a premiere, she was in Romanoff's when a party entered which included Fred Mac-Murray and his wife, June Haver. Marilyn knew Miss Haver from the days of *Love Nest*. They spoke. Marilyn introduced herself to MacMurray, shook hands with him tremulously, and told him she enjoyed his work very much.

On the set she was capable of crudity of language and cruelty of action to other actors. By the end of the filming, Don Murray had been subjected to many kinds of abuse and ridicule.

Finally, the torture of the movie-making stopped. Early in June, Marilyn returned to New York. She became openly involved in a romance which had been in progress secretly for a number of months. The man she had picked was a strange choice for her—the playwright Arthur Miller. Or was he so strange a choice? Marilyn had always been attracted to tall, craggy, even ugly men. Miller was tall and ugly, some said he was Lincolnesque. (Milton Greene believed this was the basis for the attraction on Marilyn's side.) They had met earlier, Marilyn said, they had met five years earlier, and when Miller was visiting Hollywood they had managed a brief affair even though Johnny Hyde was then in Marilyn's life.

When Marilyn and Miller began meeting in the spring of 1955, they were very quiet about it. Marilyn was not yet finally divorced from Joe DiMaggio; she was still seeing him frequently at that time. Miller was not divorced at all, although his relationship with his wife had developed from one of dependence on her to a kind of independence.

Miller was very much a woman's man. He revered and leaned on women; apparently he needed their strength. For such a man, a liaison with Marilyn could mean nothing but a disaster. For Marilyn, a man who needed strength and could not offer it could be nothing but disaster. But how could two people know this? Each seemed bedazzled by the other. Marilyn placed intellectual accomplishment very high. She might not read every word of the heavy works she purchased for her personal library, but she held the books in a respect that was more an awe. Miller, she had said earlier, was her favorite playwright.

Miller was also a favorite playwright of the Stanislavsky coterie among whom Marilyn chose to settle. For several years

Miller and his wife had gone their own ways, trying to stay together because of the two children, although Miller maintained his private social life, and it was thus that he met Marilyn in New York.

It would be dangerous, particularly for the new Marilyn, to be courted by a married man, and so they met at the Wallachs', at the Greenes', and at the homes of other friends. Greene and Miller knew one another and had for many years; Miller's father had once worked for Greene's father in New York City.

When Marilyn went west to make *Bus Stop*, Miller went west also. He went to Nevada, where he holed up in a cabin not far from Reno for the six weeks that it would take him to secure his divorce. When Marilyn returned to New York in June, 1956, Miller was waiting for her and took her to meet his mother. It was already decided that they would marry as soon as possible. Marilyn was thirty years old. She was a company president and seemed on her way to becoming a wealthy woman. She maintained an apartment in Sutton Place, one of the most fashionable streets of New York. She could buy all the champagne she wanted and she could bathe in the Chanel No. 5 she wore. She now would take another fling at marriage and see if she could not have her career and family life as well. She wanted children. She was certain that the career of this new husband would be more compatible with her own than that of her last one, for while Marilyn revered the theater, she did not really like baseball.

Chapter Eleven

TEN years after Marilyn entered the world of glamour and publicity she reached the apex of her movie career. The year was 1956. It was the year in which Marilyn Monroe Productions began to produce. It was the year that Twentieth Century Fox made *Bus Stop*, wherein Marilyn gave her most professional performance as an actress up to that time. It was the year in which she joined the gallery of notables and the notorious to become a cover girl for *Time*, one of the weekly news magazines. *Time* did not choose at random the subjects for what were called its "cover stories." It was required that the subject be newsworthy and with a continuity of newsworthiness, that is that the subject be in the news reports of the press over a period of time, and with normal expectation of continuing to be newsworthy. After Ezra Goodman of the *Time* editorial staff in Los Angeles spent several weeks in research on Marilyn and her past, *Time* came forth in May with its rags-to-riches cover story of Marilyn Monroe.

Marilyn had told the story of her life the way she wanted it to be known. She emphasized the misery of her childhood. She revealed that she had been enticed by a lodger in one of her foster homes and that he had deflowered her. She said it happened at the age of six. (Sometimes she said that it had happened at other ages.) She said that she had scrubbed floors and slaved during her childhood and referred to her stay in the Los Angeles orphanage as though it were a prison. The *Time* article was very sympathetic to Marilyn. Partly as a result of this article, Ezra Goodman and *Time* parted company. Goodman later indicated that the article was one-sided and an inaccurate portrayal of his research on the subject.

This was also the year in which Marilyn Monroe married playwright Arthur Miller. Marilyn, the woman, at thirty, was in love again. She was seeking happiness with a man who moved in the higher, more cultured arena on which Marilyn had begun to gaze from the outside. Once in a while she stepped onto this stage, joining the circle, but for the most part Marilyn stood back and watched the actors and actresses of the theater, and the eastern writers and directors who seemed so much different from the movie colonists among whom she had grown up. She was tolerated at dinners and parties. She was humble. She was quiet. A handful of people in the East made the effort to know her and to learn that one real charm of this woman was her wistful seriousness. She did not wiggle her hips or expose her bust or exude sex appeal when she was not playing a role. She had never done so. The surprise in people who met Marilyn outside the world of motion pictures and publicity was that she was so unlike the public Marilyn.

Marilyn and Miller hoped to be married without fanfare, but they could not escape Marilyn's press. When the news of the coming marriage broke, the reporters and photographers set up a watch before Marilyn's Sutton Place apartment. Each time Marilyn or Miller appeared, the reporters clustered around pestering them with questions, and the photographers blinded their eyes with flashes. When they applied for passports the uncomfortable question of Miller's political background popped into the open. In his youth, in the 1930's, Miller had been attracted to the Communist Revolution, along with many other youngsters who saw the need for social reform and who played hopefully at intellectualism. In the 1940's Miller continued to go against the tide, joining and backing various groups which sought accommodation with the Soviet Union when the temper of the nation was quite the opposite. He was regarded as the playwright of the left wing. He had written a number of plays into which were read much political significance. In the 1950's Miller had withdrawn silently from his espousal of unpopular political beliefs, and he had not really been in trouble with the government until this point in 1956.

In Washington the news that Arthur Miller would marry Marilyn Monroe and that they would go to England coincided with one of the Congressional investigations of communism in high, low, and median places, and Miller was summoned to Washington on the obvious principle that it is best to investigate *prominent* left-wingers because that keeps the investigation on the front pages of the newspapers.

In the months that were to come, Marilyn was to do something for Arthur Miller that no other woman in America could have done. She was to protect him, nurture him, and rescue him. Simply by being Marilyn, the love-goddess, the Venus of the American motion picture world, Marilyn was able to prevent what might have been personal disaster for Miller. It was a time of danger for anyone who had ever espoused the causes of the left wing, and particularly for those who had the taint of "red" about them. Senator Joseph McCarthy and his followers were riding high. Miller, the outspoken playwright of liberalism, was a prime target for Congressional investigation, and when he refused to answer questions before such a committee, he was cited for contempt of Congress. Had Miller been married to his first wife, the temper of America might have been very different toward him in the months to come, But Miller was to marry Marilyn.

How could such a man be all bad? He could not, decided the newspapers. Even the most right wing elements of the press treated Miller more gently than he could have expected had he espoused any other woman in the land.

The marriage of Marilyn, the love-goddess, and Arthur Miller, who was represented as the intellectual Joe DiMaggio of America, brought together strange groupings of interested parties. There were the taxi-drivers who whistled as they watched Marilyn's movies and would have patted her hip had they been given a chance. There were the brooding intellectuals who saw in the marriage a hopeful wedding of the avant garde and the masses. There were the open-mouthed who saw in the marriage the combination of the ridiculous and the sublime—and there were two varieties within this grouping.

At the age of thirty, with one unhappy marriage behind her, and another, her first, which she did not even like to talk about, Marilyn, the woman, threw herself wholeheartedly into her hope for a happy marriage. Marilyn's first husband, James Dougherty, had come home from war, married again, and settled down to life as a policeman in Van Nuys. He had been interviewed several times by reporters, and always he maintained that Marilyn had been a willing and happy bride. That was not how Marilyn recalled her marriage. She said it was everything but a love match. She had no such comment to make about the marriage to Joe DiMaggio, although she mentioned television often in discussing it, and privately she blamed herself for many of the failings that had brought about its collapse.

Marilyn's enthusiasm for this new marriage led her to embrace the bridegroom and his mother and father and his religion. Some said that Marilyn quickly recognized Miller's emotional dependence on his mother and capitalized on it. Perhaps, but Marilyn needed a mother of her own, even a second-hand one.

Wanting a family, Marilyn embraced the Jewish Millers with expressions of love and willingness just as she had the Catholic DiMaggios. She announced that she would become a convert to Judaism. She began talking of gefüllte fish and matzoh balls and chopped chicken liver and borscht. There is no reason to doubt the sincerity of these enthusiasms. By leaping into the Jewishness of the family and emphasizing it, Marilyn was making of this new marriage a unique experience, trying to rid herself of the doubts and recollections carried by a person who has gone through the marriage process twice before.

The last stages of the Monroe-Miller courtship were carried out in a hectic wrestling match with the press, which finally was brought to a close when they agreed to meet the newspaper men and women for a conference on June 29 if they could be left alone until that time. The newspapermen agreed and did leave them alone, generally speaking. The couple went to Miller's house in Roxbury, Connecticut, to retreat, and Mrs. Miller went with them, as chaperone. Marilyn chattered with her future mother-in-law and practiced Jewish cooking.

Their wedding day began with tragedy. The press appeared, swarming over the Miller property. Hundreds of newspapermen and photographers came to see the happy couple and to record their bliss. There was an accident. A car carrying a photographer and a girl reporter for *Paris Match*—the girl happened to be a Russian princess—crashed as it speeded up to follow Miller, Marilyn, and Miller's cousin, who were coming back to the house for the meeting with the press. The girl reporter was thrown out into the road. The Millers rushed to the house and telephoned for help, but the girl reporter died that afternoon in the hospital. For Marilyn, who could not contemplate the death of even a snake without anguish, the death of this girl was an unnerving experience. It had happened before her eyes.

There was no time for shock. The press gave no time. One soldier was down, but the rest pressed forward, shoving cameras, pads, and pencils in the faces of the lovers. Marilyn had knelt beside the injured girl and had blood on her sweater.

She changed for the press, for the public would not understand a spotted sweater. She emerged. Before she and Miller were mobbed, Milton Greene stepped forward and took charge. He allowed twenty minutes for the newsreels, twenty minutes for the still photographers, and thirty minutes for the reporters.

For more than an hour the pair stood and moved, puppets pushed into position by the inquiring press, until the inquisition was finally over. Miller was solemn and stiff and stern. He was, in fact, behaving very much like Joe DiMaggio.

They were married that day by a judge in White Plains, New York. Two days later a religious ceremony was performed by a rabbi at the home of Miller's agent. Marilyn's drama teacher, Lee Strasberg, gave the bride away.

Two weeks later, Marilyn and Miller flew to London, where Marilyn would begin work with Sir Laurence Olivier on the movie that would finally be titled *The Prince and the Showgirl*. At the airport Marilyn was at her best as the great lady of the motion picture business. She would remain in England for four months, and so it would have been a simple matter to have her heavy luggage shipped by sea. But not Marilyn. Her twenty-four suitcases and Miller's three pieces of luggage were weighed in and loaded, while the reporters babbled and the photographers flashed their bulbs. Only the *really* heavy and unwanted luggage had been sent by sea.

At London's airport the next day the scene was a repetition of the one they had left a few hours before at New York International Airport. If anything, the representatives of the English press tended to be more unrestrained than their American brothers and sisters. One photographer was trampled and one motion picture camera was damaged in the struggle.

The honeymooning pair were followed to their Georgian house in Windsor, and there they held a brief press conference in the dining room. Marilyn was quizzed about her sleeping habits and her underwear and her intellectuality. She responded to the questions about her sleeping habits and underwear. She had to respond. For had it not been for Marilyn's creation of her image as a girl who wore no underwear and slept in the raw, the press would never have begun asking such impertinent questions. Who asked Bette Davis how she slept, or Jane Russell, for that matter? Marilyn, the new Marilyn, was the captive of the old.

Marilyn and Miller soon discovered that the British press had all the tenacity of the British bulldog. Soon a squad of policemen were posted outside the Georgian house and the honeymooners spent the remainder of their stay behind the gates and walls, coming out to work on the movie set, to make social calls, and occasionally to meet with the press.

The British reporters did not like Arthur Miller very much. They considered him to be a cold fish. Perhaps the Millers had been given too big an advance billing or had persuaded the press that Marilyn was larger than life, for she made a bad impression in some quarters. She told Cecil Smith a few weeks before that she did not have any ambitions to play Lady Macbeth. Marilyn reversed herself and told a group of British newspapermen that it was the role she would like most. They snickered. It was Marilyn's lot forever to have newspapermen snicker when she made serious statements about serious subjects. It had been occurring with regularity since the early days in Hollywood when she would mention Jean Paul Sartre, or Proust, or Rilke. Nobody believed that anyone who looked like Marilyn could have any brains. Particularly they did not believe that Marilyn had any intellectual capacities. Her publicity men knew that she coined her own jokes, but they never convinced the press that this was true. The newspapermen thought she was a sexy blonde, and they were rather amused, at first, by what they considered to be her pretensions. Her producers and directors tended to be more annoyed. Sir Laurence Olivier was one of the latter.

Almost immediately after production began, the Monroe-

Miller household became the home of an invalid. The invalid was Marilyn. For when the shooting started, the president of Marilyn Monroe Productions, Incorporated, found herself in opposition to the director and leading man that she employed.

Olivier had been primed for this professional meeting. Josh Logan kept him informed during the filming of *Bus Stop* and had given words of caution. He must be very careful with Marilyn because she was undisciplined and untamed. If he handled her properly, he could draw a fine performance from her, but if he antagonized her anything could happen—and by that Logan meant anything negative.

Sir Laurence Olivier was an English actor who tended, by American standards and the standards of his popular press, to be stand-offish. Some said he was haughty. Hauteur is not easy to contain when one is successful and rich. Sir Laurence tried.

Marilyn became nervous the moment the production began. Paula Strasberg was there to quiet her and Lee Strasberg was sometimes there, too. Milton H. Greene was there. Arthur Miller was there. Everyone was trying to coax a performance from Marilyn.

It was probably not very bright of anyone to conceive of the plan of a leading man in a motion picture also taking the role of director. Motion pictures are very much unlike stage productions. The fact that a stage play can be converted into a motion picture is disarmingly misleading; a novel can be converted into a motion picture, too.

The leading man of a stage production can function as director, although whatever extra value is obtained by the actor's sensitive feeling for the play may be undermined by the loss in the over-all or back-row view. But in the play there is continuity, it is a whole, and the actors play it before a living audience. The motion picture is made on an entirely different principle. It is often filmed back end first or entirely out of sequence. The director is the only one who can see the scenes as they are being played. Even after it is filmed, the control of the picture remains in the hands of the director; he can leave an actor gasping on the cutting-room floor if he so desires; the director who is also actor sacrifices one role or the other to some extent.

Olivier apparently chose to sacrifice the acting role to that of director, or perhaps was forced into such position by the terrible demands made upon his patience by his leading lady.

Marilyn did everything she had ever done before. She was late. She came to the set coked up on sleeping pills. She forgot her lines. She blanked out. Olivier tried at one time to persuade her to calm down by advising her to count slowly: one ... two ... three ... before saying her lines. She muffed the scene again and again. Finally he was driven to exasperation.

"Can't you count, either?" he is reported to have said.

Perhaps Olivier did not say that but only thought it. Some who worked with him on *The Prince and the Showgirl* said that he never lost his temper with Marilyn, at least not publicly.

Marilyn lost her temper enough for both of them. When she felt she was being particularly abused, she sometimes said that she did not have to take this—that she could go back to work in the plane factory.

What Marilyn referred to in these bleak moments (and she often did this in her movie career) was the brief employment that served as a connecting link between the life of Norma Jean Baker Dougherty and Marilyn Monroe. When Dougherty went to sea during World War II, Marilyn found their tiny Van Nuys bungalow small and tiresome, and she went to work in the Radio Plane Parts Company in Burbank. The company, owned by motion picture actor Reginald Denny, made various components of airplanes, among them parachutes. Marilyn worked in the parachute room for a time as an inspector and then was transferred to another department. It was in this job that she first became a "pin-up girl" in pictures taken by company photographers and other photographers. Even in those old still pictures Marilyn's special quality began to appear, although she had not developed the sexy look that was later to be part of it. It was ridiculous, of course, for Marilyn to talk about going back to such a simple role in life; in another way it was an indication of how much rejection made her feel lost.

Olivier almost lost his mind, in a figurative sense. Later he said this production aged him ten years. He and Paula Strasberg did not see eye to eye. She took the liberty of telling him how to correct his own performance as an actor, and he did not seem to appreciate it.

Lee Strasberg said that Olivier was not having trouble with Marilyn—Marilyn was having trouble with Olivier. And of course this was true. It *was* Marilyn's production.

The Stanislavsky Method had something to do with the difficulties. Marilyn did hand exercises and other special exercises and practiced her lines constantly, Paula Strasberg hovering over her. Billy Wilder later compared those exercises to shaking the hands dry in a washroom. Marilyn took pills to hop her up and pills to calm her down and vitamins and other strengtheners. She drank champagne in one scene, drinking more and more as she kept muffing her lines. For a proletarian actress it might have been suspected that the muffing was on purpose to keep at the champagne and caviar, but not for the Queen of the American Movies. She had cases of champagne in the Georgian house if she wanted it.

Had it not been for Milton H. Greene, the production of *The Prince and the Showgirl* might never have been finished. Olivier took an intense dislike to Paula Strasberg and asked that she be sent home. Mrs. Strasberg was sent home, but it did not seem to help matters very much. Olivier would confer with Greene. One day while waiting for Monroe, the pair desperately conferred over most of a bottle of whiskey. Milton H. Greene's anxiety lest the movie not be finished might well be construed as partisanship; and with Miller in loving attendance, Marilyn in a state of emotional paralysis, Paula Strasberg appearing to know what was wanted, and the actions of diverse other characters, such as the wife of Miller's best friend who came to comfort Marilyn, it was not long before the weight of distrust and conflict of interest was added to the other burdens the principals had to bear.

It was probably unfortunate that Milton H. Greene and Arthur Miller knew each other from days of yore. They had never been friends. Greene had not known that Arthur Miller was going to enter Marilyn's life when he went into business with her. At the time of the marriage the press had asked the wise and obvious question about the future of Marilyn Monroe Productions. Marilyn had said her business and her husband would be kept apart. But she was constitutionally incapable of keeping them apart. Early in the production of *The Prince and the Showgirl,* Miller was called back to America by the illness of his daughter by his first marriage. Marilyn became distraught. She fell ill and could not perform. When Miller returned, she clutched him to her fiercely. She must have his protection in these unfriendly surroundings.

One day, during the production, Milton Greene walked into Marilyn's dressing room and found Miller working with a book of Marilyn's press clippings. At that moment, he said later, he sensed that he was on the way out as a participant in Marilyn's affairs.

Marilyn quarreled with many people on the set, not just Olivier and the other actors, but the wardrobe mistresses and the technicians to whom she had always been so friendly in the past.

In the intrigues that occurred, Greene fell under suspicion for taking Olivier's part against his own corporation president. Greene was trying to bring the movie to a conclusion at an expense level at which they might be able to show a profit. Marilyn was in no condition to examine such fine points.

Marilyn met Queen Elizabeth and comported herself gauchely. The house the Millers rented was located on the edge of Windsor Park, and they had the right to use the park. The Queen noted that they were neighbors. Marilyn obviously did not understand that the Crown owned Windsor Castle and that it was used as a residence or that the Crown also owned Windsor Park. She fumbled and bumbled until the Queen desisted in that line of small talk. The press reported it. The press discovered the extent of the bad blood that flowed on the set of *The Prince and the Showgirl* and began to attack Marilyn. In any relationships between Americans and British cousins there was an underlying tension, and Marilyn and Miller were the victims of a sudden case of Americanophobia as much as anything else. They had not behaved so badly to the press. Marilyn had appeared on opening night for the English production of Miller's *A View from the Bridge* in a Hollywood gown, low cut and skintight, but that was a Monroe public costume, like tails for Sir Laurence. They had refused many social invitations and secluded themselves, for Marilyn was working, and she was ill half the time and unwell the rest of it.

Her public performances brought about accusations that she was snubbing the British people—pure pique on the part of the newspapermen. Her performance on the set was such that at the end she knew what she had done. She braced herself and made a public apology to the entire assemblage as the production ended. Then Marilyn and her husband went home to the United States.

It was November 1956 and *Bus Stop* was playing in the theaters of America. The movie had been released in August. It had proved Marilyn's contention that she was an actress. Bosley Crowther in the New York *Times* said exactly that.

"For the striking fact is that Mr. Logan has got her to do a great deal more than wiggle and pout and pop her big eyes and play the synthetic vamp in this film. He has got her to be the beat-up B-girl of Mr. Inge's play, even down to the Ozark accent and the look of pellagra about her skin."

(That look of pellagra was achieved by Marilyn through the use of a chalky makeup instead of the usual flesh tone. She insisted on it as a part of her role. Although Twentieth Century Fox officials were worried lest it destroy the movie, Marilyn was proved to be right in her judgment.)

"He has got her to be the tinselled floozie," Crowther said, "the semi-moronic doll who is found in a Phoenix clipjoint by a cowboy of equally limited brains and is hotly pursued by this suitor to a snow-bound bus stop in the Arizona wilds. And, what's most important, he has got her to light the small flame of dignity that sputters pathetically in this chippie and to make a rather moving sort of her."

Other reviewers agreed that Marilyn had proved herself capable of giving a serious performance, although most of them indicated that they saw nothing wrong with the old Marilyn Monroe as contrasted to the new Marilyn.

It was several months after the new year (1957) began, before Sir Laurence Olivier pulled together the thousands of feet of film, takes and retakes and re-retakes, that Marilyn had driven him to exposing, and *The Prince and the Showgirl* was released through Warner Brothers.

Marilyn was already thirty years old when this motion picture was filmed, yet there is a scene in the picture, when Marilyn is in the presence of the Dowager Queen, played by Dame Sybil Thorndike, in which Marilyn is the image of a grown-up Shirley Temple. At thirty most people's faces have hardened into a pattern; Marilyn's face was still soft with a suggestion of what appeared to be baby fat. It was hinted that in *Bus Stop* one of Marilyn's problems in casting had been that she feared looking ancient as opposed to her leading man. The performance in *The Prince and the Showgirl* should have ended such speculation. Marilyn was still opalescent, she was still the baby doll, the essence of innocent sensuality.

The reviews of *The Prince and the Showgirl* were generally favorable. Some criticisms were made concerning Olivier's performance, and this was unusual, for Olivier was recognized as one of the great actors of the day. Bosley Crowther was not as enthusiastic over *The Prince and the Showgirl* as he had been over *Bus Stop*, but the critic for the New York *Herald Tribune* praised Olivier and found no serious fault with Marilyn's portrayal of innocent sex. John McCarten, the *New Yorker*'s critic, never did have much favorable to say about Marilyn's performances. He was a hard man, McCarten, and he found this motion picture to be largely a waste of time.

In 1956, the peak year of Marilyn's career, she worked in two motion pictures, and the net results of both were satisfactory, although the pain of production was growing worse. That autumn Josh Logan saw serious problems ahead for Marilyn when he spoke to reporters about her performance in *Bus Stop*. Hollywood had wasted Marilyn's talents shamefully, Logan remarked. "The girl has a brain. She has the makings of one of our greatest comediennes. She has immense subtlety," he added, "but she is a frightened girl, terrified of the whole film-making process and self-critical to the point of an inferiority complex."

Marilyn's public appearances increased her self-criticism. She knew, once she had come away from England, that she had ruined nearly every public scene there. She had not gone to England with the intent of alienating the technicians of the British film industry or Sir Laurence Olivier or the English people; yet she knew afterwards that she had done all of these.

Marilyn and Miller returned to New York and took up residence in an expensive apartment on East 57th Street. Marilyn employed decorators to furnish the rooms expensively. She introduced Miller, who was very careful with his money, into the ways of high life. Miller never seemed to embrace the champagne existence with a wholehearted air. Marilyn earned a great deal of money, but she spent it with a lavish hand on her household and on her friends. She said many times in her life that she cared nothing for money or possessions and she proved it. She gave away nearly everything she owned.

In January, 1957, Marilyn and Miller went to Jamaica for a vacation. On their return the worst fears of Milton H. Greene began to be realized. He wanted credit as executive producer of *The Prince and the Showgirl,* and for some reason or other Marilyn was led to believe he should not have it. If anyone on the set of that motion picture functioned as producer it was Greene. He spent most of his time trying to keep Marilyn in some semblance of discipline, babying her and talking seriously, but never harshly, to her. She was so sensitive, he said, that her whole attitude could be changed in a moment by a tone of voice, and the change was almost always for the worse except on one occasion that Greene recalled.

Marilyn was in her dressing room, throwing a tantrum. Greene came in and began to talk to her. She said something about her next picture. He said something about the picture they would do with Charlie Chaplin some day. Marilyn brightened, the tantrum was forgotten, and she floated out onto the set with a smile.

The two years after the English experiences were relatively happy ones for Marilyn. She learned to entertain and did so frequently in New York. She and Miller went out to be entertained. They became part of the New York theatrical set. They lived in New York in the winter, in the expensive apartment. In the summer they moved to Roxbury, where Miller was creating what the newspaper people began to refer to as "an estate."

But life was not quite as simple as it seemed. There were constant offers of employment for Marilyn's talents: television shows, motion picture scripts, and there was even talk of Broadway parts. Marilyn Monroe Productions, Incorporated did not prosper as much as had been hoped. *The Prince and the Showgirl* had been expensive to film, and it did not do as well at the box office as Marilyn and Greene had expected. And so difficulties began to emerge.

Marilyn Monroe Productions, Incorporated was not three years old when it collapsed. In 1957 and early 1958 Marilyn and Miller on the one hand quarrelled constantly with Greene on the other, and it became apparent that Miller was playing a role in his wife's affairs. Greene had hoped that Marilyn would hire her own independent lawyers and make her independent decisions, but this was far too much to hope for from Marilyn. One of the reasons for the arguments between Marilyn and Milton H. Greene was mutual suspicion that underground negotiations were being carried out by both parties to injure the other. The company had only one asset: Marilyn Monroe. Many people in the amusement industry were eager to use Marilyn's services, and some of them seemed to believe that the way to persuade Marilyn was to first persuade Arthur Miller.

In the summer of 1957 Marilyn and Miller rented a house on the south shore of Long Island and spent the lazy, warm days on the beach or fishing or walking. Marilyn was playing at being the housewife. It was not exactly playing; this was one Marilyn, who wanted children and a husband and a home and the simple life. She went shopping in the village of Amagansett and worked in her garden. Her husband was struggling with his writing. He was working on a play, but not very successfully. Too many things seem to have happened to him too fast, including Marilyn, for him to have rearranged his principles. A look at later published work would indicate that the old principles of *Death of a Salesman* and *The Crucible* no longer worked for Arthur Miller, and, since he was a very serious playwright, the lack of principles was a matter of concern. He certainly appeared to be a writer in the process of trying to find himself.

Marilyn became pregnant that year, and it seemed that her

fondest dreams had been realized. She had a husband who loved her. She had a home (at that moment, including the rented house on Long Island, she had three of them), she had success, and now she was going to have a child. But the pregnancy proved abortive, and one of her dreams of happiness was destroyed that autumn.

Marilyn spent the autumn of 1957 and the spring of 1958 alternatively in the New York apartment and the house in Roxbury. Miller was working on a screenplay based on a short story he had written for publication in *Esquire* in the autumn of 1957. The genesis of the short story had been in Nevada when Miller was completing his six-week residence for the divorce that would let him marry Marilyn. He had encountered some cowboys who made a precarious living capturing wild horses, noble, snorting mustangs, which were hauled off in trucks and sold to companies that ground them up for dog and chicken food.

The horror, the hopelessness of it, the commentary on inhumanity and the human condition that it stated would appeal to a writer. The short story was written. Then Miller expanded it to include a love story, in the form of a motion picture script. He did nothing with it, however, at that moment.

Lee and Paula Strasberg read this screenplay and found it to be a strong, compelling work. The fault, at that time, was that it was not a screenplay at all. Miller was a playwright, and he had produced a play for the movies, a work that was talky and paid little attention to the more important medium of the film. It was a matter of no consequence at that particular moment, because other affairs had to be settled first.

In the spring of 1958 matters came to a head between Marilyn and Milton H. Greene regarding Marilyn Monroe Productions, Incorporated. There was a meeting between Greene, Marilyn, and Miller with a representative of Miller's New York law firm. After some sparring the lawyer began

[200]

to get down to the basis on which the difficult situation might be settled. Greene asked Marilyn what she wanted. Marilyn broke into tears and ran out of the room, unable to face the conflict. Greene said he looked at Miller.

"Don't look at me," said Miller.

Greene looked at Miller again.

In April, 1958, Greene sold his 49.5 per cent of Marilyn Monroe Productions, Incorporated, to Marilyn for a little more than eighty thousand dollars. It was said that Greene had rejected an offer of a half million dollars for the stock in the happier days before the Monroe-Miller marriage. Marilyn said that she did not intend to sit by and let Milton Greene collect nearly half her earnings for seven years.

And so Marilyn Monroe Productions, Incorporated, was reorganized and was given a new board of directors. It was never to produce another movie.

In the summer, after the struggle with Milton Greene, Marilyn and Miller moved to Hollywood to undertake a new motion picture commitment. Perhaps the arrangement had been made earlier, because such matters do take time in Hollywood, as a rule. Billy Wilder had been in touch with Marilyn for some time about a motion picture that he wanted to make. It would be called *Some Like It Hot*. It would have a background set in the gangster days of 1929. A gangster, played by George Raft, leads his gang in the massacre of another gang, and two musicians, played by Tony Curtis and Jack Lemmon, see the killing and run away. They are frantic to escape, and so they dress as women and get jobs with an all-girl orchestra. They go to Florida on a train with the girls and have a drinking party in an upper berth. Tony Curtis falls in love with Marilyn, who plays a ukulele player and singer with the band. She is also an alcoholic who loves millionaires. Tony Curtis borrows a yacht from millionaire Joe E. Brown and uses it to impress Marilyn. The gangsters come back and discover the two male musicians, who hide under a table. The gangsters are wiped out by another gang in the nick of time, and Marilyn decides she loves Tony Curtis even without money.

Marilyn Monroe Productions, Incorporated, was not concerned directly with *Some Like It Hot*, but the movie was still a very independent production. It was labelled as an Ashton Picture presented by the Mirisch Company. It was filmed on the lot of the Goldwyn studios in Hollywood and was released through the United Artists Corporation. Marilyn did not simply go to work for the producers, she became a partner in the venture.

Marilyn and company had hardly gone to Hollywood when the difficulties began. She arrived at the Goldwyn studios for color tests one day to learn that the motion picture would be filmed in black and white. Marilyn did not like this at all. She had a very strongly developed sense of self-preservation. She knew how she looked and how she was at her best—on a wide screen in full color. Billy Wilder was concerned about the color problem not so much because of money as because of the nature of the film. He was producing broad slapstick. In full color Jack Lemmon and Tony Curtis would be accused of transvestitism if their makeup was light, and of impossible vulgarism if it was heavy. Marilyn gave in, but not with very good grace.

When the filming began, Marilyn was up to all her old tricks. Marilyn was late. Marilyn was bad-tempered to other players—worse than ever before. Marilyn was nasty to an assistant director. One day on the set, this underpaid, overworked man came to Marilyn's dressing room to tell her that her presence was needed on the set.

"Drop dead," said Marilyn, looking up from her book for just a moment.

Marilyn was more difficult than Marilyn had ever been before in the production of a motion picture.

On the first day she set the tone for the production.

The other players had been on the set since eleven o'clock, but, knowing Marilyn's proclivity for late arrival, Billy Wilder had set her call for 1:00 p.m. She arrived at three-thirty and then swished into her dressing room and shut the door. She did not appear outside that door until after 6:00 p.m.

For once she got what was coming to her. Billy Wilder dismissed the cast just before six, and just after six he left himself, which made Marilyn ready for action and with no one to record it or play with.

Did this solve the problem?

It did not.

Marilyn continued to be late. She muffed her lines when she carried the action properly. On one scene fifty-nine takes were required, many of them by Marilyn's dictum, before the film could be printed.

Always before, Marilyn had shown redeeming features on the set. This time she did not show them to the cast or the director. Billy Wilder was a genial man, and he admired Marilyn as an actress, or at least for the luminescent quality which Paula Strasberg defined as "star quality," as did just about everyone else in Hollywood.

Wilder commented on one of Marilyn's characteristics: that of the night-blooming Cereus. She came late on the set, and sometimes she was not very well organized when she finally emerged from her dressing room. But she warmed up as the work continued. At about the time that the other actors were ready to quit, she was going strong. Wilder noted that on some of her multiple-take scenes she played better in each scene, while the player who was opposite her began to tire and played successively worse. This created tensions on the set, and eventually it led to a blow-up with Tony Curtis, her leading man. One night, as the rushes were being shown, someone asked Curtis what was it like playing with Marilyn Monroe, and particularly what was it like kissing her?

"You want to know how it was?" Curtis said, standing up. "Okay, I'll tell you. It was like kissing Hitler."

This stupid remark was widely quoted, and it annoyed everyone around Marilyn. She deserved it, however, if an actress ever did, because she showed so little concern or consideration for any of the other players. She was so much concerned with herself that she could not worry about any others. Had she been a minor actress it might not have been so important, but in *Some Like It Hot* Marilyn was the star, the picture revolved around her, and everyone except her personal staff suffered from her actions.

Arthur Miller met his trouble with Congress in 1957 and 1958: he was cited for contempt for refusing to answer questions about people with whom he had been involved in his days of flirtation with the communist movement.

While Marilyn was on the set of *Some Like It Hot,* Miller was on trial in Washington. This was enough to explain part of Marilyn's anxiety—Miller's absence was bad enough, but the reason for it was frightening.

On August 7 a reporter came to see her on the set to give her a bit of good news, and she kept him waiting for forty minutes. Arthur Miller had been acquitted, he said, when she finally saw him. How did it strike her? asked the reporter.

She never had the slightest doubt, said Marilyn, "because I have been studying Thomas Jefferson for years, and, according to Thomas Jefferson, this case had to turn out this way."

She picked up the white ukulele that she used in the motion picture and walked away from the reporter casually, strumming "Happy Days Are Here Again." The reporter noticed that she was quite flat.

Thomas Jefferson would have been pleased, but to others it seemed that Marilyn Monroe, America's Venus, could be given as much credit for that acquittal as the drafter of the Constitution.

[204]

At the end of the production of *Some Like It Hot*, Billy Wilder made several remarks in an unguarded moment about Marilyn's performance and indicated that he did not want to work with her again. "I have discussed this project with my doctor and my psychiatrist, and they tell me I'm too old and too rich to go through this again," he said. The remarks brought a stiff demand from Arthur Miller for apology, because, said Miller, Wilder had insulted his wife. Wilder tried to patch it up, for he was by nature a friendly man, although given to off-the-cuff remarks. But the breach was not healed. Billy Wilder's name was removed from Marilyn's list of acceptable directors.

Marilyn had reasons to be upset during the later phases of the filming of *Some Like It Hot*. She was pregnant again, but again the pregnancy ended in tragedy: she lost the child by miscarriage.

Chapter Twelve

THE first three years of Marilyn's marriage to Arthur Miller brought her a degree of happiness she had not known before except for very short periods: in the early months of her marriage to Joe DiMaggio, when she dreamed of becoming an Italianate housewife; and at the peak of her affair with Fred Karger in Hollywood, when she dreamed only of love.

She was accepted as a person by Miller's friends in New York and by strangers whom she met at parties. In New York she could walk the streets without being recognized, or if recognized she was greeted with a cheery wave or a delighted grin. Hollywood was the home of the star-chasers, not New York, and a motion picture personality might stroll the entire length of Park Avenue without causing more than a few heads to turn.

The Actors' Studio, with which Marilyn remained associated, continued to give her a feeling of belonging. Lee Strasberg was her friend and teacher. Paula Strasberg, who earned large sums of money on the pictures in which she coached Marilyn, was available, and yet not the same personal problem that Natasha Lytess had become. Mrs. Strasberg was ready to work on Marilyn's movies, but she had a life of her own.

There was no suggestion of conflict between Marilyn

and her husband. She was accepted by his children, and she doted on them. He seemed to live for her, to cherish her, and, as one person said, to value her above all else. Cynics noted that Miller's creative processes seemed to be hanging in abeyance, and some concerned themselves when they saw him taking an ever-increasing interest in Marilyn's business affairs. These onlookers believed that Miller ought to busy himself instead at the playwright's task. Some newspaper busybodies speculated that being married to Marilyn was sapping Miller of his creative talent, quite forgetting that Miller had also been going through a difficult bath of fire in the Congressional cauldron.

The only apparent cause for unhappiness in this period of Marilyn's life was her inability to bear children. Marilyn wanted a child of her own. She sought the advice of doctors in her efforts to conceive and carry a baby to birth. But she could not do so, at least not then.

Money was no problem for Marilyn and Miller. They lived more ostentatiously than he might have liked, but Marilyn never saw any reason to hoard money. Her attitude was that either there was more available or there was not. Marilyn lived in the present, not in the future. She was singularly unmarked in that respect compared to other players who had known privation and poverty. She was always the creature of *Now*. Marilyn demanded constant reassurances and constant consideration. All this demand must have been trying for a husband who had always been immersed in his own affairs. Marilyn was totally honest in all matters except the little matters which concerned facts. How difficult this must have been to live with, especially for a man whose background suggested love of intrigue and who had been hurt enough in the world to protect himself at all times.

Marilyn demanded much. She demanded something that Miller, or one like him, alone could give. To her he came from the world of books and letters and she came from the gutter.

Marilyn wanted assurance that she was somebody, that she could become an actress, that she had talent other than the ability to swing her hips and jiggle her breasts and charm the world through a blaze of dusty light by means of that opalescence she flashed across the screen. She had the gift—Billy Wilder called it genius—but this was not enough for her. She wanted triumph, not through her body, which was simply trade goods to her, but through her soul. For Marilyn owned a soul, a shining soul, of the kind that is found in the believing priest, the honest harlot, and the kindly outlaw. She was a hermit living among men. Her loneliness showed through to anyone who could step aside from egotism long enough to talk to her. She had been used by many, she had been a laughingstock of Hollywood. When it came to the only thing that counted in Hollywood—money—Spyros Skouras, a Greek businessman, who spoke the American language brokenly, was the one to recognize her value to her industry and the first important man who did not laugh at her. No one laughed at Marilyn in 1957; the laughter had grown progressively more hollow in each year after 1951. No matter how bad the casting, no matter how rushed or incompetent the direction, no matter how scathing the criticism, the motion pictures in which this girl appeared often prospered even when worthless; and when the total effect was miserable, Marilyn still showed through, her shining quality leaving the image of her face and body in the souls of movie-goers.

Miller brought to Marilyn a little confidence, a little hope, a little love. If he was not sure of his own motivation, and if he was uncertain in his assurances to Marilyn that she had great talent, perhaps he did not know that she felt she must become a great actress. And, of course, she was a great actress in the sense that she could portray herself at all times convincingly. There were many on stage and screen who essayed more and accomplished less. To become a great actress, to be respected for her accomplishments alone, was Marilyn's overweaning desire. To laugh at her was to pound nails in her coffin. To encourage her was no better. To accept her and to love her meant to be with her, supporting her, day and night, month in and month out. None but a saint could bear the weight of two souls for long. Something had to give.

How they failed one another was the secret of Marilyn and Miller, and it was not explained even when it was exposed by Miller in his play *After the Fall*. Other things were explained: the constant pulling and tugging of people on Marilyn, people who wanted money. She was the most important commodity in the motion picture industry, and there was scarcely a person involved who could control his avarice when he considered her "potential." Miller's own problems relative to Marilyn were not explained, nor was his own interest in money so revealed. But since money meant so little to Marilyn for its own sake, it threatened nothing in their relationship.

Sometime before the middle of 1960 the decay of the marriage began. It was not apparent in that wonderful summer of 1957 on the coast of Long Island. Even the troubles of making *Some Like It Hot* did not bring about the end—although on this movie Marilyn behaved worse than she ever had behaved before. The money earned by *Some Like It Hot* was a soothing unguent: the movie's gross return reached ten million dollars in 1959; in 1960 it was up to twelve million dollars. It had cost nearly three million dollars to film, and some said that a million dollars of that cost was directly attributable to Marilyn's didoes; but the net profits were huge, and this motion picture was owned by the principals. Marilyn had taken a guarantee, not a salary, and was to have a percentage of the gross profits. The experts predicted that the movie would make her a millionaire.

Marilyn was known the world over, and more favorably every year. In Italy a popular opinion poll put her at the top of the list; she was more popular than any other actress and better known than Nikita Khrushchev in 1958. (The next year she met Khrushchev at a party given in Hollywood by Twentieth Century Fox.) In 1959 she received the Italian movie industry's DiDonatello award for her screen work. It was not an Academy Award but it was an indication of respect.

Marilyn's possessiveness and insecurity seemed to grow in spite of her triumphs. *Some Like It Hot* was released early in 1959. It received excellent reviews, and Marilyn's role was not denigrated even by the most sophisticated critics. She was called a talented comedienne for the part she played as a naive blonde who liked men.

Late in 1959 it was agreed that Marilyn would begin work on the second of the four movies in which she was to appear for Twentieth Century Fox Films. The picture was to be called *Let's Make Love*. It was another light comedy. In it a billionaire learns that he is to be satirized in an off-Broadway revue, and he goes to the theater to see what it is all about. He sees a beautiful singer (Marilyn), and, because he looks like a billionaire, he is hired to play the role of the billionaire who is to be lampooned. Well, one thing leads to another, and Bing Crosby, Gene Kelly, and Milton Berle all play themselves for a moment. In the end Marilyn agrees to marry the billionaire and all ends happily.

The beginning of the production was not so very happy. Marilyn had virtual control of the script, and apparently she did not believe that her part was large enough for her. And so it was expanded at the expense of the part of the billionaire. Arthur Miller's name did not appear on the script, but he was asked to write some of the additional dialogue to pad out Norman Krasna's original part as written for Marilyn. The contraction of the part of the billionaire caused Hollywood actors to walk away from the role as not being big enough for their talents. Hedda Hopper said that Yul Brynner, Gregory Peck, Cary Grant, Charlton Heston, Rock Hudson, and James

Stewart all turned down the role of the billionaire for that reason.

The part was accepted by Yves Montand, a French singer and actor who was touring the United States. Montand looked very much like a Gallic Joe DiMaggio.

Once the script problems of *Let's Make Love* were solved, Marilyn was amenable to discussions of the details of production. George Cukor, the director of the movie, went to New York with Lionel Newman, the musical director, and Sammy Cahn and James Van Heusen, the song-writers. They came to the 57th Street apartment to audition the musical score for Marilyn and thus to be sure there would be no difficulties on the set.

When the four men came into the room, Marilyn and Miller and Miller's son were there. She introduced them to the boy proudly. Then she made certain that ashtrays were available for the smokers and that they were comfortable. The song-writers began to play their songs.

In the middle of one of these the doorbell rang. Marilyn jumped up to answer the door, not wanting a servant to answer it because the caller was a friend of the son, and she wanted to make him welcome. The disturbance caused some strain among the important visitors from Hollywood, but they accepted it. Later Newman said it was not out of "disrespect" to Cukor and the composers, but because she was eager to greet the boy personally. When the two boys left the apartment, Mrs. Miller asked if the younger Miller had his keys and when he would be home. She sat down and the audition could then continue.

Marilyn liked the songs, but she wanted Miller's judgment too because she still could not trust her own. Not one word or note had to be changed in these songs, which allowed the musicians to go away happy. They knew that Marilyn was quite capable of making huge demands if she felt they were in order. Newman said that her own judgment about songs for herself was excellent. "She had an innate sense of what was good in a song, and what was good for her in a song," he said.

What difficulties the Millers had were not known publicly. Marilyn demanded a great deal from Miller. She must have judged his every act in relationship to herself. Miller characterized this aspect of Marilyn in an interview with British Reporter Henry Brandon which began with talk about Marilyn as a goddess-symbol.

"I don't regard my wife as a symbol," he said. "I know she certainly doesn't regard herself that way. She is the most direct human being I ever knew.

"I don't know what explains it, if anything does, except that she has had a life as an orphan that left her unprotected from danger and from others around her, in a way that people who have lived in secure families never know. From way back she's had to estimate her situation in life on the basis of the sternest realities, and not to allow sentiment to mislead her. The net result of it is that she responds to the most elemental aspect of the human being near her—that is, his propensity for hurting or helping—and he is immediately stimulated by the fact that he is really being looked at."

Broadway wits, making play with words, sometimes said that the Miller-Monroe marriage could be characterized as "Death of a Playwright." Miller was singularly unproductive in the four years of the marriage. Some, who obviously did not like him, said that he had nothing more to say; others, who did like him, said that marriage to Marilyn had sapped him.

In matters of emotion Marilyn was especially demanding. She insisted that Miller be with her at all times. He insisted that he have some privacy in which to create. At times, such as the summer spent at Amagansett, they might both have their wish: Miller could write quietly in one part of the house while Marilyn gardened outside. But when Marilyn must go to Hollywood or on location to make a movie, problems would arise.

The problem arose toward the end of 1959.

Marilyn had employed the public relations firm of Arthur Jacobs and John Springer to represent her. She knew Arthur Jacobs. She did not know John Springer. From Los Angeles Jacobs called Springer in New York and told him that Marilyn would be leaving for the West Coast on a certain flight. Would Springer meet her and discuss future affairs? Marilyn was always nervous about assuming a new relationship, and both she and Springer approached the meeting somewhat anxiously.

Springer met Marilyn and Arthur Miller and May Reiss, Marilyn's secretary, at the apartment on 57th Street. A limousine was waiting to take them to the airport. Outside the apartment house a group of teenagers in a car spotted Marilyn and began blowing kisses at her and laughing. She blew kisses and laughed in return. The teenagers followed them all the way to the airport, playing this game, and Marilyn played with them, in a thoroughly good humor.

They all adjourned to the bar and had a drink, Marilyn drinking champagne. After a few minutes of small talk, Marilyn told Springer that she was very pleased to know him and to have him working with her. The moment of crisis was past.

Then, until plane time, they sat and talked about nothing in particular. Springer noticed how affectionate Marilyn was to Miller. He would have sworn that there was nothing wrong between them—had anybody even thought of asking.

Marilyn and Miller flew then to Hollywood, to stay in a bungalow at the Beverly Hills Hotel. Some Hollywood observers expressed surprise to see Miller with Marilyn, not knowing how complete he found her need to be and how it was impossible to refuse her. Miller had changed. He now stood with Paula Strasberg on the set, watching Marilyn as she sweated and strained to bring across that effortless style. He was taking a serious interest in motion pictures and was in the process of developing the short story he had written for *Esquire* from a play into the movie script, *The Misfits*, for

Marilyn. It could be a very profitable venture for both of them.

The Montands were staying at the Beverly Hills Hotel in a bungalow, too. Not too long after the production of *Let's Make Love* began, Marilyn and Miller invited the Montands to a spaghetti dinner. Montand and his wife came, dressed in old clothes as were the Millers, and sat on the floor, ate spaghetti, and drank red wine. It was the first American family party they had ever attended and they were charmed. Madame Montand was a handsome European woman, a motion picture actress herself, who worked under the name of Simone Signoret and had appeared in Hollywood roles before. She knew her way around the film capital. She was very much married to Yves Montand and he to her, but during the filming of *Let's Make Love* something happened between Marilyn and Montand.

Perhaps a spark was kindled at the cocktail party that Twentieth Century Fox gave for the press in January, 1960. Marilyn was there with Miller, and Montand was there with Simone Signoret. Marilyn wore a low-cut revealing light dress. Miss Signoret was dressed conservatively in black. Montand and Miller wore conservative suits, and one might have thought from looking at them that they were related. (Montand was almost the image of Joe DiMaggio.)

Marilyn was slim and svelte. No suggestion of tension or unhappiness showed in the pictures that were taken of her that night. But then, or shortly afterward, something happened. Among other things, Miller went abroad for several weeks to work on the screen play of *The Misfits* with director John Huston. Then he spent some time in Nevada, looking over locations.

Perhaps it was Marilyn's resentment at being left alone. Perhaps it was Montand's natural Gallic proclivity for conquest. Perhaps, as some suggested, it was Marilyn's attempt to use Montand to make Miller jealous and sorry that he had been so unkind as to leave her alone in Hollywood while he went racing around the world on business of his own.

Whatever it was, it scarcely would have occurred as far as Marilyn was concerned had there not been some difficulty in the Monroe-Miller household. Marilyn was not a tramp. She did not fall in love until she had first fallen out of love.

It was deadly serious for Marilyn; she never took love lightly. It could have been serious for Montand, until his wife pulled in the reins very tightly. But that was much, much later, unfortunately for the marriage of Marilyn and Arthur Miller.

Marilyn was still afraid of the camera and the director and the unknown. An actor on the set of *Let's Make Love* discovered a most revealing commentary on Marilyn's entire life. One day this player picked up a notebook in which Marilyn had been writing between scenes and discovered the following, as she had written it:

"What am I afraid of? Do I think I can't act? I know I can act but I am afraid. I am afraid and I should not be and I must not be."

But the fact was that she was afraid and she would always be afraid and it would grow worse, not better. The fear sapped her strength and reason. It drove her to nightmares and sleeplessness. She took more and more sleeping pills, became foggy and drowsy, and created more problems in her personal and professional lives. The countless hours of waiting for Monroe continued, and when the leading lady appeared on the set, it was retakes and more retakes. Marilyn quarreled with Director George Cukor, and so did Miller when he was there. The argument began over the rushes of the day's shooting. Marilyn would express her preferences and Miller would give his opinions. Often they disagreed with Cukor's. So Cukor quit watching the rushes with them. (But when he edited the film he returned to his original judgments.)

Marilyn turned inward when she found that a director either disliked her or was insensitive to her. Film directors in

Hollywood, by and large, did not regard the problem of acting for the movies as one that should take great amounts of study or time. Many directors believed that if the actor could register elementary emotion, learn his lines, and do as he was told, everything would be fine. The contempt of many directors for players was well known, and it worried Marilyn constantly.

During her entire career, Marilyn's reaction to this was to enlist the services of all the other technicians and specialists who could and would work with her. For them she turned on every bit of charm.

Lionel Newman, who worked on *Let's Make Love* as musical director, recalled that they had a new boom man, one who handled the microphone on the sound-recording stage. This man was a Monroe fan and was nearly overcome with awe when he learned that he was going to work with her. He asked if it would be all right if he used his personal camera and took pictures of Marilyn while she was recording her songs. As a rule, photographers were not encouraged on the music recording stage because their presence and the lights distracted the players from their singing.

But in this case Newman asked Marilyn if she would mind, and she laughed and said she would not mind at all. So she entered at the appointed time, or as close to it as she could manage, and the amateur cameraman began. She was relaxed. She was wearing tight capri slacks and no makeup. She sat on a high stool and began to rehearse. The boom man snapped pictures, and Marilyn did not bat an eye except to smile at him.

With her extraordinary sensitivity to people, Marilyn recognized that she had made an enemy of George Cukor, and this made her more nervous than ever. She began to eat too much and drink too much, and she grew very flabby. It showed on the set, if less drastically in the motion picture photography.

In this motion picture, however, Marilyn did not antagonize the other players. Montand loved her. So did Wilfred Hyde-White, a British actor who played the part of the billionaire's lawyer in the movie.

"I've never known anyone with such spotty attendance," Hyde-White told the Twentieth Century Fox Press agents. "She held us up almost as much as the strike. (There was an actors' strike during the movie production.) Not only she doesn't come, but she doesn't do anything when she gets there. But I love her. I love big stars, kings and queens, very rich people, and the very famous." He once heard of a man who told a head-hunter in Africa that he came from America, and the savage said: "America—Marilyn Monroe."

Her internationalism was unquestioned now. She was banned in Kansas, where censors cut large pieces out of *Some Like It Hot*, and in Baghdad, where *Bus Stop* frightened the protectors of public morals. She was loved in Paris and in Rome and in London, in spite of her unfortunate press relations with the English newspapers. She was known everywhere. Montand called her the universal movie star. She and Montand were very close. On the set of *Let's Make Love*, on Marilyn's birthday, June 1, the cast and crew gave a birthday party which included a huge cake. Marilyn and Montand were photographed together. Arthur Miller was not in the picture.

Chapter Thirteen

THE filming of *The Misfits* was to be the very next item of business in Marilyn's life. She left Hollywood directly after the last scenes of *Let's Make Love* were filmed and spent a few whirlwind days in New York City in fittings for costumes and for film tests. It would not take too much film testing, because *The Misfits* was to be shot in black and white like *Some Like It Hot*. If Marilyn objected to the black-and-white film, she said nothing about it publicly.

The Misfits was not a normal Hollywood production. It began more as an Arthur Miller production. Miller wrote the screenplay, obviously to use Marilyn's talents. He consulted about it with Frank E. Taylor, a book publisher in New York City whom he had known for a number of years. Taylor had been Miller's first book editor. He had also spent several years after World War II in Hollywood. He was a dilettante with an Ivy League background and a large acquaintance in the entertainment world. He was a man of quick enthusiasms, and he saw vast possibilities in the combination of script, playwright, and actress. He suggested that Miller send his script to John Huston. When the script reached Huston in Europe, he, too, became enthusiastic over it. Huston found a producer in the Seven Arts Productions, which was a subsidiary of United Artists. And then came the negotiations. Marilyn and Miller were represented by Marilyn's agents at MCA. Frank Taylor suggested that Clark Gable be secured for the male lead, and since MCA also represented Gable, the communication was brief and, as it turned out, happy and positive.

So the motion picture took form. Taylor became producer. He and Miller and Huston began to put together the rest of the cast and the nuts and bolts, which included establishment of one of the greatest fanfares ever accorded a motion picture. They hired Magnum Photos Inc. to take still pictures and worked out their plans so that a picture book would be published. They made arrangements with Miller's publisher to publish the screenplay. Taylor would publish it in paperback. A reporter named James Goode planned a book on the making of the movie. All the magazines would be given coverage by Magnum—*all* the magazines, in America, Germany, France, and elsewhere. In the end the cast included Marilyn, Clark Gable, Montgomery Clift, Eli Wallach, Thelma Ritter. Paula Strasberg was hired to coach Marilyn. Taylor paid her fifteen hundred dollars a week and said that Marilyn paid her a similar sum. It was indicated that this would be one of the great motion pictures of all time.

There were delays and problems involving the commitments of various members of the group, but in the summer of 1960 all were assembled in Reno. The quarters of Marilyn and Miller were to be in the Mapes Hotel, along with many of the others of the unit. Half the hotel was in the hands of the movie-makers.

They comprised a colorful scene which ought to have helped the tourist business in Reno that summer. Taylor brought with him a wardrobe which delved heavily into the exotic: red-and-yellow trousers, electric-blue trousers, plaid silk shirts, and Tyrolean hats. John Huston wore a kind of uniform consisting of modified bush jackets and trousers in matching colors and perhaps a silk scarf about the neck. Taylor had a Thunderbird of fire-engine red. The rest of the important people had Cadillacs. None of this, except possibly

Taylor's electric-blue trousers, would have caused much stir in Hollywood. It was a welcome change for the citizens of Reno.

Miller wore khaki cotton trousers and blue workshirts. Paula Strasberg wore a costume of black dress, black shoes, and black veil, and carried a black parasol.

By July 19 everyone of importance was on location except Marilyn. She arrived that day from the East on board an airliner and kept her welcoming committee waiting for half an hour, while Sidney Guilaroff, an old friend, did her hair and she changed her clothes and made ready to greet the press that was assembled at the site. Her press agent and Miller escorted her out of the plane, and she was greeted by the wife of the governor of Nevada, given flowers and driven to the Mapes Hotel in Frank Taylor's new Thunderbird. She disappeared into the hotel.

On Sunday Miller joined Huston, the Frank Taylors, and others around the swimming pool and tennis court of one of Reno's more prosperous citizens. Marilyn did not appear. Late in the afternoon she did appear at an official cocktail party which was given for the press and notables of the area. Then she disappeared again.

Marilyn showed up on location for her first scenes just before noon on Monday, escorted by her entourage, which included Miller, her press agent, Paula Strasberg, hairdresser Guilaroff, Allan Snyder, the makeup man, and Agnes Flanagan, another hairdresser; Bunny Gardel, her friend and makeup girl, Evelyn Moriarty, her stand-in, Ralph Roberts, her masseur; a secretary, wardrobe girl, seamstress, chauffeur, and Hazel Washington, her maid.

Then, making ready for the scene, which was with Clark Gable, she took a deep breath and said in a very small poignant voice, loudly enough so that Agnes Flanagan could hear:

"Rhett Butler, to think I'm working with him."

Marilyn could not pull herself together to get to the sets be-

[220]

fore noon, so the filming was arranged around her. She was sick for two days at the end of the first week, and soon the first question the principals asked among themselves every morning was, "Is Marilyn working today?"

It was apparent that Mr. and Mrs. Arthur Miller were going in separate directions. Marilyn would ride out to the location in her Cadillac with Paula Strasberg, and Miller would ride with Huston.

There were takes and retakes. Marilyn's retakes created problems, even for her. In one scene she is eating eggs that Gable cooks for her. Before Huston got the right shot, Marilyn had eaten two dozen eggs.

Marilyn was her usual self, preoccupied and literal. One day Taylor brought a man to meet her in her dressing room, a representative of the firm that would produce a screen "trailer" or advertising short, which would be distributed to the motion picture houses which would contract to lease prints of *The Misfits*. He introduced the man as someone who had come to see about "the trailer."

"Am I glad to see you," Marilyn said, sitting in her trailer dressing room. "The air conditioning doesn't work in here."

And so another little misunderstanding was added to the story of the dumb blonde actress.

It was hot in Reno and Marilyn's lateness began to get on people's nerves, but every one of them realized that she was the central point of interest in the motion picture. So the struggle continued. Huston complained. It was beyond his comprehension that Marilyn would not be ready to start work by nine o'clock in the morning. But that was the way it was.

The story was current about Hollywood that Marilyn and Yves Montand were having an affair. Florabel Muir referred to it in an article in a weekly Hollywood publication which Miller saw. Marilyn deserted the set on August 27 and flew alone to Hollywood. A few days later the word came back that she had entered Westside Hospital for a week, suffering

[221]

from exhaustion. At about the same time, Hedda Hopper reported that Yves Montand was in Hollywood, but that he would not answer Marilyn's telephone calls. Not long afterward, Simone Signoret told the press that she was sorry about Marilyn but that Marilyn was not very wise to get mixed up with Simone Signoret's husband. Montand had no desire to engage further in the matter, apparently, for this was almost the last that was heard of it except in reverberations. He and Simone Signoret left for Paris the next week.

Marilyn came back to the set early in September, but the coolness with Miller was noticed by the press, and particularly by James Goode, who had more than usual press access to the set since he was writing a book about the filming of the movie. He noticed that Marilyn rarely spoke to the cast or crew. She was very friendly with Clark Gable and John Huston and with Montgomery Clift. But she was not nearly so friendly with Eli Wallach, who represented the Miller days.

Marilyn and Miller shared a hotel suite, but she almost always went to bed early and Miller worked late. They were seldom seen together unless there was an official motion picture reason for such an appearance. Paula Strasberg stayed with Marilyn, alternating her costumes on the set between black and brown.

Marilyn kept everyone guessing. One night she went out for a walk with Miller and the next day was very cheerful, and he seemed more concerned with her than usual. Then she was "ill" for several days again.

The reason was sleeping pills, or at least part of the reason was the constant heavy dosage of drugs. In *After the Fall* Miller indicated that Marilyn had tried to commit suicide—or had taken overdoses of sleeping pills in an apparent attempt to commit suicide—more than once during their marriage. She had tried, or had made every indication of trying, during her marriage to DiMaggio. She once said that she had tried to commit suicide during her first marriage to James Dougherty.

Sleeping pills and sleeplessness accounted for many of Marilyn's illnesses and collapses. With hostility to Arthur Miller established, Marilyn's nervousness increased and the difficulty of performing became intensified.

Marilyn was never satisfied with herself or her performance, in this movie as in all the others. Allan Snyder, her makeup man, would begin making her up in the morning. She would argue with him, wanting to be sure that the makeup was light enough. But when the job was done, she invariably said something about wishing she really looked that way, as she had said to Agnes Flanagan earlier.

Marilyn was very much concerned with death, but she did not seem to be terribly frightened by it. Snyder told one story of saving her life on the location of *The Misfits*, or at least saving her from a bad fall.

They were shooting in the corral at a ranch and Huston had Marilyn working a horse. Marilyn was not a rider but she got on the horse anyhow. Someone had left some loose wire at the side of the corral and the horse became tangled in it and shied, then headed straight for the camera. Marilyn hung on, and then Allan Snyder managed to grab the horse by the reins and the ears while Marilyn slid off.

The script of *The Misfits* was worked over during the movie. It was reported from Hollywood that there was much trouble with the script, but this did not seem to be the case. It seemed to be more a matter of John Huston, the director, making his desires clear to Miller, and the two of them working out the details.

There was a good deal of social life in the evenings in Reno. Miller engaged in some of it, Marilyn in practically none. John Huston spent many hours at the gambling tables, losing and winning thousands of dollars. Visitors came to see him from New York and from Europe. There were parties for the other players. But Marilyn remained in her suite.

Marilyn consented to be interviewed by James Goode, and he began the interview at lunch one day on a set on the edge of a dry lake. She did not want to talk about the Stanislavsky Method or about what she was trying to do with her part of Roslyn, the divorcee who falls in love with Gable. She feared that talking about the part would dilute her screen presentation. And as for the Method: "It makes work more possible." More possible. A strange phrase, but one that described clearly the agonies that Marilyn suffered in the making of a motion picture.

She expected to be nervous, however, and accepted it. Huston had once told her—on the set of *The Asphalt Jungle*—that attacks of nerves were part of the actor's trade.

In this interview, as she drank buttermilk and borscht, and even as she was interrupted by stage hands who caused a Coca-Cola to spill on the table and on her blue jeans, Marilyn was unafraid. And here she stated more clearly than anywhere else, or to anyone else, her credo as an actress.

She made no apologies for her tardiness. "What matters is what you get up on the screen—the art." What Marilyn got up on the screen, at such terrible cost to herself, mattered more to her than anything else in the world. Frank Taylor was later to say that Marilyn consciously produced tensions and conflicts because it was necessary for her to have these conflicts—that she thrived in an atmosphere of hostility. It was an odd view of a woman who could be made sick by conflict.

Marilyn sometimes tried to arrive early for work. One day she came onto the set at ten thirty, saying that she had enjoyed a straight, uninterrupted six hours of sleep, a triumphant announcement. But that same day she collapsed after lunch and could not resume filming. With very few interruptions save those she created herself, Marilyn had been under the strain of picture making since December, 1959, and this was mid-September, 1960. Besides this, a marriage was in the process of destruction, and another man had come into her life and out of it. With her usual nervousness and now facing the need to cut herself loose and build life anew, alone again, it is more wonder that Marilyn was able to concentrate on work at all than that she did so little. John Huston later said that at this period Marilyn was using as many as twenty sleeping pills a day, taking them three and four at a time with alcoholic drinks. He said later that the trip to Los Angeles had been made at his request—that she went into the hospital to be taken off sleeping pills and, after the withdrawal symptoms passed, to be put on tranquilizers.

As the shooting moved into October the entire cast became edgy. Miller's script was being rewritten in the most painful fashion day by day, and this was disconcerting, to the actors most of all. Clark Gable finally put his foot down and sent an official wire to John Huston, stating that he would accept no more script changes. It was most difficult for any actor to learn lines and adopt attitudes and then have them stricken out by the writer or director. Producer Taylor noted moodily that the script had been around for some three years in case anyone wanted to make changes in it.

Had Gable stuck by his guns, the others would have been in serious trouble because the script was now like a torn-up road. Gable received three quarters of a million dollars for his performance. Marilyn and John Huston each received $300,000 for their work, and Miller received $225,000 for his script and rewriting of it, but the others would profit if the movie profited, and Marilyn might earn as much as Gable over a period of time.

Location shooting was completed late in October and the unit moved to Los Angeles for the last work at the Paramount studios. The constant script changing and Marilyn's lack of communication with her husband cost her huge emotional waste. One scene was rewritten. Marilyn learned on the night before it was to be filmed that she should be ready with a new set of lines and action on the following day. She stayed up all night to learn her scene. The next day she was exhausted, and her face was blotchy with fatigue, but she played the scene.

Near the very end of the production, Marilyn took one afternoon to pose for still pictures which would be used to promote the movie. She had a makeup man, a body makeup girl, and secretary with her. Pat Newcomb, who would work from now on as her personal press agent, was with her. Marilyn brought along her collection of Frank Sinatra records and played them as she changed from one costume into another, from bikini to white terry-cloth robe, to a simple black dress, to a sheet. Frank Taylor sent six magnums of champagne to help while away the afternoon. At the end, five hours after the photography began, Marilyn was ready to collapse again.

The movie was finally completed on November 4, at a cost stated to be $3,955,000—so high for a black-and-white movie that if it was not the greatest work of art that had ever been produced by motion picture camera no one felt up to saying so at that moment. But money seemed to mean less and less in the industry. It meant nothing to Paula Strasberg, and she had considerable influence on Marilyn in a professional way.

"What I tell her is," said Mrs. Strasberg, "*you* are the one who gets on the screen, not the others who make the movie. You are the star. Only amateurs watch production costs—that already makes a Grade B movie."

Marilyn and Clark Gable appeared in the last scene in the motion picture, and it was so well done in one take that there was no repetition. Then the crew and part of the cast held the traditional party to celebrate the end. Clark Gable went home immediately. His wife had announced during the making of the picture that she was expecting a child, and he wanted to spend his time with her. Marilyn stayed on the set to attend the party. Arthur Miller drove back to the Beverly Hills Hotel alone.

Collapse seemed to be the watchword of *The Misfits*. Less

than thirty-six hours after playing his last scene, Clark Gable went to the Hollywood Presbyterian Hospital with a massive heart attack. Five days later, Marilyn, in New York City, announced that she would separate from Arthur Miller. Pat Newcomb told reporters. Miller, who was staying at a hotel, indicated that their differences concerned her demands on him, that she insisted that he remain with her, and that he could not—that he must have periods of seclusion in which to work. Certainly this had become the pattern of their marriage, particularly after Milton H. Greene had left the scene, and Marilyn had no one on whom to lean professionally.

Marilyn refused to attend the special screenings of *The Misfits* when Frank Taylor held them early in 1961, but Taylor and the others expressed themselves as delighted with the results. The movie was well reviewed, although not as well reviewed as the producers had hoped. It was not as successful financially as they had hoped either. Perhaps it suffered from the most common blight of any attempt to produce a group work of art: an overabundance of ballyhoo. Frank Taylor and others associated with the film were expert publicists. Having brought together a number of important names in the entertainment world, they indicated that on the flats outside Reno was being produced the greatest movie ever made—and whatever *The Misfits* proved to be, it did not deserve that title.

Clark Gable and Marilyn, in particular, were praised for their portrayals in the motion picture, but from the moment that the last scene was filmed they had obviously been entirely out of it. All the subsequent decisions—the cutting and the dubbing of sound, and the refinements that make up a movie from three hundred scenes—were directorial and management decisions. Miller, as the writer, could still be heard, but the work of Marilyn and Gable was done the moment they left Sound Stage 2 on the Paramount Lot on that November 4.

The tragedies of *The Misfits* continued to their climaxes.

Clark Gable died on November 17. Arthur Miller and Frank Taylor flew to Los Angeles on November 20 to attend the funeral, along with two hundred of Gable's dearest other friends. It was held at Forest Lawn's Church of the Recessional. Thousands would have come to the funeral had they been asked.

Marilyn did not go to the funeral. She respected Clark Gable, but she had known him a very short time and made no attempt to push her way forward. Marilyn's was always a private grief. She need not display it.

Her marriage ended in fact; Marilyn set about the task of attending to details. She closed out her affairs with Arthur Miller. In January in the border town of Juarez, Mexico, Marilyn filed suit for divorce.

Chapter Fourteen

HOW long can one human being survive on a diet of alcohol, barbiturates, and worry? Whom can one trust? How long can one trust any person? Must one give up alcohol and barbiturates and friends? How can one survive at all? These were key questions in Marilyn's life in 1961.

There comes a time in the life of a disturbed person when there seem to be no answers to such questions. Marilyn reached that moment shortly after the breakup with Arthur Miller.

She had sought psychiatric help before from Marianne Kris, Arthur Miller's psychiatrist, and had begun a program of psychoanalysis. She sought help again, this time by entering the Payne-Whitney Psychiatric Clinic at New York Hospital under the name of Faye Miller. But at Payne-Whitney the doctors and administrators treated Marilyn as a serious case, and this frightened and angered her. After three days she left the hospital and moved to Columbia Presbyterian Medical Center, where she was said to be suffering from a nervous ailment, and remained there until the first week in March. She was discharged, then had another shock: Miller's mother, for whom Marilyn had developed considerable affection, died suddenly. She attended the services.

Marilyn joined Joe DiMaggio in St. Petersburg, Florida, for a vacation late in March. The Hollywood and Broadway columnists speculated that there would be a reconciliation between them and that they might remarry. But this was not to develop, although they resumed the friendship that had ended when Marilyn married Arthur Miller. The four and a half years of marriage to Miller were years that Marilyn found difficult to discuss. She could not avoid discussion. Every reporter asked her about the marriage and about the divorce. She protected herself as best she could, but was not always able to refrain from revealing her emotions.

Marilyn's view of her life was an exceedingly negative and gloomy one. She felt that she had been used by nearly everyone in whom she had placed her trust. Had Miller used her? A reporter once asked her the question, and she came as close to criticizing Miller publicly as she had ever done. The reporter noted that Max Lerner had said that Miller sought out Marilyn because "he sensed he had come to a dead end in his writing." Marilyn was asked to comment on the Lerner remark. First she insisted that the reporter promise to print her comment in its entirety. He did so.

"No comment," said Marilyn.

Looking back, Marilyn saw few bright spots in her life. If she had a chance to make her decisions over again—the important ones—she would make them all differently, she told another interviewer.

Such a state of mind could hardly be conducive to tranquillity. There was no tranquillity anywhere she looked. She went to various psychiatrists and clinics, hoping that the doctors could cure her nervousness and the basic causes of her insecurity. But perhaps she might better have listened to Paula Strasberg.

"You cannot worry about unhappiness," Mrs. Strasberg told her. "There is no such thing as a happy artist. They develop understanding of things that other people don't understand."

Marilyn would not accept her coach's view of the life that lay before her, and she could not accept life as it was. So her misery continued.

In her four years away from Hollywood, Marilyn had achieved what was once her major goal: she was now the most important woman in Hollywood.

The people she had played with in *The Misfits* praised her, in spite of the trouble she caused them. Many magazines had published articles about the making of that motion picture. *Esquire* sent Alice T. McIntyre to Reno, and she returned bearing notes for an article which ran in March, 1961, entitled: "Making the Misfits, or Waiting for Monroe or Notes from Olympus: This Is the Way It Really Was." Yet, in spite of the faintly disparaging note of the omnibus title, Miss McIntyre was impressed by Marilyn Monroe, and, after asking Paula Strasberg if Marilyn could act, Miss McIntyre dutifully printed the answer: "Of course she can act. What do you think she is doing?"

Coronet magazine, in February, 1961, printed an article whose genesis lay far back in the days before the press sensed any strains on Marilyn's marriage to Miller. "Mosaic of Marilyn," it was called. The five most important men on *The Misfits* set (discounting Frank Taylor, who was not regarded as a professional) were asked to comment on Marilyn.

John Huston had this to say: Marilyn was ready to undertake serious, complex roles, like the one she played in *The Misfits*. He did not need to direct her very much because she had keen instinct about lines, words, and gestures. He had asked her to play Anna in his next picture, *Freud,* and he planned to make *Lysistrata* with her in the future.

Eli Wallach, a Method actor, said this: Marilyn was far from the dumb blonde. She had courage. She saw herself drowning in Hollywood in 1955 and told her studio that she was not going to continue to be exploited for sex alone. She was unique because she caused people to sense something real and helpless in her and made them want to protect her. She made them ashamed of their lasciviousness.

Clark Gable described everything Marilyn did as unique

[231]

among women, strange and exciting, from the way she talked to the way she used her body. He and she had much in common: the public expected sexy scenes in their movies. He had played opposite Jean Harlow and in some ways he could compare Marilyn to her, particularly since both made their reputations in comedy. But the differences were vast: Harlow was relaxed and made no effort to be funny. Often she did not know that she was funny. Marilyn was high-strung, worried about her lines, appearance, and performance, and constantly tried to improve as an actress.

Montgomery Clift's response was less thoughtful, but revealing (Marilyn and Clift had become friends during the filming of *The Misfits*, and he may have been closer to her at that point than anyone else in the world, although there was no question of romance involved.): Marilyn listened and wanted and cared, using an amazing intuition and razor-like perceptions. They had talked about New York and Hollywood. She had planned to continue to live in New York. Hollywood, to both of them, was a false society where one could preserve oneself only through a sense of humor. Clift saw that humor in Marilyn, but he also caught the feeling that she was so much *alive* as to be terribly vulnerable to hurt from others.

Arthur Miller said that he had based much of the character of Roslyn on Marilyn. Marilyn's extraordinary embrace of life was mingled with great sadness. To understand her one would have to watch her with children and to compare, to see that her whole approach to life was theirs: simplicity and directness. He had not helped Marilyn as an actress; she had perfected herself. Marilyn could imply the world in a look. She had become a fictional character for writers, for each saw her through his own set of pleasures and prejudices, said Miller.

So the compendium had it that Marilyn was an accomplished actress, courageous but afraid, exciting, inhumanly perceptive, ultrasensitive, and very sad.

[232]

Marilyn spent the spring and part of the summer of 1961 trying to recover her health. A minor operation was performed on her in Cedars of Lebanon Hospital in Los Angeles in May. At the end of June she returned to New York for more serious surgery—the removal of the gall bladder. When she emerged from the hospital she was mobbed by the press. She had not lost her appeal. She recovered nicely and quickly, for physically Marilyn was in quite good form. She looked her old self, having lost the extra pounds she put on during the emotional storms she suffered in the filming of *Let's Make Love*.

In spite of all the money she had earned in the last few years, Marilyn now had relatively little capital. It did not make very much difference to her, because at that point she did not wish to buy a house. She preferred to live at the Beverly Hills Hotel where she had lived temporarily many times before. She had not made any serious plans for the future.

In Hollywood Marilyn visited her friends and worked with her secretary and press agent to handle the many calls for pictures. She was never upset by requests that she pose for still pictures; always she seemed to enjoy the process, and she knew very well how essential they were to her success.

Nor was Marilyn confined now to Hollywood. She did not give up the Fifty-seventh Street apartment. She had discovered the world of New York, the world of the serious theater, and it could no longer be said of her, as she herself had said in 1956, that her home was in Hollywood. She was now living both in Hollywood and in New York, and her inclination was to move entirely to New York at some future time.

Marilyn and Lee Strasberg talked often about the possibility that she would appear in a serious theatrical production—*Anna Christie* was the one most mentioned. She would not do the movies *Freud* or *Lysistrata* now with John Huston, for Huston's changing of *The Misfits* story had served to change Marilyn's part to something she did not like. This was the reason for much of her upset during the filming; it was the reason for most of the cost excesses; it was the cause for the hollow sounds of back-patting that producer, director, and writer were heard to make on the evening of the film's release. So changed was the film from the original concept that each tried to convince the other that it was good.

Marilyn's response was to wash *The Misfits* and those responsible for it from her life. She would not do another film with John Huston, she said. Marilyn did not go back—ever. Her face, like that of any goddess, was pointed proudly to the sun.

Marilyn was wistful. One day she drove out to visit Agnes Flanagan, whose husband had been an electrician at Warner Brothers Studios for twenty years. The Flanagans had two children, and Marilyn sighed as she sat with the family, wishing aloud that she had a family of her own. Agnes Flanagan offered Marilyn a place in her household, but Marilyn became embarrassed.

Often she called for Billy Travilla, the designer, when she wanted to take some still pictures. The pictures had always been in great demand. One day there was a bit of experimenting going on during the portrait work at the gallery on the Twentieth Century Fox lot. The photographer was trying out a new sensitive Eastman film, and a quiet little man was sitting, watching, waiting for the film so he could take it away. Marilyn posed in very little clothing, short nightgowns and drapes. The Eastman man was half choked with embarrassment and half popeyed with interest. Marilyn teased him unmercifully, asking on adopting each new pose:

"Is this all right for you, Mr. Eastman?"

The little man shrank, on each question, just a little lower in his chair.

Marilyn had met the members of the Rat Pack here and there in Hollywood. She had traveled on the fringes of the Pack a little when Milton Greene was squiring her in Hollywood after the divorce from Joe DiMaggio. She became especially friendly with Frank Sinatra. Some in Hollywood said that she fell in love with him and wanted to marry him. Others said she used Sinatra to make Montand jealous—but Montand was long gone then, hauled in on a short rein by Simone Signoret.

There was involvement with Sinatra, and there was always the residue of possession for the other men she had loved. When Miller married again, Marilyn suffered an attack of what Nunnally Johnson called "the vapours." She locked herself in her room. She would see no one and would not answer the telephone. Whether it was love, possessiveness, hurt pride, or remembrance of personal failure, Marilyn was deeply affected by the news.

By the end of the year 1961 it was apparent that neither of Marilyn's last two films had been as appealing to the public as *Some Like It Hot*, and Marilyn was looking for a script to become a movie which would strengthen her position. She was acutely conscious of the Hollywood axiom that an actor is only as good as his last picture, and only that if the picture was within the last year. Overexposure in Hollywood was bad, but the actors and actresses feared underexposure even more. And *The Misfits* had been a failure.

Under Marilyn's contract it was time in 1962 for her to make another movie for Twentieth Century Fox.

She did not want to make another motion picture for the studio. She and Lee Strasberg were talking seriously now about a play. They were talking seriously about television productions. But Marilyn still owed Twentieth Century Fox two films or at least another year of contract. If she did not live up to the contract, she could be compelled to do nothing until the time ran out. She would receive only one hundred thousand dollars for the film she might make for Twentieth Century Fox, where she had commanded three hundred thousand. As usual, the money was really the least of it.

Marilyn was not happy with the scripts proposed. Finally, however, she was persuaded.

There were undeniable advantages to having a studio which would bear the administrative expenses connected with the making of a picture—particularly since Marilyn now had neither producer nor writer at her side.

At Twentieth Century Fox, producer Henry Weinstein began casting around for a story for Marilyn. It was to be a light comedy, filmed in color. Weinstein found a story and asked Nunnally Johnson to write the script for the movie, having settled on the title *Something's Got to Give*. Johnson agreed, but said that he did not think it would be a very good idea for him to discuss it with Marilyn before he set to work. Johnson recalled that Marilyn had turned down his script for *How to Be Very, Very Popular*, which he had conceived after two experiences with Marilyn in pictures, and which was really made for her talents. Also, while Johnson had moved to England to live, he had heard the stories from the set of *Some Like It Hot*, and they were very frightening stories. Johnson was a professional with a stern attitude toward professional responsibility, and what he heard from Billy Wilder, Jack Lemmon, and Tony Curtis indicated what he considered to be inexcusable behavior. Rudeness was one matter. There had been many stars before Marilyn who were rude to their co-workers. But Marilyn's performance was very much like that of the girl-under-water that Johnson remembered from *We're Not Married* a decade before. He did not really want to talk to Marilyn.

Weinstein told him that Marilyn wanted to talk with him, although she had said she was sure that Johnson would not write the script. Why? Because she thought Nunnally Johnson did not like her since she had turned down his earlier script.

This apparent humility intrigued Johnson. He felt that he should reassure her on that point; if he had disliked every leading actor and actress who had turned down one of his scripts, he told Weinstein, he would not have a friend in Hollywood.

Johnson met Marilyn in the very comfortable and very expensive Polo Bar at the Beverly Hills Hotel.

"Have you been trapped into this, too?" she asked.

He said no, this was not the only story that had been offered to him for scripting, but that he had liked it very much and thought it would make an excellent movie.

Marilyn stared at him.

Johnson grew uncomfortable. He did not know what she was thinking. So to ease the tension he ordered champagne.

They sat in the Polo Bar for three hours, drinking three bottles of champagne. Johnson mused to himself that Marilyn had come a long way since the night she came to his house and the premiere at which she mixed bourbon and water and a sewed-on gown.

He discovered that Marilyn's initial concern had been lest her own judgment be completely wrong. She suspected that it always was wrong. In the conversation she made statements, but if he disputed one she backed off completely, without argument. He felt that she did not believe in herself at all.

At the end of the three hours and bottles Marilyn was excited by the project, and Johnson, who confessed that up until that meeting he had no use at all for Marilyn Monroe, was converted, did a complete somersault, and regretted every harsh word he had ever said about Marilyn. He was astounded to learn that she had real humor. He was shocked to learn that she had real perception and was able to probe weak points in the story line. He was delighted to learn that she was not stupid, but very quick, and that she was not sullen, but very gay.

Johnson learned that Marilyn knew exactly what she was up against on this motion picture. The director who had been selected to do the picture disliked her intensely and had said so in enough places around Hollywood that the news had gotten to Johnson in London. Marilyn did not need him to tell her. The director was George Cukor, the famous women's director of Hollywood. She and Miller had fallen out with Cukor on the set of *Let's Make Love*. Perhaps she had insulted him by being unmanageable and shredding his reputation of being able to handle any female player. No matter the cause, the damage was done, and there would be trouble ahead. Marilyn confessed that she was terrified of working with Cukor. Yet there was nothing she could do about it. He was written down on her list of directors who were acceptable to her.

Marilyn and Nunnally Johnson parted as friends, and they were to remain so for the few remaining months of Marilyn's life.

Johnson went off to write his script, and when it was completed copies went to Marilyn and to Dean Martin, who was to play opposite her in the movie. Martin had not signed to play and did not until he had read fifty pages of the script. Then he said he wanted to be a part of it. He telephoned Marilyn, and Marilyn decided, on the basis of Martin's judgment, that she liked the script, too. She had read all of it. She had been excited by it, but she had not called Nunnally Johnson until she had some backing for her own unrespected opinion.

Marilyn then told Johnson what she had done and confessed to him that she believed she had slipped with her public since the days of *Some Like It Hot*. She was delighted with the script, looked forward to working in the movie, and was convinced that this picture would make her more popular than ever. When they met she was so excited, she wanted to talk to Johnson about casting, although he was not concerned, and about fine points in the script—not critically, but from the point of view of the player. She was as excited as a little girl. She forgot for a while her terror of George Cukor. They worked together, then, to complete the details so that Nunnally

Johnson could return to his home in England that spring, and the motion picture could get into production.

As had every other woman involved with Frank Sinatra, Marilyn discovered that his interests were broad and varied. One day Johnson picked up the Hollywood newspapers and saw an announcement by a girl named Juliet Prowse that she was going to marry Sinatra. Marilyn saw it too. She suffered "the vapours" again, and it was several days before Johnson could bring her back to earth to read and concentrate on the script at hand.

She did recover. She did get down to work again.

All the details were settled and Nunnally Johnson prepared to return to England. His job was done. On the evening before he left, Marilyn telephoned and asked if she could see him in the morning.

"I have some other business engagements first thing in the morning before I leave," he said.

"Where will you be?" she asked. "I'll go there any time you say."

"That's wonderful," Johnson replied in his Georgian accent, and gave her the room number and the name of the hotel where he was due for a meeting the next morning. "I'll see you there at seven thirty."

"I'll be there at seven forty-five."

"Honey," said an unbelieving Nunnally Johnson, who knew his movie actresses, "goodby and good luck."

At 7:45 the next morning Johnson's meeting was interrupted by a telephone call.

Marilyn was in the lobby of the hotel, but the alert management agents would not let her ascend.

"Tell them you're a call girl and we sent for you," said Johnson.

Marilyn giggled. She told the clerk just that. The words "call girl" changed everything. She was allowed to ascend.

Marilyn came up to the room in tight capri pants, a blouse,

[239]

without makeup, and carrying two bottles of Dom Perignon. Johnson was not inclined to champagne at eight o'clock in the morning so he handed them back to her.

Marilyn had nothing on her mind. She simply wanted to drive Nunnally Johnson to the airport, her way of thanking him for having been kind and helpful to her.

It was late spring when the filming of *Something's Got to Give* began. Everything was settled. Marilyn was playing the role of the leading lady. Dean Martin was playing the husband. Phil Silvers was playing the lawyer, and Wally Cox had a role, as did Cyd Charisse.

Marilyn looked beautiful and ten years younger than she had in the filming of *Let's Make Love*. She came to the studio for fittings in high spirits. Fittings were difficult with Marilyn because she wandered around the dressing room, leaving her designer with pins in his mouth and no actress. She could not stand still. She went from mirror to telephone, stopped and looked in the mirror and walked over to her handbag, pulled out a lipstick and applied some, and then returned so that the fitter could put in more pins. She apologized, but she did not stand still.

She had purchased the house on Fifth Helena Drive in Brentwood and was making a surprisingly strong attempt to readjust her life. There were lapses, and they grew worse as the summer wore along. Her emotional involvements were quick and erratic. The rumor in Hollywood was that she sought the company of prominent people like the Robert Kennedys in order to make Frank Sinatra jealous. Her involvement with Sinatra, in any event, had become much less noticeable than before, although she described him as "a friend of mine."

She had made her trip to Mexico, purchased furniture, and seemed to be on the road to some kind of recovery—although there was always that champagne bout in Mexico City to remember. She was alone, although she did not seem as lonely as before. She was drinking far more than was good for her. She was not as healthy as she ought to be. She was suffering from anemia and was taking shots for it, but the illness was apparently not regarded as too serious by her general physician. No, what happened to Marilyn on the set of *Something's Got to Give* was not because of physical illness.

She appeared on the set to work in good spirits. Her costume tests showed her slim and radiant. Then things began to go wrong.

Shortly after Nunnally Johnson left Hollywood, Director George Cukor began rewriting the script of *Something's Got to Give*. The script had been approved by the producer, by the stars, by everyone but the director. But he did not like it. Apparently there was to be the same kind of rewriting, reworking, and directorial attitude that was exhibited in *Let's Make Love*. Marilyn was not prepared to undergo the experience again. She did what she had done so many times before: she reported sick.

Cukor continued to make his changes. The changes were made on blue sheets, and they were to be substituted for the other sheets of the script as they came in. Day after day the changes arrived at Marilyn's house in Brentwood. Finally, there were only four pages left in the original script.

Clark Gable had been able to throw real fear into John Huston, Frank Taylor, and Arthur Miller when he announced that he would accept no further changes in the script of *The Misfits*. Marilyn did not have a clear-cut script clause in her contract. What Cukor's rewriting meant was that she would no sooner get set on an attitude toward her character than she was thrown off by drastic changes.

Of course it was calamitous.

The changes in the script drove her to excess after excess. When she went home from the lot she would not relax but would begin studying for the next day's filming, learning the lines, planning each gesture. Instead of becoming sleepy, as she contemplated the changes in script, she would grow wide awake. Then she would begin to take sleeping pills, perhaps washing them down with liquor.

She would awaken when the alarm rang and might get to the studio on time, but Marjorie Plecher and Allan Snyder would take a look at her and send her to lie down for half an hour. Then they would awaken her and begin making her up and dressing her. Even with extra sleep, Marilyn was woozy day after day. Hazel Washington made black coffee and made Marilyn drink cup after cup, but she still moved and dressed as though she were hypnotized.

On the set everyone saw the condition into which Marilyn had fallen, and her producer, at least, knew the reasons for it.

There were several reasons.

For one thing, Marilyn annoyed the officials of the Twentieth Century Fox Studio considerably by her behavior. She reported sick at the end of May and then appeared in New York City, where she sang "Happy Birthday" before thousands at the mass rally to celebrate President John F. Kennedy's birthday at Madison Square Garden.

Marilyn spent much time in New York in this period. John Springer escorted her to various parties and appearances. She was to appear at a party for the Actors' Studio at nine o'clock one evening. She did not manage to get there until midnight, but when she arrived she was radiant and charmed everyone there almost into forgetting how late she had been.

But the studio in Beverly Hills was not charmed.

Another reason for Marilyn's difficulty was that the Hollywood studios were finally rising in counter-revolution against the stars who had rebelled against the studios a few years before. In the MGM production of *Mutiny on the Bounty*, Marlon Brando had cost the studio millions of dollars by insufferable, mutinous behavior. Mario Lanza had ruined a score of performances and had finally killed himself with his excesses. The studios had money problems, and those of Twentieth Century Fox were very serious. The Pico Boulevard studio was about to be closed down. Only one sound stage was in operation—to produce *Something's Got to Give*. Everyone at the studio, from production chief to messenger, was nervous and upset, particularly since Twentieth Century Fox's other important female player, Elizabeth Taylor, was cutting up and creating far worse trouble than Marilyn ever had. At that point, the studio's contract with Marilyn made her less important to the stockholders than was Miss Taylor, and they had far more riding on the latter. There was an air of distinct hostility towards performers, and it focused on that performer nearest at hand: Marilyn.

Another reason still for the problems between Marilyn and her studio must have been that George Cukor was a successful director who had been around Hollywood for as long as Hedda Hopper, and that was a long time. Cukor believed in the axiom that the film was the director's responsibility. He brooked little interference in the making of his movies, no matter how sweet the tongue or how soft the glove.

The effect of Cukor's orders for rewriting of the script was immediate and catastrophic on Marilyn. Producer Henry Weinstein had tried to soften the blow by having the new pieces of script transcribed from blue to white paper before they were sent to Marilyn's house, but Marilyn was not fooled.

There was one final reason for the deterioration of Marilyn's relations with Twentieth Century Fox: Spyros Skouras, her most important supporter, was seriously ill.

Skouras spent much of the months of June and July in the hospital in New York. While he was gone Marilyn's struggle with the studio came to a climax.

What happened to Marilyn, was the question; what critical, vital, final blow was struck?

Nunnally Johnson had this to say:

"I don't believe for one moment that Marilyn paid the slightest attention to the revisions. That is, to decide whether they were better or worse than the script I had given her. That wasn't what sent her to bed and eventually to the pills and the booze. What sent her to bed was still another, and this time a final, blow to her poor frail confidence in herself. This time she *knew* she had formed a right decision, a certain judgment. That was what made her so happy with me. Not with me as a person, really, but with me as perhaps the agency of the opportunity to make a decision that had turned out to be right. With me as the nearest sympathetic person with whom to enjoy this rare and exalting thrill. And then to have the whole illusion destroyed by the one person an actress like Marilyn stands in awe of, the director. Who always knows all. Once again, after all, she was a dope."

Marilyn went to the studio when she felt able, but it was an agony for her now. Paula Strasberg was there to help her, but, even with her coach on the set, she could not concentrate.

Since she could not work on her lines, Cukor and the others suggested that she work on the swimming sequence, in which Marilyn takes a swim in the pool while Martin watches from above in the house. Marilyn tried to please. Cukor asked her to do the sequence nude, and she said she would do so.

She got Allan Snyder, her makeup man, to stand beside the camera and be sure that not too much of her showed. She wanted the outline of her body to show—nothing more. She was not satisfied with Cukor's approval of the scene alone, but demanded the protection of Marjorie Plecher, her wardrobe girl, and Allan Snyder.

Marilyn wore a bathing suit when she went into the water, then slid it off, and did the nude swimming sequence.

There were still photographers on the set that day, and Marilyn let them photograph the sequence, too, as publicity for the film. Later she gave them the rights to the still photographs, rights estimated by some to be worth half a million dollars.

Marilyn was able to work enough to produce much more

film than the studio first indicated when the dispute began. Someone said she appeared only often enough and worked only enough to produce seven and a half minutes of film. Spyros Skouras and others in New York saw some twenty minutes or so. Paula Strasberg remembered that a great deal more than that was accomplished. But whatever was accomplished, it was all done by June 1, Marilyn's thirty-sixth birthday.

She came to the studio that day in a happy mood. She lunched at the studio commissary wearing a pale-blonde wool suit with a blonde mink collar, blonde mink hem, and blonde mink beret to match. Usually the wardrobe girls frowned on the players who wanted to wear studio costumes to lunch, because it created more work for them and endangered the costumes, but Marjorie Plecher this day suggested that Marilyn wear the suit. Marilyn was childishly grateful. She asked Miss Plecher if she was *sure* it was all right.

Marilyn lunched with Paula Strasberg. At the end of the day's filming, the crew gave a surprise party for her on the set. She was as gay as before. Earlier, when an interviewer asked her if she was happy, she was evasive, saying that she could be very, very gay.

When the birthday cake was brought to the set, Marilyn turned to Bunny Gardel and said, "How many years have we been together?" Bunny Gardel, knowing it was more, said vaguely, "About ten." Marilyn laughed. "That's a nice round number," she said.

It was another private joke. Bunny made it a point to keep telling Marilyn what a nicely rounded figure she had.

A little later on the night of her birthday, Marilyn left the birthday party and walked to her Cadillac limousine with Wally Cox. The chauffeur drove them away. They went to dinner and then to Chavez Ravine to Dodger Stadium, where she made an appearance in behalf of the Muscular Dystrophy Association.

[245]

Marilyn went home that night from the baseball park. The next day was Saturday. On Monday, June 4, she reported in ill. She never did return to the set of *Something's Got to Give*.

Marilyn tried desperately to escape the trap she felt she was in. She tried to get Nunnally Johnson to return and take over the movie. He would not. It was impracticable for him at the moment, but in self-preservation he would not do it anyhow. He knew that she could have, and may have, convinced herself that he was the only one who could save the movie, but she might become just as convinced, when he had accepted, that was out to destroy her. Johnson now liked Marilyn enormously, but he also knew that she was neurotic and too unstable for him to work with.

Nunnally Johnson tried to persuade Joe DiMaggio, who was in London for a few days, to go to the West Coast and see if he could not help Marilyn. DiMaggio said he was very sorry, but that there was nothing he could do to help her. He promised to call Marilyn on the telephone, but he did not want to go to Hollywood. He said it would not do any good.

During the week that followed, Peter Levathes, vice president in charge of production at Twentieth Century Fox, let it be known that he was going to fire Marilyn.

From his hospital bed Spyros Skouras tried to prevent Levathes from taking so strong an action. But he was too far away, and too weak at the moment, to engage in the kind of negotiation it would have taken to prevent a breach.

Dorris Johnson cabled Marilyn, suggesting that she come to London to visit them for a few days, hoping that a change of scene would resolve some of the problems. The cable arrived just as the news came out that Marilyn was discharged from the picture and would be replaced, and that Twentieth Century Fox was filing suit against her for violation of her contract. Marilyn cabled back: "Thank you both but it was not my fault, Nunnally."

The Johnsons learned what Marilyn meant when they

picked up the next editions of the London newspapers. The set was closed. Twentieth Century Fox had filed suit against Marilyn for a half million dollars. Lee Remick was to replace Marilyn in the film. Marilyn wired the stagehands and the others on the set that she was sorry.

A battle began then. The next day Dean Martin paid his respects to Miss Remick. Although the Monroe costumes fit her very well, he would not play opposite her. He had signed to play opposite Marilyn and that was the way it was.

On June 12 the set was truly closed down and the crews laid off. A week later Twentieth Century Fox filed suit against Dean Martin for nearly three and a half million dollars, but released Lee Remick from her contract, realizing that the matter was far from settled.

On June 25 Dean Martin filed a countersuit for nearly seven million dollars against the studio. Two weeks later Cyd Charisse filed suit against the studio and Martin for unpaid salary.

The legal battles continued.

Marilyn tried to pick up the strings of her life. It took time. She went to her physician, Dr. Engelberg, for her nerves and for anemia shots. She went to see her psychiatrist or he came to see her daily to help treat her anxieties.

But she was not idle, and she was not bottled up alone in her house.

Late in June Marilyn began posing for a series of photographs which would be used in the high-fashion magazine, *Vogue*. She was to be completely and tastefully clothed in ensembles created by a fashion designer.

Marilyn conferred with photographer Bert Stern, and they made arrangements to take the pictures in an improvised studio at the Bel Air Hotel. Allan Snyder, her makeup man, prepared her with very little makeup, and she settled down to be a model for three evenings, beginning June 23. Food was brought in and quantities of champagne were consumed, and the pictures were made. One night Marilyn apparently consumed a little too much of the champagne and reverted to nature. She went into the bedroom, stripped off her clothes, and posed for photographer Stern in diaphanous pieces of cloth which exposed nearly all her body. She was very beautiful. Only, her eyes seemed a little glazed, sultry, like a sleepwalker or an Eastern harem girl loaded with hashish. The nearly nude photographs were later reproduced in *Eros,* a short-lived magazine which said it was dedicated to art but which was banned by postal authorities and went out of business.

Marilyn showed no objection to the use of these photographs. Contact prints were submitted to her, and she crossed out certain pictures she disliked—but she did not cross them out because of any modesty over exposure of her body, only because she did not like the facial expressions.

Modelling, exposure in the magazines, was Marilyn's weapon against obscurity. She posed for pictures which were taken for *Cosmopolitan* magazine over a three-day period. She posed for pictures taken for *Life.* To do this she employed Allan Snyder and Agnes Flanagan to make up her hair and face, and she sat for hours as they worked on her to fabricate the public Marilyn.

She attended a party for United States Attorney General Robert Kennedy at the Lawfords' on June 26, and she met twice, once in late June and once in mid-July, with officials of Twentieth Century Fox in an effort to settle their difficulties.

In July Marilyn spent several hours with *Life* Associate Editor Richard Meryman, who made a tape recording of their interview. She discussed her hopes and dreams and ideas as fluently as she had ever done. She seemed pleased with herself, if a little vague. At one point in a long day she suggested that she go into the kitchen and cook a steak for Meryman and herself, but when she looked in the refrigerator it was virtually bare. And yet—it was not totally Marilyn's responsibility to know what was in the kitchen. She did not keep house for herself—she employed a housekeeper. But apparently Marilyn had not made it clear to the housekeeper that she was to maintain food in the house above the daily requirements.

The entire *Life* venture with Marilyn had been an edgy affair from the beginning. When Marilyn was in New York in May, John Springer had persuaded her to meet Meryman to discuss the possibilities of such an interview. The idea of being taken seriously as a person appealed to Marilyn, but one of the representatives of *Life*, a woman, did not. The woman attempted to move in on Marilyn too rapidly. She said they would be "friends." Marilyn, ever exact in her use of words, said she did not have many friends. She grew cold, and Springer feared that Marilyn would not consent to the interview at all.

But Meryman persevered, the offensive woman was removed from the picture, and the interview was finally arranged.

Meryman was given an insight into Marilyn's life at this period which was not accorded many outsiders. The purpose of his interview was to etch Marilyn's personality into the pages of the magazine. In taped recordings that he made during two long sessions, Meryman did just that. He was able to transcribe her speech patterns and her language onto the printed page. Marilyn's speech patterns and language were later to be carefully reproduced for purposes of the theater, into Arthur Miller's *After the Fall*. Meryman, the expert in personality interviews, spoke in a most complimentary fashion of Miller's ear, if not of his taste.

When Richard Meryman entered the house in Brentwood, he felt the impact of Marilyn's fears. "The house was saturated in paranoia," he said.

Marilyn lived alone most of the time. Her housekeeper came to the house in the mornings and left in the evenings. Her secretary was there during the day, and Pat Newcomb, her press representative, spent a considerable amount of time at the house. But at night, or on most nights, Marilyn was alone.

There were two different telephone lines into the house; both were unlisted, in the Hollywood tradition. One of these lines was more private than the other, but even with both of them Marilyn did not always answer the telephone. She concealed her telephones, hiding them under cushions in the furniture.

Marilyn was very nervous during this period, and Meryman felt as though he were walking on eggs during the interviews. During the first taping he had begun to relax a bit. He was never alone with Marilyn; Pat Newcomb was there. They were drinking champagne that first evening, and Marilyn, too, seemed relaxed. But there was an undercurrent of suspicion. Marilyn was talking at one point about the misunderstanding by businessmen and others of the actor. She said that actors and actresses are not machines, as so many people thought, but that a performance depended on many factors. The conversation drifted from the point for a moment, and Meryman wanted to bring it back.

Now what was it like, Meryman asked, confidentially, when Marilyn was "cranking up" for a scene?

Marilyn froze. The room suddenly became a refrigerator. "I am not a machine," she said.

Meryman nervously made a joke of his *faux pas*, and his lame explanation was accepted. But from that moment on he chose his words cautiously. He felt that if he made another slip with her he would get nothing at all.

Like so many others who encountered Marilyn after reading her press notices, Meryman was surprised to discover that she was not "sexy." He did not find her particularly beautiful either, because of the large head and jaw. He was totally entranced by her, however, by her innocence and also by her excellent taste. Meryman is the son of an artist and is married to an artist. He examined the few pieces of Mexican furniture which had arrived and was impressed. He saw a Chinese horse carved in wood, which she had picked up in

San Francisco's Chinatown, and knew it for a work of real art. He examined the paintings on her walls, moderns of the semi-abstract school with recognizable objects, and found them to be tasteful and attractive. To him, her good taste was the most surprising thing about her.

During this period Marilyn's tension was apparent even to a stranger. She had drinks all evening with Meryman—champagne one night, vodka the other. Both times she complained of fatigue and hoped the liquor would "help." And she was not eating; on one of the days, at lunch time, Meryman sat by while Marilyn and Mrs. Murray negotiated—and that was the description of the conversation—about what Marilyn would eat for lunch. Mrs. Murray was cooking hamburgers. Marilyn did not want any lunch. She finally consented to eat half a hamburger.

There was an eery, "me-against-the-world" quality about the household which was disturbing. One day Meryman happened to be in the neighborhood, and he stopped at the house. It was around ten o'clock in the morning. He rang for some time, but there was no answer, although he could see someone waiting on the little glass-enclosed sun porch. Another time, an evening, he came by to leave some material. Two cars were in the driveway, but again no one answered his ring.

On the second night of the interview, Marilyn got off the subject at hand for a long period and it was difficult for Meryman to get her back on. She began talking about the mistreatment she had received from Twentieth Century Fox. She was particularly incensed about the script changes in *Something's Got to Give*. She said that the changes had wrecked the script, and Meryman felt she knew what she was talking about.

Meryman's task in the interviews was to make Marilyn expose herself, her mind, to the readers of *Life*. Once the interviews were completed and the transcript was made, he re-

[251]

turned to New York to prepare the article as it was to appear in the magazine.

The first installment appeared in the issue of August 3, and it proved that Marilyn was a person to be taken seriously, for she showed that she worked at her art and thought about it:

Goethe said, "Talent is developed in privacy," you know, and it's really true. There is a need for aloneness which I don't think most people realize for an actor. It's almost having certain kinds of secrets for yourself that you'll let the whole world in on only for a moment, when you're acting.

But everybody is always tugging at you. They'd all like sort of a chunk of you. They kind of like to take pieces out of you. I don't think they realize it, but it's like *"rrr do this, rrr do that."* But you do want to stay intact—intact and on two feet.

But when you're famous you kind of run into human nature in a raw kind of way. It stirs up envy, fame does. People you run into feel that, well, who is she—who does she think she is, Marilyn Monroe? ...

I don't understand why people aren't a little more generous with each other. I don't like to say this, but I'm afraid there is a lot of envy in this business. The only thing I can do is I stop and think, "I'm all right but I'm not so sure about *them.*"

For instance you've read there was some actor that once said about me that kissing me was like kissing Hitler. Well, I think that's *his* problem. If I have to do intimate love scenes with somebody who has these kinds of feelings toward me then my fantasy can come into play. In other words, out with him, in with my fantasy. He was never there ...

Sometimes it makes you a little sad because you'd kind of like to meet somebody kind of on face value. It's nice to be included in people's fantasies but you also like to be accepted for your own sake.

Fame to me certainly is only a temporary and a partial

happiness—even for a waif and I was brought up a waif. But fame is not really for a daily diet, that's not what fulfills you. It warms you a bit but the warming is temporary. It's like caviar, you know—it's good to have caviar but not when you have it every meal and every day ...

I now live in my work and in a few relationships with the few people I can really count on. Fame will go by and so long, I've had you, fame. If it goes by I've always known it was fickle so at least it's something I experienced, but that's not where I live.

These were Marilyn's expressed philosophies. They fit, entirely, the character she had lived these thirty-six years, two months, and three days. They had very little to do with the Marilyn that was seen on the silver screen.

Marilyn was relaxed when Meryman was at the house. She charmed him immediately—after, of course, keeping him waiting interminably. She appeared at one time in brilliant yellow slacks with a loose blouse. She appeared at another time in a brassiere and panties. Either way, her appearance was entirely satisfactory.

There were other indications of Marilyn's difference from the Marilyn known to screen fans. Her garden was one of them—a brilliant garden, loaded with blooming flowers, a garden that Marilyn tended herself.

And Meryman was impressed with the range and depth of emotions Marilyn exhibited: anger, humor, wistfulness, bravado, tenderness, ruefulness, sadness—and that breathy voice, and the laugh that rose to a happy squeak. She was, he said, utterly cheerful on that first day of the interview. Once she had a half-hour telephone conversation with Wally Cox, during which she lay on the floor and giggled and rolled around, dragging the telephone and its long cord with her.

Meryman had never met a more delightful person, he said, nor one who would be more impossible to live with. Some said she had little energy, but Meryman found her energy limitless, and he could sense that her emotional demands on anyone close to her would also be limitless.

The tensions that were apparent to Meryman were not apparent to Marjorie Plecher, the wardrobe girl from Twentieth Century Fox, who came to see Marilyn three different times after the set of *Something's Got to Give* closed down. The last time was around August 1. Marilyn seemed happy and pleasant on that occasion.

She had several ideas and several plans in motion. One was to produce a picture under the Marilyn Monroe Productions imprint using as producer Arthur P. Jacobs, her former public relations man. Jacobs had some experience in studio publicity, although none in production. Marilyn kept urging him to find her a good story and said that then she would arrange for him to produce it.

Jacobs found a story, persuaded a pair of script-writers to write a complete script, and presented it to Marilyn. She liked the script and told Jacobs to go ahead with his plans. Jacobs talked to J. Lee Thompson, who had directed *The Guns of Navarone*. At first Marilyn did not think Thompson could do comedy, but Jacobs showed her prints of two previous comedies, and she agreed to meet Thompson and discuss the matter.

"Unless I hate him when I meet him you have a deal," Marilyn told Jacobs.

Thompson was in Canada, and Jacobs said it would be a few days before he could come to Los Angeles for the meeting.

So matters stood. Marilyn had other offers, for stage plays, Las Vegas appearances, and other motion pictures. Her plans were to go ahead.

She had her difficulties. One night Billy Travilla went to dinner at La Scala. A friend came to his table to talk for a moment, and, when the friend left, Travilla noted that he went across the room to speak to a girl who looked very much like Marilyn. As he looked again, he saw that the girl was with Peter and Pat Lawford and a man he did not know, and that it was Marilyn.

Travilla had found it difficult to recognize Marilyn because she was wearing a quiet blue chiffon dress, no makeup, and did not look at all like the motion picture Marilyn he usually saw. He recognized her, really, by her child's laugh. He went to Marilyn's table and said hello. She did not seem to recognize him, and his feelings were hurt. Then she came out of what he said was a *haze* and introduced him to the Lawfords and the other man. Travilla went back to his own table, still disturbed.

Later, Travilla told studio publicity representatives, he gathered that Marilyn had been in a haze from sleeping pills. But this was Travilla's assumption. It might well have been something else—liquor, perhaps, or Marilyn's embarrassment at seeing and being greeted by a man whose services she was no longer using. Marilyn had discovered a new designer whose clothes pleased her more: Jean Louis, and this designer was used on *Something's Got to Give*. Marilyn was always uneasy with people she had once known well and had discarded.

Around the first week in August, Twentieth Century Fox officials decided they had too much money tied up in Marilyn to lose all. Spyros Skouras had been talking since he saw the partial film, and he said that Marilyn was never better, never more appealing. His advice prevailed. The others may even have recognized the intelligence of Nunnally Johnson's comment that movie-goers came to see Marilyn and not any of the disgruntled officials.

Plans were made to resume production of *Something's Got to Give*. On the last visit of Majorie Plecher to the house in Brentwood, she and Marilyn talked about the fittings that Marilyn would have in a few days with Jean Louis for the rest of her wardrobe, and then Marilyn showed Marjorie around the house and explained where she would put the various pieces of Mexican furniture that were soon to arrive from the south.

Director J. Lee Thompson was to arrive in Los Angeles on Monday, and Marilyn had an appointment with him and with Arthur Jacobs for that day. They would discuss plans for the comedy *What a Way to Go*. Marilyn had scheduled an appointment with her Los Angeles attorney, Milton Rudin, for that same day. They hoped to come to final terms with Twentieth Century Fox.

Toward the end of the week, Marilyn telephoned the Strasberg apartment in New York. The Strasbergs were out but she told their secretary to be sure that her maid had a key to the 57th Street apartment and that she came in to clean and dust, because Marilyn would be in New York on Monday or Tuesday.

Then came the weekend of August 4.

At the end of it, the handsome Spanish house on Fifth Helena Drive was just another house. The garden was just another garden. The furniture and paintings and bric-a-brac were just so much used equipment. Even Marilyn's small white French poodle, Moff, was no longer at the house. He had been taken to Pat Newcomb for protection. There was one who could not be protected: Marilyn.

Chapter Fifteen

AND so Marilyn Monroe was dead. So alone was she that there was no one to take the responsibility for seeing her decently buried, no one but Joe DiMaggio. Arthur Miller had married again; he had found in one of the photographers who worked on the set of *The Misfits* the strong woman he needed. He had been suckled by his first wife, smothered by his mother, cleansed by Marilyn, and now had found a mature woman to support his need.

Miller had sacrificed much. The failure of the marriage could not be laid at his door; he had not wandered and he had borne with fortitude the secondary role of consort to the queen. It had not begun that way. On the trip to England, Marilyn had been making a movie, but Miller had the gratification of attending the opening night of his play, *A View from the Bridge*, in a London production. But as time went on, the consort role became more the public one. There are scenes of Arthur Miller pasting clippings about Marilyn Monroe in Marilyn Monroe's scrap book. There is nothing wrong with the scene, but some found it indicative of the course of the marriage.

Miller himself was to paint the authoritative picture of the demands that Marilyn made on him in *After the Fall*.

When Nunnally Johnson saw the play in London, he liked

it. He recognized two Marilyns: the lovely one he knew, and the ugly one emphasized in Miller's portrayal.

The Strasbergs hated it. Nearly everyone close to Marilyn hated it, and most did not believe it. In this compendium of masochism and sadism, all sought some sign of reassurance that it could not be their Marilyn. But Miller was merciless. They searched among Marilyn's wardrobes to match her clothes; they sought out her wigmaker to be sure that the hair was right; on the set in rehearsals Miller worked to be sure that the actress who played Marilyn used Marilyn's gestures. Then, having purged himself, Miller had the effrontery to deny that this creature he had created was Marilyn.

The denial was obviously truthful. It was not Marilyn, it was Marilyn's marriage to Miller there on the stage, Miller's rationale to the world and to his new wife of what had been.

Those who knew Marilyn well—people like Fred Karger and John Springer, the Strasbergs, Spyros Skouras—knew that this was not their Marilyn. What Marilyn was it, the woman who took so much of Miller's time that he logged it—40 per cent, he said—who took so much of his emotional strength as to leave him weak?

There was such a Marilyn—Richard Meryman had drawn a glimpse of her. So had Nunnally Johnson.

Miller gave Marilyn much during their marriage, in self-respect and attention as a person. Marilyn gave Miller much, in love and safety and physical possessions. The marriage, not the failure of it, was the real tragedy.

Miller, married again, had no desire or right to come to Los Angeles to sort out the affairs of Marilyn in those grim days of August. He could not even reveal himself when reporters gave the news. How can a man be asked to say flat outright how he feels about the death of the past, when the future stands by his side? He can be asked. Only a Marilyn would give an answer to such a question; an innocent alone would feel bound to answer.

DiMaggio, who could not come to Marilyn before, knowing to himself that it would do no good, now came in grief and fury.

Hollywood—the movie colony—was prepared to give Marilyn a motion picture funeral. It was presumed by many that she would be taken to Forest Lawn, the Olympus of the movie gods and goddesses, and that a shrine would be erected at the usual huge cost, where Monroe worshippers could come to pay their homage.

But DiMaggio had no such plans. The movie colony was rigidly excluded from the funeral service. Joe DiMaggio said that the movie-makers had killed Marilyn, and therefore they were not coming to the funeral. Some, including such notables as Patricia Lawford, sister of the President of the United States, had flown across the country to pay their respects. DiMaggio was unbending. The Rat Pack and other voluble representation of Hollywood snarled their resentment. DiMaggio paid no heed.

Marilyn had joked from time to time with Allan Snyder about making her up. "... As long as the body is warm," she had said. Then in some moment of despondency she had asked him to promise her that he would make her up even when she was dead. Snyder and Marjorie Plecher accomplished the task that was for them especially gruesome, thinking always of the living Marilyn as they touched the cold flesh. Then came the funeral and burial in a simple grave at Westwood Memorial Park on the west side of Los Angeles. A few friends of Marilyn's who were not in the motion picture business were invited to the funeral. Anne and Mary Karger were there, and so was Inez Melson, a guardian of Marilyn's mother. Agnes Flanagan came, and Allan Snyder, and Marjorie Plecher, and May Reiss, Marilyn's secretary. Only those from the film colony who had served Marilyn personally and were her friends were invited. Her two lawyers came, and a handful of others. There was not a name that suggested Hollywood or notoriety in the list, except Joe DiMaggio's.

He and his son, one of Marilyn's favorite foster children, were the principal mourners, and their grief was real. So was the grief of Marilyn's friends and co-workers who came to pay their last respects around the coffin. Lee Strasberg gave the funeral oration.

A few days after the funeral, Marilyn's New York and Los Angeles lawyers began the routine gathering of bills and claims against the estate and the settlement of Marilyn's affairs. To whom did the bequests go? Small amounts went to her secretary and the half-sister Marilyn did not really know, and to the widow of her old drama coach Michael Chekhov. A small bequest was made to Norman and Hedda Rosten, Arthur Miller's friends, in behalf of the education of their daughter. Marilyn's personal effects went to Lee Strasberg. A large sum of money and eventually an income went to Dr. Marianne Kris, Marilyn's New York psychiatrist. The remainder, the residuary estate, went to Lee Strasberg. Joe DiMaggio was not remembered in the will. Once again he gave much and took nothing from Marilyn. His gifts were a goodby kiss and the whispered words, "I love you."

Marilyn's affairs were not easily settled. There could be no decent burial and then quick forgetting. Financially, her estate would drag on for years until the last few motion pictures in which she appeared ceased to be shown on the screen. In death, Marilyn was a more disturbing woman to society than she had been in life, for although the city and county of Los Angeles neatly shelved its corporate responsibilities by declaring her the victim of her own hand, the world at large was not nearly so certain of the validity of this verdict. And the moral issue remained: not *how* Marilyn Monroe died at the age of thirty-six, at the peak of her career, but *why*.

For one so beautiful, one so much photographed, one so

well known to the world in face and figure, Marilyn was disturbing in that she was so little known.

In his funeral address, Lee Strasberg differentiated between the legendary Marilyn Monroe and the Marilyn he knew. He did not speak of the legendary creature, but of the student and artist who had reached for perfection and who had not attained it.

This was the real Marilyn, the one so few believed in.

The other Marilyn, the correspondent member of the Rat Pack, the creature of the publicity photographs, the nude pin-up girl of *Eros*, this was the fabricated Marilyn, the Hollywood Marilyn that she had created and maintained for sixteen years. One was as much a part of her as the other. They could not be separated, and she would not have separated them if she could. That much she showed on the night that she threw off her couturier dresses and false modesty in the Bel Air Hotel and posed wantonly for photographer Stern.

Marilyn was wanton. She was amoral. She was free. She was shining. She was nature's own creature, and although she violated the mores of her culture, ignoring them, she always appeared small and clean and frail.

Marilyn was a goddess. The moralists said as much, mournfully. They lamented the need of humanity to worship at such shrines.

Marilyn was Opportunity. In the world at large she aroused emotions that ranged from manly lust to the yearning to protect her and from womanly jealousy to feminine sympathy. With those around her she aroused the same feelings, and another: avarice. So many sought so much from Marilyn, and she gave it so freely that there was little left.

Marilyn was strong. She sought success in the movie industry and she achieved it, working against the greatest odds, using any and every weapon at her disposal not excluding that fatal weapon, her sex. Having achieved success on one level, she yearned to transfer it and to prove that she was actress as well as Sex Goddess and Personality. She did prove that she was an effective film comedienne. A dozen important critics said as much. Lincoln Kirstein, in the *Nation*, claimed that "as a classic comedienne of grace, delicacy, and happy wonder, she certainly has had no peer since Billie Burke or Ina Claire."

Marilyn was dedicated. She would stay up all night long to learn her part and perfect it. She cared for nothing short of perfection. She worked twice or three times or four times as hard as any other player in her scenes.

Marilyn was weak. She had no self-confidence and she developed none. Partly, this can be attributed to the arena in which she sought to struggle for success. There is no security in art or what passes for art or pretends to be art. There never was. There never will be. Insecurity and creativity are bound up one within the other. Masterpieces are not created by time clocks, gray flannel suits, or in housing developments.

One of Marilyn's great weaknesses was her trust. She trusted everyone until everyone betrayed her. The others might not admit to betrayal, but they had not examined the bargain, and Marilyn seldom stated it. She thought everyone should know the bargain. She gave her total commitment, expecting theirs. But the total commitment of others was not forthcoming. To DiMaggio she said: All right, we will go and live in your house in San Francisco and I will become wife and cook and go fishing with you and help you tend the restaurant. She was happy to do this when she was playing Mrs. DiMaggio. But when she and DiMaggio came to Los Angeles, her arena, she expected him to show the same commitment to her and her enterprise that she showed to his. People, Marilyn did not know, do not work that way. At least, people that Marilyn knew did not work that way, and neither she nor anyone else knew many people who are ready to make total commitment.

Marilyn believed too much. She trusted those who told her

they, too, believed. Of her drama teachers, the one best for her must have been Michael Chekhov, because he had a sense of humor. That is not to denigrate Natasha Lytess or Lee Strasberg. Only Marilyn could know what she owed Strasberg, and she felt that it was very, very much.

One of Marilyn's old acquaintances, a script supervisor on a number of her pictures, said after Marilyn's death that she believed Marilyn's weakness was in allowing too many people to attach themselves to her, to take too much advice, to depend on her own judgment only in the judging of people. The judging of people is the task at which all people are least likely to succeed. Marilyn's judgment of her own actions, of the quality of a script, of a song, of colors and textures—all these senses of judgment were highly developed in her. She did not trust herself. She gathered people around her and let them make judgments and accepted them. When the judgments proved wrong, or she was convinced that they were wrong, she moved away from the people, who then could not understand why.

Was Marilyn the victim of "ballyhoo and sensation," as Sir Laurence Olivier charged?

In a sense she was. The ballyhoo and sensation were her own doing from the beginning. She posed for the pin-up pictures, right until the last semi-nude photographs and the swimming scene in *Something's Got to Give*. The ballyhoo and the sensation created the Love Goddess and the Love Goddess must keep the creation in motion.

And yet, Marilyn was at her happiest when she was posing for cheesecake pictures. She was proud of her body, not ashamed of it. She had nothing to hide, and she never learned shame, except the shame of being ridiculed, of being scorned for something you have done. She never learned to be ashamed of being a beautiful woman and of loving it. It was not the process of ballyhoo that frightened her. The making of the movies frightened her.

Was Hedda Hopper right when she said all—meaning all in Hollywood and all in the business of publicity—were guilty of Marilyn's death, that they built her to the skies and loved her, but left her lonely and afraid when she needed them most?

Perhaps, but then the publicists built Marilyn to the skies to serve their own selfish motives. Marilyn caused the building. She had the materials, to begin with, and she created the need. She would never have blamed the publicists of the world for her death. She loved them and what they could do for her, except on those infrequent occasions when they turned against her as at the press conference with Olivier in New York or the press conferences in England.

Was Marilyn the Sacrificial Lamb destroyed on the altar of capitalism, as *Izvestia* claimed?

Something can be said for this theory, but not very much. Certainly Marilyn was exploited by Twentieth Century Fox, particularly in the period in which she held the first seven-year contract and earned perhaps forty thousand dollars in a year in which she brought fifteen million dollars into the studio's coffers. Exploitation is a part of the capitalistic system; eventually Marilyn was convinced by Milton H. Greene that the exploitation of her talents was a little too severe. So Twentieth Century Fox lost by being less than generous. If Marilyn did not gain, it was not because of the leeching corporation—not after 1955. More can be said about the exploitation of Marilyn by others, and perhaps even the corruption of others by the avarice she so unwittingly aroused in the souls of men.

Marilyn signed a contract with Milton Greene which would make him almost half participant in her income for a seven-year period, and as her executive producer on the one movie the company made, were Greene's services worth so much? It became a point for quarreling. Marilyn and Arthur Miller decided they were not. What were these services worth? At what point would Marilyn not be exploited but assisted? No one in American society works for another without consideration of financial gain. Any contract, save the marriage contract, that is drawn on any other basis is looked upon with grave suspicion. The capitalistic society depends for its existence on exploitation. But then, what society does not, no matter how it is termed?

And in the twentieth century all societies in the civilized world seem to be moving to become more alike. Arthur Miller discussed this in an interesting way one day in that celebrated two-way interview (Miller and Marilyn) with Henry Brandon of the *London Sunday Times*. Miller was talking about culture:

> A thing gradually gets to be judged solely for one thing—for its mass appeal, its ability to be merchandised. That goes for a novel, it goes for a poem, it goes for a movie. The older idea that a thing had an intrinsic value which gave it the right to exist even though it could not gain a tremendous mass audience is going by the board.
>
> In England you support your BBC because it has value, you think, which can't be translated into money. And now you've got commercial television standing alongside it, which is a beautiful American invention, and it's eating up the audience. In my opinion you will soon have to make a decision based on some old cultural values, and it will have nothing to do with economics. They are going to tell you that democratic ideology says that this is what the people want and therefore they have a right to get it: who are you to tell them what they should listen to? If this country's experience is any guide, it's going to be very difficult to withstand that argument because it lends an ethical justification to naked avarice.
>
> I don't mean that it's altogether bad that this should be, but just relying on the so-called majority vote is a way of divesting yourself of responsibility. If popularity is the single determining thing that establishes value, it will be harder and harder to do anything but repeat the tried and untrue. A

genuinely new idea must meet great resistance. That is its definition. Whereas the art of selling is the art of evading resistance.

Marilyn obviously kindled avarice no matter what she touched, and *The Misfits* was obviously the result of it.

She was used by many. She created profit and financial benefits for many who were close to her. She changed her will many times, and each time left her money to a different group of beneficiaries. The last group represented but the latest period of her life. Had she lived she would have gone on, and the beneficiaries might have changed again.

As Spyros Skouras noted, Marilyn did not die rich. She did not stay still long enough, remain in Hollywood long enough, or make enough pictures at her peak to become truly wealthy. Always, in every way, Marilyn represented an unrealized potential.

Was Marilyn an ambitious, designing female, struggling to the top by any means available, and then taking the quick way out when she found herself aging and alone, as Clare Boothe Luce indicated in the article she wrote for *Life* two years after Marilyn's death?

Certainly Marilyn was ambitious. She was one of the most ambitious women in history. Designing? Not at all. She was so far from artful in her approach to life and her environment that she lived in pain. Had she been artful she would not have been dead at thirty-six. Had she been designing she would have created a way of life that would have allowed her to survive.

Marilyn certainly did use many available means in her struggle to the top in Hollywood. She used her sex openly. Yet her goal was an honest one: achievement. It was not money. She turned down the money of Johnny Hyde. So Marilyn did not use every means: she might have taken Hyde's money and then bought her way up. Such an idea would never have occurred to her, for it was outside the frame of her existence.

Clare Boothe Luce was quite wrong when she suggested that Marilyn was driven to suicide because she saw herself aging and alone. Mrs. Luce compared Marilyn's plight to that of the painter who discovers he is going blind or the pianist whose hands are stiffening. Mrs. Luce ignored the Twentieth Century Fox production called *Marilyn*, which showed her more beautiful and radiant than ever before, even regal, in scenes taken from the unfinished *Something's Got to Give*. And Mrs. Luce had not bothered to look at the cover of the autumn 1962 issue of *Eros*, which showed the wanton, beautiful, youthful Marilyn.

Alone, yes. But by now Marilyn was used to being alone. She had been used by many men, she might have been used by many more; she was not one to stop looking for happiness because misery lurked always around the corner. Marilyn was settling down with loneliness for what might be a long siege.

Was Marilyn the creature of her times, the image of Everywoman and what she might become, given her fill of the heady brews of success in our America?

Yes, she was that creature: the poor girl who struggles up the ladder of success, in the manner that the poor little boy of the nineteenth century came to success in the Alger stories, fighting her way in a business society. Horatio Alger would not have approved of Marilyn's use of sex—but he did not live in the last half of the twentieth century.

Marilyn's plight was worth examining because she was the most spectacularly successful woman of the twentieth century in the business world. Saying that, one's mind leaps to consideration of Jacqueline Kennedy and Mrs. Franklin Delano Roosevelt—but these women achieved success through the reflected glory of their husbands, and it is beside the point to discuss their accomplishments in society after they had achieved success. Madame Curie was not in the business world.

[267]

Couturiers, perfumers, and women investors such as Hetty Green were not to be compared with Marilyn.

Marilyn had a quality shared by only one other product of Hollywood, and that was Charlie Chaplin; it was the quality of international appeal. Clark Gable became tremendously wealthy and popular, but he did not have it. Marilyn and Charlie were the geniuses of their times. Charlie Chaplin was the greater because he was controlled. Marilyn did not direct and write and compose for her movies; the best she could ever hope for was that she could gather around herself a group of loyal, generous people who would do these things for her, to bring her forth at her best. She did not know how to accomplish this task of organization, and this was her primary failure.

Yes, Marilyn was Everywoman. First of all, she was Everywoman in Hollywood, where there is not a successful, happy female queen, and there never will be. As an actress, Marilyn was far from great, and far from fulfilled. As a Hollywood player, Billy Wilder's appraisal of her as genius struck very close to the mark.

One of the problems of success is learning to live with it. There is nothing unique in Hollywood excesses: excesses were the byword of the Goulds and Fisks, Vanderbilts and Morgans. The elder J. Pierpont Morgan, in particular, was a man given to the pleasures of the flesh. His mistresses remain uncounted. Lechery and drunkenness and avarice have always been present at the successful levels of society; Hollywood, as Long Branch, Long Island, and Saratoga once did, suffers from too much money too newly earned, too much leisure, and no natural code of behavior. But these are extremes; the woman in society who finds success pays a heavy price for it in New York or Nashville or Naples as a woman, if she persists.

And also, Marilyn's story is unique. The indictment Marilyn left us in her death is not the indictment of Hollywood, or the indictment of the capitalist society, or of the Western world. It is far more, it is the indictment of humanity's progressive inhumanity. Marilyn was a *natural*, an innocent soul who lived for thirty-six years in a corrupt and corrupting world. She was not an idiot or a person born without the powers of reasoning, as the definition of the word *natural* is sometimes given to be. She was bright, she was witty, she read widely although without discipline. She sought success in the one field in which she could attain it: through the use of her body. The use she made of her body was in all naturalness; she saw no sin or harm in sex: the evil was in the eye of the beholder. Marilyn's soul was untouched by her own actions. She was at one with animals and birds and children, which are also innocent. She gave love freely, reaping contempt in return. She was hurt far more than hurting. She abided, far more than one might expect any human being to do, by the impossible strictures of the Golden Rule.

Marilyn's failure was not even the failure of one who manages to be born into the wrong century. Had she been born two centuries earlier, it would have been the same for her. Her success, then, would have been as a mistress to the king, the closest form of feminine success which one might equate to Hollywood Queen. But even then, she would have been destroyed by the excesses of others against her—or not even against her, but involving her because she stood in their way to achieve what they wanted.

Jonathan Swift exposed Marilyn's society as well as his own in *Gulliver's Travels*, when on his second voyage, to Brobdingnag, the English traveller Gulliver is caused to discourse on the customs and habits of his people with the King of Brobdingnag.

The King remarks that ignorance, idleness, and vice seem to mark the legislators of Gulliver's land. That laws are "explained, interpreted, and applied by those whose interest and abilities lie in perverting, confounding, and eluding them."

He sees no standards, no reward for virtue, learning, valor, integrity, love of country, or wisdom.

"I cannot but conclude the bulk of your natives to be the most pernicious race of little odious vermin that nature ever suffered to crawl upon the surface of the earth."

Harsh words from an eighteenth-century moralist; should they be applied to twentieth-century society and particularly to the Hollywood of Marilyn Monroe? They could be, and were so applied in essence by twentieth-century moralists. But the sins of Hollywood, which begot and perpetuated Marilyn Monroe, are also bound up in its virtues. Life is measured by the capacity of men and women to inherit or achieve leisure and splendor. Hollywood is like the Wall Street of the nineteenth century and the gold mines and diamond mines and oil fields. It is as full of sharks and scalpers and muckers as all places where riches come quickly and easily through combinations of luck and shrewdness. Hollywood is long on new riches and short on manners; so such arenas always were and always will be; they are the monuments of our volatile society.

Marilyn was unique in one way, and not at all unique in another. She was alone in that she was Marilyn, but elements of her story have been repeated a dozen times in Hollywood. The Kim Novak story in some aspects is a case in point. Miss Novak was a poor Chicago girl. She came to Hollywood and became a box office favorite. She began to run late, quarrel with her studio (Columbia) about money, have headaches, dizzy spells, unaccountable illnesses. She knew nothing about acting but studied constantly. Like Marilyn, if ambition and effort were the keys to the arts, she would have been a master of all she surveyed. Like Marilyn, Kim Novak rushed from nowhere to stardom; the only appreciable difference is that she did so much more quickly than Marilyn, having been given more help from her studio in the form of more important roles in the beginning of her career. After all, Marilyn did not receive second billing, even, until her fifteenth film—if one forgets the forgettable *Ladies of the Chorus*.

Two years after Marilyn's death, Billy Wilder had reversed his opinion. He wished she were back, he said. The sound of the cash register is the loudest in the land. Like everyone else in business, Wilder could hear it plainly.

As long as the sound rings loud and clear there will be more Marilyns to strive for fame and fortune above all else, throwing all else aside as they move along, and in the end wondering why the money and power they have amassed so suddenly have not automatically brought them contentment. Money without power buys happiness very easily, and power is happiness for certain types of people. But money and power together are heavy weapons, not suitable for ignorant, uncultured, innocent women. Regal queens of nations and empires had difficulty enough in exercising royal power, and only a few of them managed to protect themselves from excesses. Marilyn was innocent, innocent of intent to do evil and innocent of understanding of the world's ways, and this was her tragedy. It will be repeated endlessly in human affairs.

Index

[274]